Dos For Dummies

P9-EDG-489

Cheat Sheet

For those times when you're even too lazy to read DOS for Dummies, here is a quick reference of a few essential items.

General stuff

This is the DOS prompt: C>

The DOS prompt may also look like this: C:\>

You can use upper- or lowercase to type at the DOS prompt.

Press Backspace to erase.

Press Esc (Escape) to cancel.

Press F3 to repeat the last DOS command.

Press Enter to send the command to DOS.

Lost and found

Where am I?

To find your current drive and directory, type the CD command (by itself). That displays the full name of your current drive and directory:

C> CD

C:\123\BUDGET

Above, the CD command tells you you're on drive C in the \123\BUDGET directory.

Where is it?

To find a lost file when you don't know its name, type this DOS command:

C> DIR /P

Look carefully at the list of files displayed. Is yours in there?

If you do know the file's name, type this command:

C> DIR \FILE1 /S

Press Enter and watch the screen for your file (named FILE1 above). DOS will display the directory where the file is located. You can then use the CD command to change to that directory.

To find a lost directory, type this command:

C> DIR *.* /A:D /S | FIND "SUBDIR"

Carefully type in that command, substituting SUBDIR above with your directory's name.

Sneaky DOS guide

To do this . . .	Type this . . .
Cancel a DOS command	Ctrl-C
Pause a long display	Ctrl-S
Turn on DOS's printer	Ctrl-P
Turn off DOS's printer	Ctrl-P
Clear the screen	CLS
Log from drive C to drive A	A:
Log from drive A to drive C	C:
Change directories to \DATA	CD DATA
Change to the root directory	CD \
List all files	DIR
List files in the wide format	DIR /W
List files with a page/pause	DIR /P
List a specific file, FILE1	DIR FILE1
Make a duplicate of a file	COPY FILE1 FILE2
Copy a file to another drive	COPY FILE1 A:
Copy a file to another directory	COPY FILE1 \OTHER\DATA
Copy a group of files	COPY *.DOC A:
Delete a file	DEL FILE1
Delete a group of files	DEL *.DOC
Delete all files	DEL *.*
Rename a file	REN FILE1 FILEONE
Rename a group of files	REN *.DOC *.BAK
Move a file (part 1)	COPY FILE1 C:\NEW
Move a file (part 2)	DEL FILE1
Display a file's contents	TYPE FILE1
Format a disk in drive A	FORMAT A:
Format a disk in drive B	FORMAT B:
Format a low-density 5¼-inch disk	FORMAT A: /F:360
Format a low-density 3½-inch disk	FORMAT A: /F:720

IDG BOOKS

. . . For Dummies: #1 Computer Book Series for Beginners

Dos For Dummies

Cheat Sheet

For those times when you're even too lazy to read DOS for Dummies, here is a quick reference of a few essential items.

Filenames

Filenames have two parts: The first part (the filename) can be from one to eight characters long. The second part (the extension) starts with a dot (period) and can be from one to three characters long.

The first part of a filename should be as descriptive as is possible with eight characters.

The second part of a filename should tell you what type of file it is: TXT for text files; DOC for documents; etc.

Filenames can contain letters and numbers, and can also start with a number. Filenames cannot contain spaces. The following characters are also forbidden in a filename:

. " / \ [ ] : * | < > + = ; , ?

The ? wildcard is used to match a single character in a filename.

The * wildcard is used to match a group of characters in a filename.

The *.* wildcard matches all filenames.

Pathnames

The root directory on every disk is named \ (backslash).

A pathname starts with the drive letter, a colon, and then the root directory:

C:\

Directory names in a pathname are separated by backslashes:

C:\123\AGENDA

A pathname never ends with a backslash (see above).

A filename can be the last item in the pathname; it must be separated from the last directory by a backslash:

C:\PROCOMM\DOWNLOAD\PROJECT.ZIP

Helpful info

- Always quit an application when you're done with it; return to DOS, then start your next program.

- Never turn off the computer when a disk drive light is on.

- Always turn off the computer when you're at a DOS prompt (C>).

- "Bad command or file name" means DOS doesn't recognize the command; check your typing, check for errant spaces, and then try again.

- "File not found" means DOS can't locate the file you've named; check your typing, check for errant spaces, and then try again.

- "Abort, Retry, Ignore" means something's amiss. If you can fix the problem, then do so (such as inserting a disk into the drive), then press R for Retry. If it's beyond hope, press A to Abort. Never press I for Ignore (or F for Fail if that option is listed).

. . . For Dummies: #1 Computer Book Series for Beginners

More Words from the Critics

This "is a light-hearted survey of the operating system everyone loves to hate, with plenty of sugar coating on its information."
–L.R. Shannon, *The New York Times*

"*DOS for Dummies* delivers DOS essentials to DOS-phobics in a lively, witty, style....The book's liberal warnings, helpful tips, reminders, and technical note sidebars greatly enhance the basic instructions."
–*Publishers Weekly* Magazine

"How do you become 'computer-literate' if you're not 'literate' to begin with? Answer: you find a computer instruction book that's the equivalent of the Cliff's Notes version of the DOS manual. You're holding that book in your hands."
–Joe Bob Briggs, Nationally Syndicated Columnist
& Drive-in Movie Critic

And <u>Many Words</u> from the <u>Thousands of Satisfied Readers</u> of *DOS for Dummies*:

"I loved every page of it. I've been looking for a computer book like this for 6 years."
–Anita Ramig, Racine, WI

"First PC related book I've been able to read cover to cover. Informative and entertaining."   –Gerard Grenier, Potomac, MD

"Simple and funny–you're communicating! With the masses!...If you make computers knowledgeable to everyone then where will the gurus go?"
–George Akob, Chesapeake, VA

"Easy, funny book on a horrid subject...*Great* book–within something like 10 minutes, I am now able to copy disk[s] to [the]hard drive, delete files, use software switches, use directories and other things! Great from a "Mac" point & click user!"
–Wayne Yoshida, Huntington Beach, CA

(More comments on next page)

More Reader Comments from Those Who Have Purchased *DOS for Dummies*:

"Love this book–constant reference piece. Helped me get over the new computer jitters!"
–Charles Ramstack, Waukesha, WI

"Takes the pain out of DOS (It's the aspirin of computing)...Absolutely superb....Best book yet on the subject."
–Jerome Valentine, M.D., Tamarac, FL

"Excellent! Thanks. I feel human again."
–Roz Brown, Lakewood, CO

"It's in English–not in 'computerease.'"
–William Reimers, Ontario, CA

"This is the best, readable book for survival on computers!"
–Joann Tillberg, Virginia Beach, VA

"Clear and concise...This is a fine book, useful, honest, well produced. I certainly got my money's worth."
–Howard M. Schott, Boston, MA

"I just think it's great."
–Charles Gray, Holbrook, MA

"Forbidden commands! That alone made it worth the price. This book more than fulfilled its goals. Good going!"
–Carlos DelRio, Houston, TX

"Dan Gookin cuts the fat and gets to the point...I really found his approach delightful and helpful. I will recommend it to friends and business acquaintances."
–Vicki Kendall, Virginia Beach, VA

"It has been mentioned by [an] experienced computer owner that this book should be given out when any computer is bought....Understandable, clear and simple wording–distinctive what-to-do and what *not to do*....Thanks many times over."
–Georgina Strueby, Campbell River, British Columbia

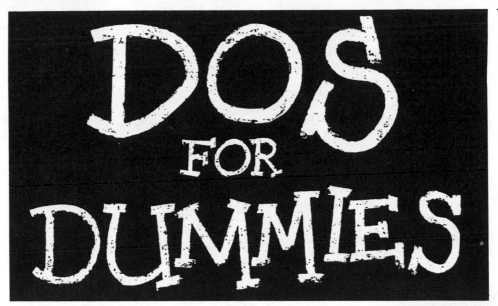

TM

by Dan Gookin

IDG Books Worldwide, Inc.
An International Data Group Company
San Mateo, California 94402

DOS For Dummies

Published by
IDG Books Worldwide, Inc.
An International Data Group Company
155 Bovet Road, Suite 610
San Mateo, CA 94402
(415) 312-0650

Library of Congress Catalog Card No.: 91-75965

ISBN 1-878058-25-8

Printed in the United States of America

15 14 13 12

Publisher and President: John J. Kilcullen
Project Editor: Jeremy Judson
Publishing Director: David Soloman
Copy Editor: Rafe Needleman, Executive Editor Reviews, *InfoWorld*
Production Director: Lana J. Olson
Text Preparation and Proofreading: Shirley E. Coe
Indexer: Ty Koontz
Editorial Department Assistant: Dana Sadoff
Book Design and Production: Peppy White and Francette Ytsma
(University Graphics, Palo Alto, California)

Distributed in the United States by IDG Books Worldwide, Inc.
Distributed in Canada by Macmillan of Canada, a Division of Canada Publishing Corporation; by Woodslane Pty. Ltd. in Australia; and by Computer Bookshops in the U.K.

For information on translations and availability in other countries, contact Marc Mikulich, Foreign Rights Manager, at IDG Books Worldwide. Fax: (415) 358-1260.

For sales inquiries and special prices for bulk quantities, write to the address above or call IDG Books Worldwide at (415) 312-0650.

Acknowledgements

IDG Books Worldwide would like to thank Marty Mathews, Tom Marcellus, Ray Valdés, Dr. John Lombardi, Judy Duncan, and Miles Musser for their contributions to this book.

(The publisher would like to give special thanks to Bill Murphy, without whom this book would not have been possible.)

About the author

Dan Gookin has been involved with computers since June of 1982 when he bought a TRS-80 Model III from Radio Shack.

After three years of ridicule, Dan received an original IBM PC as a gift from CompuSoft, the computer book publishing house where he worked. Though it sounds nice, the PC had two 160K disk drives and 64K of RAM. But a few months later it was up to XT speed, with full memory and a 20MB hard drive. He also bought a Macintosh in 1986 and has owned an Apple IIGS.

Dan is a writer and computer "guru" whose job is to remind everyone that computers are not to be taken too seriously. His approach to computers is light and humorous, yet very informative. He knows computers are important and can do a great deal to help people become productive and successful. Yet Dan mixes his knowledge of computers with a dry sense of humor that keeps everyone informed — and awake.

Presently, Mr. Gookin works for himself as a freelance writer. His most recent titles include *The Microsoft Guide to Managing Memory with DOS 5*, *DOS 5 User's Guide*, and *Enhanced Batch File Programming*. He has a radio talk show on KSDO AM 1130 in San Diego, and contributes to *PC/Computing* and *PC Buying World* magazines. Dan holds a degree in communications from UCSD.

About IDG Books Worldwide

Welcome to the world of IDG Books Worldwide.

International Data Group (IDG) is the world's leading publisher of computer periodicals, with more than 150 weekly and monthly newspapers and magazines reaching 25 million readers in 50 countries. If you use personal computers, IDG Books is committed to publishing quality books that meet your needs. We rely on our extensive network of publications — including such leading periodicals as *PC World, Computerworld, InfoWorld, Macworld, Lotus, Portable Office, Publish, Network World, Computer Buying World,* and *SunWorld* — to help us make informed and timely decisions in creating useful computer books that meet your needs.

Every IDG book strives to bring extra value and skill-building instruction to the reader. Our books are written by experts, with the backing of IDG periodicals, and with careful thought devoted to issues such as audience, interior design, use of icons, and illustrations. Our editorial staff is a careful mix of high-tech journalists and experienced book people. Our close contact with the makers of computer products helps ensure accuracy and thorough coverage. Our heavy use of personal computers at every step in production means we can deliver books in the most timely manner.

We are delivering books of high quality at competitive prices on topics customers want. At IDG, we believe in quality and we have been delivering quality for 25 years. You'll find no better book on a subject than an IDG book.

John Kilcullen
Publisher and C.E.O.
IDG Books Worldwide, Inc.

International Data Group's publications include: **ARGENTINA'S** Computerworld Argentina; **ASIA'S** Computerworld Hong Kong, Computerworld Southeast Asia, Computerworld Malaysia, Computerworld Singapore, InfoWorld Hong Kong, InfoWorld SE Asia; **AUSTRALIA'S** Computerworld Australia, PC World, Macworld, Lotus, IBM World, Digital World, Government Computer News, Communications World, Profit; **AUSTRIA'S** Computerwelt Oesterreich; **BRAZIL'S** DataNews, PC Mundo, Automacao & Industria; **BULGARIA'S** Computer Magazine Bulgaria, Computerworld Bulgaria; **CANADA'S** ComputerData, Direct Access, Graduate CW, Macworld; **CHILE'S** Informatica, Computacion Personal; **COLUMBIA'S** Computerworld Columbia; **CZECHOSLOVAKIA'S** Computerworld Czechoslovakia, PC World; **DENMARK'S** CAD/CAM WORLD, Computerworld Danmark, PC World, Macworld, Unix World, PC/LAN World, Communications World; **FINLAND'S** Mikro PC, Tietoviikko; **FRANCE'S** Le Mond Informatique, Distributique, InfoPC, Telecoms International; **GERMANY'S** Computerwoche, Information Management, PC Woche, PC Welt, Unix Welt, Macwelt; **GREECE'S** Computerworld, PC World, Macworld; **HUNGARY'S** Computerworld SZT, Mikrovilag; **INDIA'S** Computers & Communications; **ISRAEL'S** People & Computers Weekly and Monthly, Macintosh; **ITALY'S** Computerworld Italia, PC World Italia; **JAPAN'S** Computerworld Japan, Macworld, NextWorld; **KOREA'S** Computerworld Korea, PC World; **MEXICO'S** Computerworld Mexico, PC Journal; **THE NETHERLAND'S** Computerworld Netherlands, PC World Benlux, AmigaWorld; **NEW ZEALAND'S** Computerworld New Zealand, PC World New Zealand; **NIGERIA'S** PC World Africa; **NORWAY'S** Conputerworld Norge, PC World Norge CAD/CAM, Macworld Norge; **PEOPLE'S REPUBLIC OF CHINA'S** China Computerworld, China Computerworld Monthly, PC World China; **PHILLIPPINE'S** Computerworld Phillippines, PC Digest/PC World; **POLAND'S** Komputers Magazine, Computerworld Poland; **ROMANIA'S** InfoClub; **SPAIN'S** CIM World, Communicaciones World, Computerworld Espana, PC World Espana, AmigaWorld; **SWEDEN'S** ComputerSweden, PC/Nyhetherna, Mikrodatorn, Svenska PC World, Macworld; **SWITZERLAND'S** Computerworld Schweiz, Macworld Schweiz; **TAIWAN'S** Computerworld Taiwan, PC World, Publish; **THAILAND'S** Computerworld; **TURKEY'S** Computerworld Monitor, PC World/Turkiye; **UNITED KINGDOM'S** Graduate Computerworld, PC Business World, ICL Today, Lotus UK, Macworld UK; **UNITED STATES'** AmigaWorld, CIO, Computerworld, Digital News, Federal Computer Week, InfoWorld, International Management, International Computer Update, Lotus Magazine, Macworld, Network World, NextWorld, PC Games, PC World, Portable Office, PC Letter, Publish, Run, SunWorld; **USSR'S** MIR PC, Computerworld, Computer Express, Network, Manager Magazine; **VENEZUELA'S** Computerworld Venezuela, Micro-Computerworld; **YUGOSLAVIA'S** Moj Mikro.

Table of Contents

• •

Acknowledgements .... **v**

Introduction .... **xv**

Section One: The Absolute Basics **1**

Chapter 1: Computer 1A (for Non-Science Majors) **3**
Turning the computer on 3
   Technical stuff to ignore 5
Running a program 5
   Background information worth skipping 7
The DIR command 7
   Only frustrated typists should read this 8
Looking at files 9
   Fancy jargon section 10
   An easier, yet more advanced way 10
Changing disks 11
Changing drives 13
   Technical background and other drivel 13
Changing directories 14
   Real boring technical details — but read it anyway
     because you'll get lost if you don't 14
Changing diapers 15
Turning the computer off 15
"I want to leave my computer on all the time" 16
Resetting 17
   Trivial background fodder 18

Chapter 2: Life at the DOS Prompt **19**
Names and versions 19
The prompt, or "What do you want?" 20
Prompt error messages 21
Typing at the prompt 22
Beware of spaces! 22
Beware of user manuals and English punctuation! 23
The handy F3 key 25
Canceling a DOS command 26
Prompt styles of the rich and famous 26
Additional worthless information 27

Chapter 3: File Fitness (Stuff You Do with Files) **29**
Duplicating a file 29
Copying a single file 30
Copying a file to you 31
Copying a group of files 32
Deleting a file 33

Extra verbiage on why you would want to delete files 34
Deleting a group of files 34
"The file! I cannot kill it!" 35
Undeleting a file 36
    Additional skippable information 37
Moving a file 38
Renaming a file 38
Printing a text file 39

Chapter 4: Easier DOS: The DOS 5 Shell **41**
Starting the DOS shell 42
Do you have a mouse? 42
Quitting the DOS shell 42
Changing the display in the DOS shell 43
Moving between the different parts of the shell 45
Working with files 46
Copying files 46
Deleting files 47
Moving files 47
Renaming a file 47
Finding a lost file 48
Changing from one drive to another 48
Changing from one directory to another 48
Running programs in the shell 49

Section Two: The Non-Nerd's Guide to PC Hardware **51**
Chapter 5: Your Basic Hardware — What it Is and Why **53**
The nerd's eye view 53
The microprocessor 54
    The differences between an 80386, 80386DX, and 386SX 55
The math coprocessor 56
Disk drives 56
What are ports? 57
    The printer port 58
    The serial port 58
    Definitely skip over this stuff 59
Modems 59
    Definitions to ignore 60
The date and time 60

Chapter 6: RAM (or, Memory, the Way We Were) **63**
Don't forget memory 63
How much memory you need 64
Memory terms to ignore 65
Conventional memory 66
The 640K "barrier" 67
Upper memory 68
Expanded memory 68
    Trivial technical details 69
Extended memory 69
    More trivial, extended memory stuff 69
Upgrading memory 70

Chapter 7: The Video Display (That's the Computer Screen)..... 71

Color and mono 71
"Which do I have?" 72
Graph-a-bits soup 73
Funky displays 74
"Why doesn't my game work?" 75
    Other popular questions you don't have to read 76
"The graphics looked great in the store" 77

Chapter 8: Keyboard and Mouse
(or, Where Is the "Any" Key?) 79

Keyboard layout 80
So where is the "any" key? 81
The keys of state 82
    Interesting, yet skippable information on reverse state keys 83
Slash and backslash 83
Enter or Return? 84
Alt-S means what? 85
Ctrl-S and the Pause key 86
The WordStar cursor and cursed-at key diamond 87
Controlling the keyboard 88
"My keyboard beeps at me!" 89
Having a mouse 90
Using a mouse 90
Mouse terminology 91
    Button 91
    Pointer or cursor 91
    Click 91
    Double-click 92
    Drag 92
    Select 92
Mouse droppings 92

Chapter 9: The Printer (Making the Right Impression).............. 93

Getting connected 94
    DOS's forgettable printer names 94
    The serial connection 95
Going on-line 96
Form feeding 97
    Force a page out 97
"The page didn't come out of my laser printer!" 98
In a jam? 98
Printing on one line or massive double spacing 99
Printing the screen 99
Print Screen woes 101
Printing DOS 101
Printing a directory 102
"Why does it look funny?" 103
Those funny characters at the top of the first page 104

Chapter 10: All You (Don't) Want to Know About Disks..........**105**

Why are disks hardware? 106
Buying disks 106
Formatting a disk 108
Formatting a low-capacity disk in a high-capacity drive 109
"Why can't I 'notch' a disk to make it high capacity?" 110
How low-density disks are different than high-density disks 111
Which disk is this? 111
Label your disks! 111
What kind of disk is this? 112
Changing the volume label 114
Write-protecting disks 115
Reformatting disks 115
Duplicating disks (the DISKCOPY command) 116

Section Three: The Non-Nerd's Guide to PC Software **119**
Chapter 11: Basic Software Setup **121**

Finding compatible software 121
Installation 123
Read me first! 123
The installation program 123
The location 124
Configuring a computer application 124
The READ.ME file 125
Using your new software 126
Learning your software 126
Updating your software 127
About the darn command formats 128

Chapter 12: It Tells Me to Edit My CONFIG.SYS or
                AUTOEXEC.BAT File! **131**

Hunting down the files 132
Using the DOS 5 editor 132
Editing the file 132
Adding the new line 134
Saving the file 134
Information about the editor not worth reading 134
Quitting 135
Using EDLIN 135
Editing the file 135
Painful background information about EDLIN 136
Adding the new line 136
Saving the file and quitting 137
Reset 138

Chapter 13: The Hard Drive: Where You Store Stuff **139**

What is a subdirectory? 140
The root directory 140
You are not required to know this stuff 141
That funny "<DIR>" thing 142

What is a pathname? 143
Finding the current directory 144
    Technical background junk 145
Changing directories 145
The tree structure 146
Checking the disk (the CHKDSK command)................................147
"CHKDSK says I have lost files in clusters or something" 149
Backing up 149
Backing up the hard drive using DOS BACKUP 149
Backing up a single file 151
Backing up today's work 152
Backing up modified files 152

Chapter 14: Files — Lost and Found 153
Name that file! 153
Use these filenames — go directly to jail! 155
Significant filenames 156
How to name a directory (the MKDIR command) 156
Using the DIR command 157
The wide DIR command 158
Making DIR display one screen at a time 158
Displaying a sorted directory 159
Finding a lost file 159
Finding a lost subdirectory 161
Wildcards (or, poker was never this much fun) 162
Using the ? wildcard 162
Using the * wildcard 163
    Quirky, yet easily skippable stuff 164
Using *.* (star-dot-star) 164

Section Four: Yikes! (or, Help Me Out of This One!) 165
Chapter 15: When it's Time to Toss in the Towel
(and Call a DOS Guru) 167
"My computer's down and I can't get it up!" 167
"It's just acting weird" 169
"The computer has lost track of the time" 170
"Gulp! The hard drive is gone!" 171
    Read this if you care about your data 171
A record of your setup program 172
Steps to take for a "locked" computer 173
"I had to reset my computer" 174
    Freely skip this stuff on why you need to reset 174
When to scream for help 175
"I just spilled java into the keyboard" 176

Chapter 16: After You Panic, Do This 177
"Where am I?" 177
"How do I get back?" 178
"Where is my file?" 179
"Where is my program?" 179

The perils of DEL *.* 180
"I just deleted an entire subdirectory!" 181
"I just reformatted my disk!" 182
Restoring from a backup 182

Chapter 17: DOS Error Messages
(What They Mean, What to Do) **185**
Abort, Retry, Ignore? 186
    Tales from real life you don't have to read 187
    Skip this only if you don't take the hard drive seriously 187
Access denied 187
Bad command or file name 187
Bad or missing command interpreter 188
Drive not ready error 189
Duplicate file name or file not found 189
File cannot be copied onto itself 189
File creation error 190
File not found 190
General failure 190
Insufficient disk space 191
Invalid directory 191
Invalid drive specification 191
Invalid file name or file not found 192
Invalid media, track 0 bad or unusable 192
Invalid number of parameters 192
Invalid parameter 192
Invalid switch 192
Non-system disk or disk error 193
Not ready, reading drive X 193
Write protect 193

Section Five: The Section of Tens **195**
Chapter 18: Ten Common Beginner Mistakes **197**
Assuming it's your own fault 197
Mistyping commands 198
Buying the wrong thing 198
Buying too much software 198
Assuming it will be easy (just because it says so) 198
Incorrectly inserting disks 199
Logged to the wrong drive or directory 199
Pressing Y too quickly 200
Reformatting an important disk 200
No organization or housekeeping 200

Chapter 19: Ten Things You Shouldn't Ever Do **201**
Don't switch disks 201
Don't work from a floppy disk 202
Don't take a disk out of the drive with the light on 202
Don't turn off the computer when the hard drive light is on 202
Don't reset to leave an application 203

Don't plug anything into the computer while it's on 203
Don't force a disk into the drive 203
Never format a high-capacity disk to low-capacity 203
Never format a low-capacity disk to high-capacity 203
Never load software from an alien disk 204
Never use these dangerous DOS commands 204

Chapter 20: Ten Programs That Make Life Easier **205**
COPYCON (IQ:60) 205
Direct Access (IQ:50) 207
The DOS 5 Shell (IQ:100) 208
LIST (IQ:70) 209
Magellan (IQ:90) 210
PC Shell (IQ:100) 211
Windows (IQ:90) 212
XTree Easy (IQ:80) 213
Other cutesy shells 214
    Purpose 214
    Ease of installation 215
    Ease of use 215
    Support 216
    Price 216

Chapter 21: Ten Popular Programs (and How to Fake Your Way Through Them) **217**
Black box program rules 218
dBASE IV 220
Q&A 223
Lotus 1-2-3 228
Quattro Pro 233
WordPerfect 238
Microsoft Word 5.5 242
WordStar 246
Windows 3 250
Harvard Graphics 254
Using Procomm Plus 257

Chapter 22: Ten Otherwise Worthless Acronyms to Impress Your Friends **263**
ASCII 263
    Please don't read this 264
DOS 264
EGA 264
EMS 264
ESDI 265
FUD 265
IDE 265
SCSI 266
VGA 266
WYSIWYG 266

Section Six: DOS Reference for Real People 267

Chapter 23: DOS Commands You Can Use (the Top 10)..........269

The CD command 269
The CLS command 270
The COPY command 270
The DEL command 270
The DIR command 271
The DISKCOPY command 271
The FORMAT command 271
The MORE command 272
The REN command 272
The TYPE command 272

Chapter 24: Beyond DOS Commands You Can Use (the Other 51) 273

Commands you may occasionally use 273
Commands you may see others use 274
Commands no one uses more than once 276
Commands not worth bothering with 277
Commands no one in their right mind uses 278

Glossary 279

Index 285

Reader Response Card ....end of book

Introduction

• •

Welcome to DOS for Dummies, a book with 80 percent less fat than other books on DOS. In fact, the idea here is simple: You're a smart person, but a DOS dummy — and you have absolutely no intention of ever becoming a DOS wizard. You don't want to learn anything. You don't want to be bored by technical details or background fodder. All you need to know is a single answer to that one tiny question, and then you'll close the book and be on with your life. This is the book you're looking for.

This book covers 100 percent of the things you'll be doing with your computer. All the common activities, the daily chores, the painful things that go on with a computer, they're all described here — in English.

About this book

This book isn't meant to be read from front to back. It's more like a reference. Each chapter is divided into sections, which have self-contained information about doing something in DOS. Typical sections include:

- Changing disks
- Typing at the prompt
- Deleting a group of files
- "My keyboard beeps at me!"
- Formatting a disk
- Finding a lost file
- "Where am I?"

You don't have to remember anything in this book. Nothing about DOS is worth memorizing. You'll never "learn" anything here. This information is what you need to know to get by, and nothing more. And if any new terms or technical descriptions are offered, you'll be alerted and told to ignore them.

How to use this book

This book works like a reference: You start by looking up the topic that concerns you either in the table of contents or the index. That will refer you to a specific section in this book. In that section you'll read about doing whatever it is you want to do. Some special terms may be defined, but usually you'll be directed elsewhere if you want to learn about the terms.

If you're supposed to type something in, it will appear in the text as follows:

```
C> TYPE IN THIS STUFF
```

Always press the Enter key after you're told to type something in. In case you're baffled, a description of what you're typing usually follows.

Occasionally you may have to type in something that is specific to your system. When that happens, you'll be told how to type in the command particular to your situation, usually by replacing the bogus filename in this book with the name of a file on your disk. Nothing is ever harder than that.

If you need more information, you'll be directed to the appropriate chapter and section. And if anything goes wrong, you'll be told what to do and how to remedy the situation.

At no time does this book direct you back to the (yuck!) DOS manual. If you're into learning about DOS, then I can recommend a good tutorial on the subject. This book will help you after the tutorial is done, but it's not a substitute. (And you definitely don't need to read a tutorial before using this book.)

What you're not to read

Several sections have extra information and background explanations offered. (I just couldn't resist — after writing 20-odd books on using computers I'm compelled to do this.) These sections are clearly marked and you can skip over them as you please. Reading them will only increase your knowledge of DOS — and that's definitely not what this book is all about.

Foolish assumptions

I'm only going to make one assumption about you: You have a PC and you "work" with it somehow. Further, I'll presume that someone else set up your computer and may have even given you a few brief lessons. It's nice to have someone close by (or on the phone) who can help. But you know how unbalanced they can become when you ask too many questions (and don't have enough M&Ms or Doritos handy).

How this book is organized

This book has six major sections, each of which is divided into two or more chapters. Inside each chapter are individual sections that pertain, for the most part, to the chapter's subject. Aside from that level of organization, the book is really modular. You can start reading at any section. However, thanks to tradition, I've outlined the entire book below:

Section One: The Absolute Basics
This part of the book contains general background information on using the computer. It's the primary stuff, the things you'll be doing most of the time or will have questions about.

Section Two: The Non-Nerd's Guide to PC Hardware
Getting into a dissertation on the workings of a microchip is way beyond the scope of this book. However, information on using the hardware — and with special emphasis on not dropping it on your foot — is provided. There is also a section on using a printer, which I find lacking in most other books on DOS.

Section Three: The Non-Nerd's Guide to PC Software
Software is what makes your PC go, supposedly. This part of the book contains information about using software and working with disks and files. There is (and I apologize for this) a special section on buying and installing software. Hopefully you'll have someone else do that for you.

Section Four: Yikes! (or, Help Me Out of This One!)
Good news: Computers don't blow up in your face like they do on 1960s TV shows. Bad news: They still do horrible things that will leave your mouth agape and your soul yearning. The chapters here will sooth your frazzled nerves.

Section Five: The Section of Tens
This part of the book contains several chapters that are lists of ten-somethings: ten common beginner mistakes; ten things you should avoid; ten things to throw at the computer — you get the idea.

Section Six: DOS Reference for Real People
DOS is nothing more than a mean computer program, plus about 50 or so unusual commands and cryptic utterances. They're all listed here in various categories, with descriptions directly relating to how useful or useless the command is.

For Chapter 21 we solicited the help of different experts in the products covered. Tom Marcellus, author of the *PC World Q&A Bible* (IDG Books, 1991) and editor of *The Quick Answer* (a Q&A newsletter) wrote the section on Q&A; Ray Valdés, technical editor for *Dr. Dobb's Journal*, wrote the section on using Procomm; Dr. John Lombardi, president of the University of Florida and word processing reviewer for *InfoWorld*, wrote the Word 5.5 and WordStar sections; Judy Duncan, president of Duncan Engineering and database reviewer for *InfoWorld*, wrote the section on dBASE IV; Miles Musser, product manager at Borland, wrote the section on Quattro Pro.

Icons used in this book

This alerts you to nerdy technical discussions you may want to skip (or read — for that nerd in all of us).

Any shortcuts or new insights on a topic are marked with this icon.

A friendly reminder to do something.

A friendly reminder *not* to do something.

Where to go from here

Now you're ready to use this book. Look over the table of contents and find something that interests you. Just about everything you can do with DOS is listed here. But primarily you'll be spending your time in what Chairman Mao called "the great struggle with the computer." Do so. Toil, toil, toil. But when you hit a speed bump, look it up here. You'll have the answer and be back to work in a jiffy. Or half a jiffy if you're a quick reader.

And now . . . let's get started. Good luck!

Section One
The Absolute
Basics

The 5th Wave
By Rich Tennant

"RESPONSE TIME SEEMS A BIT SLOW."

In this section...

Don't you hate those books that have long-winded, stuffy introductions? The wannabe aristocratic author goes on and on about his/her qualifications, rattles off the names of 400-or-so people who helped with this or that, mentions his/her relatives and loved ones, all the computer industry, the lone soul who really wrote the book, etc. They tell you about this and that: These books are usually long on hot air, short on fact, and big on margins. But all you want to do is to get working (and could care less about the author's loftiness).

Well, this book is different.

Chapter 1
Computer 1A
(for Non-Science Majors)

● ●

In this chapter...

▶ How to turn the computer on.

▶ How to run a program.

▶ How to use the DIR command — and why.

▶ How to change diskettes.

▶ How to change drives.

▶ How to look at a file.

▶ How to change directories.

▶ How to turn the computer off.

▶ How to leave a PC on all the time.

▶ How to reset.

● ●

*T*his chapter contains a quick summary of some basic computer stuff and everyday things you do on your beloved PC. These items don't collectively fit into any specific category. These are things you may be doing a lot or are topics you have questions about. As with the rest of the book, everything here is cross referenced.

Turning the computer on

Turning a computer on is as easy as reaching around the side for the big red switch and flipping that switch to the ON position. Some computers may have their big red switch in front.

In keeping with the international flavor of computing, computer companies have done away with the illogical, Western culture-dominated habit of putting "ON" and "OFF" on their on/off switches. To be more politically correct, the PC's switch uses a bar for ON and a circle for OFF. You can remember this by

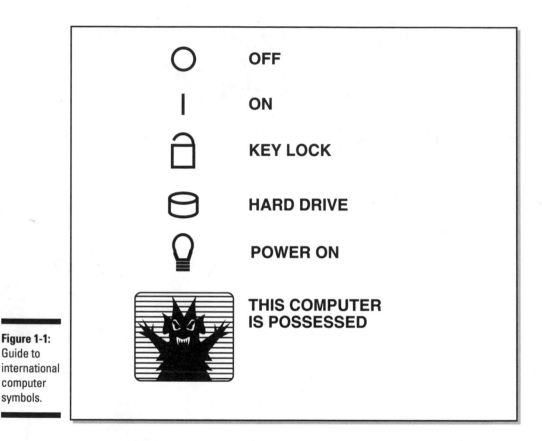

O OFF

| ON

KEY LOCK

HARD DRIVE

POWER ON

THIS COMPUTER IS POSSESSED

Figure 1-1:
Guide to
international
computer
symbols.

keeping in mind that a circle is an "O" and OFF starts with an "O." Then again, so does ON. Just don't think about it. Actually, you can hear the computer when it's on, so if the computer isn't making a noise, flip the power switch in the other direction. The following is a short list of problems (and their solutions) you may experience starting up.

✔ If you can't see the screen, wait a while. If nothing appears, then turn the monitor on.

✔ If the computer won't turn on, check to see if it's plugged in. If it still doesn't come on, refer to Chapter 15, "When it's Time to Toss in the Towel."

✔ If the computer does something unexpected, or if you notice it's being especially unfriendly: First, panic. Next, turn to Section Four of this book to figure out what went wrong.

Technical stuff to ignore

Your computer has many plug-inable items attached to it. Each one of them will have its own on/off switch. There is no specific order to follow when turning any equipment on or off, though an old adage was "turn the computer box on last." Or was it first? I don't know. But one way to save the hassle is to buy a power strip or one of the fancier computer power control center devices. You plug everything into it, then turn on the whole shebang with one switch.

Running a program

You get work done on a computer by running a program. If you're lucky, somebody's set up your computer so it automatically runs the program you need. Turn on the PC and zap!, there's your program. The only time you've got a problem is when something goes wrong and the program "crashes" or it doesn't turn on like it's supposed to (or while you were at lunch Petey from the mailroom came in and played games leaving you with "C>" to puzzle over).

If you're on your own and nothing seems to happen automatically, then you need to start a program yourself. Here's how:

First, you need to know the program's name. Then you type that name at the DOS prompt.

For example, WordPerfect is named WP. To "run" WordPerfect you type WP at the DOS prompt, then press Enter:

```
C> WP
```

Figure 1-2 lists the names of several popular DOS programs and what you type at the DOS prompt to run them. Note that you don't need to type what's listed in the parentheses; those are extra instructions or information about the program.

    ✔ If your program isn't on the list, then you'll either have to read the manual to find out what name you type, or ask someone who knows. When you find out what name you type, add it to the list in Figure 1-2 (that's what the blank lines are for).

    ✔ If your computer is set up to run some sort of menu system, try typing MENU at the DOS prompt to run it.

Program	Name to type/instructions
dBASE	DBASE
DESQview	DV (Press the Alt key to run other programs)
Excel	WIN EXCEL (This program should really be run from Windows)
GrandView	GV
Harvard Graphics	HG
LapLink III	LL
Lotus 1-2-3	123
Magellan	MG
MultiMate	WP
PC Tools	PCSHELL
Procomm Plus	PCPLUS
Prodigy	PRODIGY
Q&A	QA
Quattro	Q
Quicken	Q
SideKick	SK
Ventura Publisher	VP
Windows	WIN
Word	WORD (The non-Windows word)
Word for Windows	WIN WINWORD (This program should really be run from Windows)
WordPerfect	WP
WordStar	WS

Figure 1-2:
Popular PC
program
names.

✔ Several of the programs in Figure 1-2 allow you to type additional information after the program's name: WordPerfect allows you to type the name of the document you're editing; dBASE can be followed by the name of a database program to run. If you do this, remember to place a space between the program's name and any other information that follows.

✔ Yes, Quattro and Quicken both have the same name, Q.

✔ Other terms for running a program include: loading a program, launching a program, and starting a program.

✔ If you have DOS 5 you may find the "DOS Shell" displayed, instead of a mostly blank screen. Refer to Chapter 4 on the DOS 5 Shell — it will make life easier for you.

Background information worth skipping

Programs are also known as applications, though the term "application" is more general: WordPerfect is a word processing application. The program is WordPerfect, and it's file is named WP.EXE. You type the name of the file at the DOS prompt. DOS then loads that program into memory and executes the instructions.

Under DOS, all program files are named with either a COM, EXE, or BAT ending (called a filename extension). Don't bother typing in this part of the name at the DOS prompt, nor should you type the period that separates COM, EXE, or BAT from the file's name. Refer to "Significant filenames" in Chapter 14 for more information (worth skipping).

The DIR command

The most popular DOS command is DIR, which displays on the screen a list of files on the disk. This is how you can find which programs and data files are located on a disk. DIR is especially helpful if you're missing something; it will help you locate that document or spreadsheet you were recently working on.

To see a list of files, type DIR at the DOS prompt and press Enter:

```
C> DIR
```

If the list is too long, you can type the following DIR command:

```
C> DIR /P
```

The /P makes the listing pause after each screenful of files. (Remember, "Wait for the P.")

To see a list of filenames only, type the following DIR command:

```
C> DIR /W
```

The /W means wide and it gives you a five column name-only list.

If you want to see the files on a floppy drive, follow the DIR command with the letter of the floppy drive:

```
C> DIR A:
```

Above, DIR is followed by "A:" indicating that it should list files on any disk in that drive (and there should be a disk in the drive before you use that command). If you want to find out which files are on drive B, substitute "B:" for "A:" above.

✔ You can use the DIR command to find files by name, as well as locate files in other subdirectories on disk. Refer to Chapter 13 for information on subdirectories.

✔ The output of the DIR command shows a list of files on your disk. The list has five columns: the file's name; the file's extension (part of the name); the file's size (in "bytes" or characters); the date the file was created or last modified; and the time of the last modification. If you use DOS 5 this information can be sorted.

✔ For additional information on hunting down lost files, refer to "Name that file!" in Chapter 14. (Even more information on the DIR command is provided in Chapter 14.)

✔ If you have, or think you have DOS 5, be sure to check Chapter 14 for other ways to do this.

Only frustrated typists should read this

For being a simple three letter word, DIR is perhaps the most commonly misspelled DOS command ever. I often spell DIR as DRI — sort of a Freudian slip (or DIRL). A way to prevent DOS from spitting back "bad command or file name" at you when you do this is to create a batch file for each of your DIR command misspellings. These are called "error messages" — more about these later in Chapter 17.

What's a batch file? It's something no DOS dummy needs to know about. So, if you have a friend who knows what a batch file is, force him or her at Dorito point to build you several misspelled DIR command batch files, plus other batch files for commands you frequently mistype. It's considered socially correct to offer them a pint of Häagen Dazs in return for this favor.

Looking at files

There are two types of files on a PC: English and Greek. You can use the TYPE command to display any file's contents. You'll be able to read the ones in English (or ASCII, see Fancy jargon section below). The files in Greek — actually in secret computer code, but it might just as well be Greek — are program files or data files, or any other stuff you cannot read.

To look at a file you must know its name. (If you don't know the name, you can use the DIR command; refer to the previous section.) You type the file's name after the TYPE command and a space:

```
C> TYPE FILENAME.EXT
```

Press Enter to see the contents of the file, which above would be FILENAME.EXT. For example, to see the contents of the LETTER.DOC file, you would enter the following command:

```
C> TYPE LETTER.DOC
```

The file is then displayed on the screen.

Tech tidbits to skip

The DIR command's output may throw you. When you want to name a specific file, you glue both the file's name and extension together with a period. For example, the following is how a file may look in the DIR command's display:

LETTER DOC 2560 4-19-94 2:49p

However, the name of the file is really:

LETTER.DOC

The DIR command spaces out the name and extension to line everything up into columns. If you don't want to see files listed in this format, try the following DIR command:

C>DIR/B

And if that flies by too fast for you to see, try the following instead:

C>DIR/B/P

✔ If you get a "File not found" error message, and you're certain the file exists, then you probably mistyped its name. Re-enter the command and check your typing. Or, you can use the DIR command to verify that the file exists.

✔ Text files usually end with TXT in their filename. The DOC ending is also popular, though DOC doesn't necessarily mean it's a text file. Some common text filenames are READ.ME or README.

✔ If the file still can't be found, refer to "Finding a lost file" in Chapter 14.

✔ You won't be able to see all files, even though your application may display them perfectly. These "Greek" files typically contain special codes and functions for the computer, stuff that the program will eat and then spit back at you as non-Greek information. Unfortunately, the TYPE command just isn't that smart.

✔ In the DOS 5 Shell, just open the file displays. See Chapter 4.

Fancy jargon section

Files you can see are referred to as text or ASCII files. These files contain only regular alphabetical stuff, not computer code, and they're typically formatted in a manner that makes them easily displayed by the TYPE command. ASCII is the name of the coding scheme, and what it stands for is not important but pronouncing it ASK-ee is. (Don't pronounce it ASK-two or you'll be pelted with small rocks.)

An easier, yet more advanced way

If the file scrolls by too quickly, you can use the following version of the TYPE command:

```
C> TYPE LETTER.DOC | MORE
```

That's the TYPE command, the file you want to type, a space, and the "bar" character, followed by another space and the word MORE. This command causes the file, LETTER.DOC above, to be displayed one screen at a time. Press the spacebar to see the next screen.

The secret to this command is the MORE filter, which is just a special program that reads text and then shows it back to you one screen at a time. The prompt

" — more — " is displayed at the bottom of the screen, prompting you to press "any key" for "more" text. Another format is:

```
C> MORE < LETTER.DOC
```

The above command has the same effect as the longer version: The file LETTER.DOC will be displayed one screen at a time. Is that command cryptic looking, or what?

Changing disks

STEPS: Removing a 5¼-inch floppy disk from a drive

Step 1. Make sure that the drive light is not on. You should never remove a disk from the drive when the light is on.

Step 2. Open the drive's latch. The disk may spring out a bit, allowing you to grab it. If the disk doesn't pop out, then pinch it and remove it from the drive (just as you would snatch a stubborn piece of toast from the maws of an electric toaster — and don't use a fork either).

Step 3. Put the disk into its paper sleeve. Disks should always be kept in these sleeves when they're not in a drive. If you have a disk caddie or storage locker, put the disk in its sleeve in there.

STEPS: Removing a 3½-inch floppy disk from a drive

Step 1. Make sure that the drive light is not on. You should never remove a disk from the drive when the light is on.

Step 2. Push the button below or to the side of the drive. The disk will spring out from the drive (like the computer is sticking its tongue out at you). Pinch it, and slide the disk out all the way.

Step 3. Put the disk into its proper storage place. Unlike 5¼-inch disks, you don't have to keep the rugged 3½-inch jobbies in a sleeve.

STEPS: Inserting a 5 ¼-inch floppy disk from a drive

Step 1. Make sure there is not a disk already in the drive. If there is, remove it.

Step 2. Make sure the disk drive's door or latch is open.

Step 3. Insert the disk, label side up and toward you. Slide it in all the way.

Step 4. Close the drive door or latch.

STEPS: Inserting a 3 ½-inch floppy disk from a drive

Step 1. Make sure there is not a disk already in the drive. If there is, eject it — phooey!

Step 2. Insert the disk, label side up and toward you. (It only goes in one way.) Slide it in all the way. At some point, the drive will "grab" it, and take it in the rest of the way.

✔ Only access the floppy drive after you've inserted a disk. If you do otherwise, you'll get a DOS error. Refer to Chapter 17 for dealing with that type of error.

✔ Never change a disk while you're using it. For example, wait until you've completely saved a file before removing the disk.

✔ If the drive door latch doesn't close, then the disk isn't inserted properly; try again.

✔ Keep your disk drive doors open when there isn't a disk in the drive.

✔ Never force a disk into a drive. If it doesn't fit then you're either putting the disk in wrong, there is already a disk in the drive, or what you're sticking the disk into isn't a disk drive. (Many times disks get wedged into the space between two drives; don't be embarrassed, even the "pros" do it. In fact, the editor-in-chief of the company that published this book confessed to me in an unguarded moment that he did it, and had to practically disassemble his computer to get the disk out!)

✔ Okay, since sticking a disk between two drives is an issue, take one of those tiny, sticky write-protect tabs that came with your disks and tape one or more over the space between your floppy drives — or just about any other slot on the front of the computer into which you may someday slip a disk.

✔ For more information on disks, refer to Chapter 10.

Changing drives

The computer can only pay attention to one disk at a time. To change its attention from one drive to another, type that drive's letter followed by a colon. Press Enter to "log to" that drive. (Whichever drive the computer is currently using is referred to as the logged drive; "using" equals "logged" in computer speak.)

For example, to change from drive A to drive C, you would type:

```
A> C:
```

To change from drive C to drive B, type:

```
C> B:
```

A colon always follows a drive letter in DOS.

- ✔ Drive A is always your first floppy drive; drive C is always the first hard drive. A second floppy drive is drive B. Any additional drives in the system are lettered from D on up through Z.

- ✔ On most systems, the DOS prompt indicates which drive you're currently using, or logged to. If it doesn't, refer to "Prompt styles of the rich and famous" in Chapter 2.

- ✔ Don't change to a floppy drive unless there is a disk in that drive. Refer to the previous section.

- ✔ If you see the message "Drive not found," then that drive doesn't exist on the system. If you know this to be untrue, refer to Chapter 17.

- ✔ In the DOS 5 Shell, just click on the drive letter (see Chapter 4).

Technical background and other drivel

Using a drive is the same as being logged to it. Any time you're using your PC, you're logged to one drive or another. This is usually reflected in the DOS prompt.

The drive designator is how you tell DOS to log to another drive. It's basically nothing more than the drive letter followed by a colon (not a semicolon). Otherwise, the drive letter by itself could be mistaken for a filename or the name of a program or DOS command. So you must specify a colon whenever you're referring to a disk drive.

Even if you don't have a drive B, you can log to it by typing B: and pressing Enter. On single-floppy drive systems, drive B is a "phantom" drive. DOS will prompt you to "switch disks" when you change from drive A to B and back again. This is helpful when working with more than one floppy disk, but generally speaking it can be a real pain in the elbows. (Maybe someday Andrew Lloyd Weber will write an opera about the Phantom B Drive. Then again, maybe not.)

Changing directories

Real boring technical details — but read it anyway because you'll get lost if you don't

DOS has the ability to divide disks up into individual work areas, which are called directories. Each disk has one main directory, the root directory. The root directory's symbol is the single backslash (\). All other directories on disk are subdirectories of (under) the root directory.

Directories can have directories of their own, which can have even more directories. This is how a pathname is created. If your instructions tell you that your files are to be found in the \SCHOOL\DATA directory, that means that the directory DATA is a subdirectory of SCHOOL which is a subdirectory of the root directory. Note how the backslash is used to separate items:

\	The root
\SCHOOL	The SCHOOL directory under the root
\SCHOOL\DATA	The DATA directory under the SCHOOL directory under the root

This subject is painfully elaborated on later in this book, primarily all over Chapter 13.

To change to another directory on a disk you use the CD command followed by the name of the directory.

```
C> CD \WORD\DATA
```

Above, the CD command changes directories to the \WORD\DATA subdirectory. Note the space between CD and the directory's pathname.

To change to the root directory of any disk, use the following command:

```
C> CD \
```

✔ For more information on the root directory, refer to "The root directory" in Chapter 13; for information on pathnames, refer to "What is a pathname?" also in Chapter 13.

✔ A longer version of the CD command is CHDIR. Both do the same thing. I use CD because it's quicker to type.

✔ Directory names contain backslashes (\). This is not the same character as the forward slash (/). Refer to "Slash and backslash" in Chapter 8.

✔ The name of the directory typed after the CD command never ends with a backslash, though it may contain several backslashes. Note that not all directory names you type will start with a backslash. (It depends on "where you are" on the disk, which is elaborated on in "Finding the current directory" and "The tree structure," both in Chapter 13.)

✔ If you see an "Invalid directory" type of error, you may not be entering the correct directory name. Refer to your sources for the correct pathname. Plan ahead: Ask them for the full pathname and type that in after the CD command.

Changing diapers

This book doesn't cover the subject of changing diapers. Personally, I've never been blessed with the honor of rummaging through some tyke's soiled shorts. But watch for future editions of this book where this section may actually contain information.

Turning the computer off

Sure, turning the computer off is easy: Just flip the big red switch. The power goes DINK, the fan softly warbles away, and the hard drive spins to a low hum and then stops.

Attached to these easy-to-handle instructions is the following armada of rules, listed by order of importance:

✔ Never turn off the computer when you're in the middle of something. Always "quit to DOS" first. The only time you should safely turn off your PC is when you're at the DOS prompt. An exception to this is when your computer has gone totally AWOL. When that happens, refer to Section Four of this book.

✔ If you're running a program such as DESQview, Windows, or Software Carousel, refer to "Black box program rules" in Chapter 21 for more information about turning off the computer.

✔ Don't turn off the computer when any drive light is on. Sometimes you may have quit a program, yet the computer is busily storing away information on the disk. Wait for that DOS prompt, then turn the computer off.

✔ Wait at least 30 to 40 seconds before turning the computer on again.

✔ If possible, try not to turn off the computer more than three times a day. My advice is to leave the machine on all day and only turn it off at night. However, there is a school of thought that recommends leaving the computer on all the time. If so, refer to the next section.

"I want to leave my computer on all the time"

The great debate rages: Should you leave your computer on all the time? Well, anyone who knows anything will tell you "Yes." Leave your computers on all the time, 24 hours a day, seven days a week. The only time you should really turn a system off is when it will be unused for longer than a weekend.

Computers like being on all the time. You leave your refrigerator on all night or when you're away on trips, so why not the PC? It won't raise your electrical bill, either.

The only thing you should be careful about is turning the monitor off when you're away from the computer. This avoids the perils of phosphor burn-in, or what happens when a computer is left on too long and retains an image of 1-2-3 (or whatever you use a lot) on the screen — even when the system is off. Turning off the monitor while you're away solves this problem.

✔ Screen dimming programs are available to "black out" your monitor after the PC has been idle for a given amount of time.

✔ If you do leave your computer on all the time don't put it under a dust cover. The dust cover will give the computer its very own "greenhouse effect" and bring the temperatures inside the system way past the sweltering point.

Resetting

Resetting your computer is a way to turn your computer off and on again without having to actually do that (and it's healthier for the PC than kicking the power cord out of the wall, despite the full feeling that gives you). When you reset, you're restarting the computer while it's on.

There are two ways to reset: If your computer has a reset switch, you can punch it. Otherwise, you can press and hold the Ctrl, Alt, and Del keys at the same time. Release the keys. This is known as the three-finger-reset, or Ctrl-Alt-Del (control-alt-delete).

Now the question arises: When should you reset? Obviously at any time you're panicked! Personally, I only reset if the keyboard is totally locked up and the program appears to have gone to the mall for some Mrs. Field's cookies and a soda. (Sometimes Ctrl-Alt-Del doesn't work in these situations, so if you don't have a big reset button, you have to turn the computer off, wait, then turn it on again.)

The only other time you really need to reset is just to "start over." For example, I was experimenting with a program that made my keyboard click every time I pressed a key. There was no obvious way to turn off this annoying pestilence, so I reset.

The reason for leaving your computer on, if you care to know

There are lots of interesting reasons why you should leave a computer on all the time. One is that the initial process of turning a computer on is a tremendous jolt to the system. It's often said that you subtract one day from the computer's life for each time you switch the system off and then on. But who knows?

The truth is, leaving the computer on all the time keeps the temperature inside the box even. When you turn the system off, the electrical components cool. Turn the PC on again, and the components heat right back up. (The system's fan will keep them from getting too hot.) It's that temperature change from turning the system off and on that causes the damage. After a time,

the solder joints become brittle from the changing temperature and they'll crack. That's when the real problems occur. By leaving your PC on all the time — or just by minimizing the times you turn it off and then on — you can prolong its life.

An opposing school of thought claims that the above is true, but also that leaving the computer on all the time wears down the bearings in your hard drive and causes the cooling fan to poop out prematurely. So be nice to your hard drive's packed bearings and turn the PC off once a day. Ack! You just can't win. (I leave my two primary systems on all the time, if you care to know.)

✔ As with turning a computer off, you shouldn't reset while the disk drive light is on or while you are in an application (except when the program has flown south). Above all, do not reset to quit an application. Always quit properly to DOS before you reset or turn off the computer.

✔ Remember to remove any floppy disks from drive A before resetting. If you leave the a disk in, the computer will try to start itself from that disk.

✔ A less drastic form of getting out of a tight situation is to use DOS's cancel key, Ctrl-C. Refer to "Canceling a DOS command" in Chapter 2.

✔ If you're running a black-box type of program (Windows, DESQview, Software Carousel, etc.), refer to "Black box program rules" in Chapter 21 for information about resetting.

Trivial background fodder

A reset is often called a warm boot. This is like a cold boot that has been sitting in front of the furnace all night.

Try Ctrl-Alt-Del first. If that doesn't work, press your reset button. You only need to press it once. If your system doesn't have a reset button, you'll need to turn off the computer, wait-wait-wait, then turn it on again.

Chapter 2
Life at the DOS Prompt

• •

In this chapter...

▶ How to determine which version of DOS you're using.

▶ How to use the DOS prompt.

▶ How to enter DOS commands.

▶ How to deal with two common DOS error messages.

▶ How to read manuals and books on entering DOS commands.

▶ How to use the nifty F3 shortcut key.

▶ How to cancel a DOS command.

▶ How to change the DOS prompt.

• •

*P*erhaps one of the most disgusting ways to work with a computer is to type secret codes at a hieroglyphic prompt. But let's be realistic. What's the end result of trying to make something too easy? It becomes boring. The DOS prompt may be cryptic, but it's definitely interesting. (Okay, and physical torture can be interesting, but that doesn't mean we volunteer for it in droves.)

This chapter contains information about using the DOS prompt. These are mostly tips, though some of the items here will give you valuable shortcuts and make using the prompt — obscure as it is — a bit easier.

Names and versions

What this book calls *DOS* is really a computer program created by Microsoft. Their version is called MS-DOS, short for Microsoft Disk Operating System. The one they make and sell to IBM is called PC-DOS, short for Personal Computer Disk Operating System. Microsoft sells other versions as well. Various computer hardware manufacturers label DOS using their own names: Compaq DOS, Tandy DOS, Wambooli DOS, etc. It's all DOS.

What's the difference? Very little. MS-DOS is a general DOS for everyone. The brand name DOSs may have certain special programs included, and those programs may only work on specific computers. But generally speaking, all the flavors of DOS are the same. DOS also has version numbers. There have been five major releases of DOS, numbered 1 through 5. Each major release also has its own minor releases: There was DOS version 1.0, 1.1, 2.0, 2.1, 3.0, 3.1, etc. The minor release number is separated from the major release by a period or dot. Also, the first minor release is zero, not one.

To find out which name and version of DOS you're using, use the VER command:

```
C> VER
```

Press Enter and DOS displays its name and version number.

✔ Aside from being perhaps the simplest and most stupid DOS command, VER can be used to determine which version of DOS is installed on a computer. If you wind up using an alien computer, type VER to see which make and model of DOS is installed. That may explain why some DOS commands function weirdly, or why some commands aren't available.

✔ If the version turns out to be 5.0 or higher, see Chapter 4 on the DOS Shell.

The prompt, or "What do you want?"

The DOS prompt is how DOS tells you it's ready for your input, for you to type something, enter information, or just idly sit back and swear at the computer. In this book, the following prompt is used as an example:

```
C>
```

The prompt on your system may look like this:

```
C:\>
```

✔ The letter in the prompt tells you which disk drive you're currently using (or "logged to"). Refer to "Changing drives" in Chapter 1.

✔ The greater-than sign (>), is the all-purpose computer prompt. It means "What do you want?"

✔ Other variations of the droll DOS prompt exist. Some will contain the name of the current directory, some may show the date and time, and some may look like Bart Simpson. (Refer to "Finding the current directory" in Chapter 13 for information on the current directory; refer to the FOX television network for Bart Simpson.)

✔ You can change your system prompt using the PROMPT command. Refer to "Prompt styles of the rich and famous" later in this chapter.

✔ If you have DOS 5.0 and use a mouse, you can use the DOS Shell, you lucky dog, and skip a lot of this stuff most of the time — see Chapter 4.

Prompt error messages

Two common error messages are produced at the prompt: "file not found" and "bad command or file name." "File not found" means that the file you've specified doesn't exist. Don't panic; you may have just typed it in wrong. Check your typing. If that fails, refer to "Finding a lost file" in Chapter 14.

"Bad command or file name" is similar to "file not found," though in this case the message is really "program not found." You may have mistyped the name of a program, added a space, or forgot something. Refer to "Where is my program?" in Chapter 16 for additional information on solving this problem.

✔ Individual programs will produce their own, unique error messages for "file not found." They vary in syntax, but they all mean the same thing.

✔ Other error messages are possible at the prompt, some of which will really burn your buns. Refer to Chapter 17.

Unimportant background info

The term OEM is used to describe an enterprise that puts together a computer. IBM, Tandy, Dell, AST, Compaq, Zenith — these are all OEMs, or Original Equipment Manufacturers. Each of them may license their own version of DOS from Microsoft, then repackage and sell that DOS under their own label.

Sometimes you'll see subminor versions, typically from OEM versions of DOS. For example, the first version of Tandy DOS for the first Tandy 1000 computer was 2.11.34. That's the second major version of DOS, the 11th minor version, plus 34 tweaks by Tandy.

Usually, a minor release of DOS (or any software for that matter) warrants the printing of a new manual. To get around this expense, and usually for only very slight modifications, you'll see a tiny-minor release, such as DOS 4.01. This type of release number indicates only minor "bugs" have been fixed or subtle features changed.

If you're curious (and you wouldn't be reading this section otherwise), the OEM versions of DOS usually add programs specific to their machines, including their own custom version of the Basic programming language. If you have PC-DOS or Compaq DOS, note that the version of Basic supplied will only work on IBM or Compaq computers.

Typing at the prompt

You use the prompt by typing after it. All the text you enter at the keyboard will appear on the screen next to the prompt. Of course, what you type are DOS commands, the names of programs, or general insults to the computer.

The information you enter at the DOS prompt is the command line, which is an assortment of words, cryptic and English, that direct the computer to do something. Sending that information to DOS is done by pressing the Enter key. Only by pressing Enter is the information sent, which gives you an opportunity to back up and erase or to change your mind and press Ctrl-C or the Escape (Esc) key to cancel.

✔ As you type, the underline cursor on the screen moves forward. The cursor marks the spot on the screen where all text appears.

✔ If you make a mistake typing at the DOS prompt, press the Backspace key to back up and erase.

✔ If you want to discard the entire command line, press Esc. On some computers, the backslash (\) will be displayed and the cursor will move down to the next line on the screen. You can start over from there. (Other computers may just erase the line and let you start over.)

✔ I don't need to mention that the DOS prompt is unfriendly. In fact, DOS is arrogant and will only understand certain things. When it doesn't understand something, it spits back an error message (refer to the previous section).

✔ On the bright side, there's really nothing heinous you can do at the DOS prompt. Most of the deadly things you can do involve typing in specific commands, and then answering Y (for yes). If you accidentally stumble into one of these situations, type N (for no). Otherwise, there's little you can do at the DOS prompt that will damage your PC.

Beware of spaces!

There are three bad tendencies beginners have when using the DOS prompt: They don't type in any spaces, they do type in spaces, or they type in periods.

Always keep this in mind: The DOS prompt is not a word processor. You don't need to type formal English; punctuation, capitalization, and spelling are often overlooked. So never end a command with a period. In fact, periods are only used when naming files that have a second part or extension.

Spaces are another sticky point. You must stick a space (and only one space) between two separate items. For example:

```
C> CD \FRIDGE\LEFTOVER
```

Above, the CD command is followed by a space. You must put a space after CD or any DOS command.

```
C> WP CHAP02.DOC
```

Above, the program WP is run. It's followed by a space and the name of a file.

As with typing in a space, don't type in too many spaces. Above, there is no space in the file named CHAP02.DOC. If you're a touch typist, you may have a tendency to type a space after the period. Don't. Always type in a command exactly as you see it listed in a book, magazine, or computer manual.

- ✔ In some books and magazines, they may use a funny typeface to indicate "the stuff you type in." This may make it look like extra spaces are typed in a command, typically around the backslash (\) character. Watch out for these!

- ✔ A few DOS commands may end in a period, but only when that period is part of a filename. For example:

```
C> DIR *.
```

The above DIR command lists all files that don't have a second part or filename extension. The "*." is a legitimate part of the command. This is about the only instance in which a DOS command will end with a period.

- ✔ If you forget to type a space at the proper place, you'll probably get a "bad command or file name" error.

Beware of user manuals and English punctuation!

Manuals and instruction books often tell you what to type at the DOS prompt. But there is no established convention for doing this.

This book uses the following method:

```
C> VER
```

The DOS prompt is shown followed by the text you enter in a different typeface than the rest of the text in the book. The prompt is always going to be "C>" in this book, though it may appear in some other way on your screen.

Some manuals will follow what you type with the word Enter, sometimes in a bubble or in some other happy typeface. That means to press the Enter key after typing the command; don't type in the word Enter on the command line.

Some manuals will list what you type on a line by itself, without the prompt:

```
VER
```

Some manuals will include the command in the text — which is where this can get tricky. For example, they may say:

```
Enter the VER command.
```

Above, "VER" is in uppercase, meaning you type it at the DOS prompt. Sometimes it may be in lowercase, italics, or boldface. The worst is when they put the command in quotes:

```
Type the "DIR *.*" command.
```

Above, you can gather that you type the DIR command, followed by a space, an asterisk, a period, and another asterisk. You would not type in the double quotes surrounding the command. In this book, the command would be specified as follows:

```
C> DIR *.*
```

So far so good. But when English punctuation rears its ugly head, you may see one of the following:

```
Type the command "DIR *.*".
```

```
Type the command "DIR *.*."
```

The first example is grammatically incorrect: The period is on the outside of the double quote. Of course, the period ends the sentence — it's not part of the command you should type in. The second example is what most computer book editors will do to DOS commands. No, the period is not part of the command, but a period on the inside of a quote is grammatically correct in that circumstance.

If you type in the period as part of the DOS command, you'll see one of DOS's inflammatory error messages.

✔ DOS commands and program names can be entered in upper or lowercase. Most manuals and books, including this one, use uppercase.

✔ No DOS command ends in a period. There are exceptions, but the point here is that if you see a command ending in a period in a manual or computer book, it's probably a part of English grammar and not something you need to type.

✔ The command line contains spaces. They will follow the name of the command, separating filenames and any other options typed after the commands.

✔ The DIR command outputs filenames with spaces separating the name and the extension. When you type a filename at the DOS prompt, a dot separates the name and extension. Do not use spaces.

✔ No user manual is 100 percent correct. If you type in the command exactly as it's listed and the computer still produces an error, try it again with a space or without a period.

✔ General information on using your keyboard is covered in Chapter 8.

The handy F3 key

The F3 key provides a handy shortcut whenever you need to retype a DOS command. For example, to list files on the disk in drive A, you type the following command:

    C> DIR A:

If the file you wanted isn't on that diskette, remove it and replace it with another diskette. Then, instead of retyping the same command, press the F3 key. You'll see the same command displayed:

    C> DIR A:

Press Enter and the command is executed a second time.

If this doesn't work, then you may have a "keyboard macro" enhancement program operating. In that case, try pressing the up arrow cursor key instead.

Canceling a DOS command

The universal cancel key in DOS is Control-C or Ctrl-C. Pressing this key combination halts most DOS commands. In some cases, it may even halt a DOS operation in progress.

To press Ctrl-C, hold down the Ctrl (Control) key and type a C. Release the Ctrl key. You'll see "^C" displayed on the screen, and then another DOS prompt.

- Always try Ctrl-C first. You never want to reset — or worse, turn off — your computer to get yourself out of a jam.

- Applications programs use their own cancel key, which is usually the Escape key. (There are exceptions, however, such as WordPerfect that uses the F1 key.)

- The Ctrl-Break key combination works identically to Ctrl-C. Note that the Break key is usually a shared key; you may find the word "Break" on the front of the key instead of the top.

- The caret or hat symbol (^) is used to denote "control." So when you see ^C it means Control-C or the Ctrl-C keystroke. Likewise, ^H means Control-H; ^G means Control-G and so on. Some of these keys have significant meaning, which there's no need to get into here.

Prompt styles of the rich and famous

The DOS prompt is a flexible thing. It can really look like anything you imagine, contain interesting and useful information, and so on. The secret is to use the PROMPT command.

Other books will offer you a tutorial on the PROMPT command and how it works. Rather than bother with that, here are some popular prompts you can create. Just type in the command as listed and you'll have your own excellent DOS prompt.

The standard, boring prompt:

```
C>
```

To create the standard prompt, which contains the current drive letter and a greater-than symbol, type in the following command:

```
C:\> PROMPT
```

The informative drive/directory prompt:

```
C:\>
```

The most common DOS prompt shows the current drive, directory, and the greater-than sign. Type in the following command:

```
C:\> PROMPT $P$G
```

The date and time prompt:

```
Wed 7-31-1993
12:34:25.63
C:\DOS>
```

This prompt contains the current date, time, and then the drive and directory information found in the second example. Note that the date and time information is only current while the new prompt is displayed; it's not constantly updated on your screen. Here's the command you should carefully type to produce this prompt:

```
C:\> PROMPT $D$_$T$_$P$G
```

To make your favorite prompt permanent, you need to edit your AUTOEXEC.BAT file and place the PROMPT command into it. This is covered in Chapter 12.

Additional, worthless information

The prompt can contain any text you like. Simply specify that text after the PROMPT command:

```
C:\> PROMPT Enter command:
```

Or the ever popular:

```
C:\> PROMPT What is thy bidding?
```

You cannot directly specify the following characters in a prompt command: less-than (<), greater-than (>), and the pipe (|). Instead, use the following: $L for less-than (<); $G for greater-than (>); and $B for the pipe (|).

Since the dollar sign ($) is used as a special prefix, you'll need to specify two of them ($$) if you want $ as part of your prompt. That's okay; when money's involved, greed is good.

Chapter 3
File Fitness
(Stuff You Do with Files)

● ●

In this chapter...

▶ How to duplicate a file.

▶ How to copy a file.

▶ How to copy a file to the current directory.

▶ How to copy a group of files.

▶ How to delete a file.

▶ How to delete a group of files.

▶ How to delete a file that refuses to die.

▶ How to undelete a file.

▶ How to move a file.

▶ How to rename a file.

▶ How to print a text file.

Note: If you have DOS 5, you can perform the above functions in the easy-to-use DOS 5 Shell.

● ●

A file is basically a collection of stuff on disk, usually stuff you want to keep. One of DOS's main duties (right after confusing the hell out of you) is to work with files. For a filing cabinet, this is obvious. Under DOS, it's not.

This chapter is about working with files — duplicating, copying, deleting, undeleting, moving, and printing them — everything you want to know about files.

Duplicating a file

Duplicating a file is done with the COPY command. You need to know the name of the original file and the new name you want to give the duplicate.

Suppose the file you have is named SAMPLE1DOC. You want to make a duplicate file named SAMPLE2DOC. Here's what you type:

```
C> COPY SAMPLE1.DOC SAMPLE2.DOC
```

A common reason for doing this is to make a backup file of an original. For example, if you work on CONFIG.SYS and AUTOEXEC.BAT:

```
C> COPY CONFIG.SYS CONFIG.BKD
```

Above, the file CONFIG.SYS is duplicated and given the name CONFIG.BKD.

Both the original and duplicate files will have the same contents, but different names. This is because no two files in the same directory can be given the same name.

✔ If the operation is successful, DOS responds with the message "1 file(s) copied." If not, you'll most likely receive a "File not found" error. That's okay, you probably just mistyped the original filename. Try again.

✔ To find out which files are on disk, you use the DIR command. Refer to "The DIR command" in Chapter 1.

✔ For information on naming new files, refer to "Name that file!" in Chapter 14. Generally speaking, files can contain letters and numbers. A filename can be up to eight letters long, then you can specify an optional period and up to three more letters if you like. If the duplicate already exists, DOS will overwrite it. This happens without any notice. For example, if the file SAMPLE2DOC already existed (above), DOS would copy the original file, SAMPLE1DOC over it. Use the DIR command first to make sure your file doesn't already exist.

Copying a single file

Copying a file is handled by the COPY command. You need to know the name of the original file and the destination, or the place where you want to put the copy.

For example, to copy a file to another disk, specify that drive's letter plus a colon:

```
C> COPY SAMPLE1.DOC A:
```

Above, the file SAMPLE1DOC is copied to drive A. On drive A, you'll find an identical copy of the file SAMPLE1DOC; both files will have the same name and contents. To copy a file to another directory on the same disk, specify that directory's pathname. For example:

```
C> COPY SAMPLE1.DOC \WORK\STUFF
```

Above, the file SAMPLE1DOC is copied to the subdirectory \WORK\STUFF on the same disk.

To copy a file to another directory on another drive, you must specify the full pathname, which includes the drive letter and colon:

```
C> COPY MENU.EXE B:\MAIN
```

Above, the file MENU.EXE is copied to the MAIN directory on drive B.

- ✔ If you want to copy a file to the same directory as the original, then you must specify a different name. Refer to "Duplicating a file" above.

- ✔ For more information on pathnames and subdirectories, refer to Chapter 13. Copying? Duplicating? What's the diff and why should I care?

True, copying and duplicating a file are the same thing. In both instances, you have two copies of the same file, each containing the same information. The difference is only in the vernacular: A duplicated file is usually on the same disk in the same directory and has a different name. A copied file is usually created on another disk or in another directory.

Note that you can copy a file with a different name, which is like duplicating it. For example:

```
C> COPY SAMPLE1.DOC A:SAMPLE2.DOC
```

Above, SAMPLE1DOC is copied to drive A — but it's given a new name, SAMPLE2DOC.

Copying a file to you

A short form of the COPY command can be used to copy a file from another disk or directory to your current directory. In this format of the COPY command you only specify the original file (which cannot already be in the current directory).

For example, suppose the file DREDGE is located on drive A. To copy that file to drive C (your current drive), you would type:

```
C> COPY A:DREDGE
```

To copy the BORING.DOC file from the \WORK\YAWN subdirectory to your current location, you can type:

```
C> COPY \WORK\YAWN\BORING.DOC
```

✔ Copying a file in this manner only works when you're not in the directory containing the file. Of course, after the COPY command, the file will be in the current directory.

✔ You cannot duplicate files using this command; you can only copy them from elsewhere to the current directory. If you try this command and the file is in the current directory, you'll get a "File cannot be copied onto itself" error.

✔ For more information on directories, refer to Chapter 13; information on the "current directory" is offered in the section "Finding the current directory" in that same chapter.

Copying a group of files

You can copy more than one file with a single COPY command. This is done by using wildcards.

The * wildcard replaces a group of characters in a filename.

The ? wildcard replaces a single character in a filename.

For example, if you want to copy all files with the DOC extension to drive A, you would use the following command:

```
C> COPY *.DOC A:
```

Above, the *.DOC matches all files ending in DOC: BABY.DOC, EYE.DOC, EAR.DOC, WHATSUP.DOC, etc. Note that both the period and the DOC ending are specified after the asterisk. They are copied to drive A, as noted by the A: above.

To copy all files, use the *.* (star-dot-star, which is less of a tongue twister than asterisk-period-asterisk) wildcard:

```
C> COPY *.* A:
```

A common use of this command is when copying all the files from the floppy drive to your hard drive:

```
C> COPY A:*.*
```

Above, you're copying the files "to you" from the floppy drive. (Refer to the previous section for the gory details.) The ? wildcard is used to represent a single character in a filename. For example, assume you had ten chapters in a book, named CHAP01.DOC through CHAP10.DOC. You can copy them to drive A using the following command:

```
C> COPY CHAP??.DOC A:
```

✔ For more information on wildcards, refer to Chapter 14, the section starting "Wildcards (or, poker was never this much fun)."

✔ Refer to Chapter 13 for information on the current directory and pathnames.

Deleting a file

Deleting a file is done with the DEL command. You follow DEL with the name of the file you want to delete:

```
C> DEL SAMPLE.BAK
```

There is no feedback; the DEL command is like the midnight assassin, silent and quick.

If the file you're deleting isn't in the current directory, you must specify a drive letter and colon or a pathname:

```
C> DEL A:MEMO
```

Above, the file MEMO is deleted from drive A.

```
C> DEL \WP51\DATA\XMASLIST.93
```

Above, the file XMASLIST.93 is deleted from the \WP51\DATA directory.

✔ Never delete any file named COMMAND.COM.

✔ The ERASE command can also be used to delete files. ERASE and DEL are exactly the same command and do the same things. (I know, it's redundant. But that's what you should expect from DOS.)

> ✔ If the file doesn't exist, you'll see a "File not found" error.
>
> ✔ Information on using pathnames is covered in Chapter 13.

Extra verbiage on why you would want to delete files

Deleting a file with the DEL command seems like a drastic thing to do — especially when you've invested all that time in creating the file. But there are reasons. The first is to clean up space. Some files may contain unnecessary copies of information, some files may be old versions or BAK (backup) duplicates. Deleting them gives you more space.

Zapping extra files is also a part of disk maintenance or "housekeeping." If you've ever created a TEMP, KILL, or JUNK file, then you use the DEL command to delete them. (Oh, TEMP, KILL, or JUNK may contain information you had to save to disk, but now no longer need — stuff like today's bets at the track, the rough draft of your letter to your congressperson, or that second copy of the books before the auditor comes.)

Deleting a group of files

To delete more than one file at a time — truly massive, wholesale slaughter — you use the DEL command with wildcards. This can get nasty.

The * wildcard replaces a group of characters in a filename.

The ? wildcard replaces a single character in a filename.

For example, to delete all files with UP as their second part (the extension) you would use the following command:

```
C> DEL *.UP
```

Above, *.UP matches all files ending in UP: FED.UP, SHUT.UP, THROW.UP, etc. Note how both the period and the UP ending are specified after the asterisk.

As with deleting a single file, the feedback from this command is nil. Yes, even as a mass murderer, DEL makes no noise.

An exception to DEL's silence is when you use the *.* wildcard. Since this deletes all files in the directory, something must be said:

```
C> DEL *.*
```

DOS will heed you with the following message:

```
All files in directory will be deleted! Are you sure (Y/N)?
```

Don't be too quick to press Y here. Ask yourself, "Am I certain I want to ruthlessly destroy those innocent files?" Then, with a greedy "yes" gurgling from your lips, press Y and Enter. Boom! The files are gone.

- ✔ For more information on the wildcards, refer to "Wildcards (or, poker was never this much fun)" in Chapter 14.

- ✔ You can also delete groups of files on other disks and in other directories. Wow! Run amok! But be sure to specify the proper locations for the files, disks, and pathnames as needed.

"The file! I cannot kill it!"

Suppose that one day, when you're feeling rather spiteful, you decide to delete that useless CAREBEAR.FOO file. You type the following with wicked staccato fingers:

```
C> DEL CAREBEAR.FOO
```

But upon pressing Enter, you see that DOS tells you "Access denied." Ha! Will that spoil your mood, or what?

Generally speaking, when you see "Access denied" it means someone somewhere doesn't want you to delete the file. There are some very important files on your system. Some may not have names obvious to you. So it's never a good idea to go out stomping on files like a kid through a flower bed. Tsk, tsk, tsk.

Shhh! (Whisper this if you're reading aloud.) If you really want to delete the file, you must first type the following, using the proper filename or wildcard:

```
C> ATTRIB CAREBEAR.FOO -R
```

That's the ATTRIB command, followed by the name of the file, space, then a minus sign (–) and an R. There cannot be a space between the minus and the R.

By pressing Enter, you're removing the "access" protection from the file(s). You can now delete it (or them):

```
C> DEL CAREBEAR.FOO
```

Need I mention it again? Files are protected for a reason. Only use the ATTRIB and –R when you badly want to delete a file.

Undeleting a file

The miracle of DOS 5 is that it allows you to undelete a file you've just — whoops! — deleted. Now I'll be clear about this: Just because you can undelete a file doesn't mean you should be sloppy with the DEL command. But if you ever are sloppy (and who isn't?), then you have the UNDELETE command to save you.

Suppose you've just razed the BUBBLE.POP program. Upon realizing this grievous mistake, you type the following:

```
C> UNDELETE BUBBLE.POP
```

Essentially the UNDELETE command is the opposite of the DEL command. You simply substitute UNDELETE for DEL to snatch the file(s) back.

After pressing Enter, DOS will display some interesting and complex statistics. I have no idea what all that means, but it sure is impressive. (Read it aloud over the phone to a friend and they're certain to think you're a computer genius.)

Some background stuff I shouldn't tell you about ATTRIB

The ATTRIB command is used to modify special features of a file that are called attributes. One of these attributes is the "read-only" attribute. When a file is marked as "read-only," you can only read from the file. Any attempt to modify it, rename it, or delete it will be met with an "Access denied" error.

To make a file or group of files read-only, the ATTRIB command is used with a +R:

```
C> ATTRIB NOKILL.ME +R
```

Above, the file NOKILL.ME will be read-only protected. Of course, the protection offered here is minimal: Any dolt can use the ATTRIB command to remove the read-only protection and delete the file. Go figure.

UNDELETE will display the file's name and whether or not it can be undeleted. If so, you'll be asked if you want to undelete the file. Press Y. Further, you will need to supply the first letter of the filename.

You can also use the UNDELETE command with wildcards. For example:

```
C> UNDELETE *.*
```

You'll see the names of all recoverable files in the directory (or those that match the wildcard you've entered). Press Y to undelete each as you're prompted. You'll have to specify the first letter of each filename.

✔ The sooner you undelete a file, the better. This has nothing to do with time; you can turn off your computer, wait a few weeks, then power it back on again and still be able to undelete the file. However, if you create any new files, copy files, or do any other disk activity, then your chances of a full file recovery are remote.

✔ If you see a message that reads "The data contained in the first cluster of this directory has been overwritten or corrupted" — don't panic. That's DOS's friendly way of telling you the file cannot be undeleted. Sorry, but it happens.

✔ You cannot undelete a file if you've copied over it with the COPY command.

✔ There are several interesting utilities and third-party programs that make file recovery an art form. Refer to your local software dealer for more information or complain to your favorite DOS guru.

✔ For more information on wildcards, refer to Chapter 14; for information on directories refer to Chapter 13.

Additional skippable information

A faster way to undelete files is by specifying the /ALL switch. For example:

```
C> UNDELETE *.* /ALL
```

Above, the UNDELETE command will attempt to rescue all the files (*.*) in the directory. The /ALL switch tells UNDELETE to go ahead and undelete everything — without prompting you Y or N and asking for the first letter of the filename. Instead, each file will be given the pound sign character (#) as its first letter. You can later rename each file on its own if you like.

Moving a file

DOS has no specific file moving command. But, when you come to think of it, moving a file is simply using COPY to make a duplicate, then using DEL to delete the original. That's basically a "move" (which would be, sort of, like paying the movers to move your furniture to the new house and then having them dynamite the old one).

The first step is to copy the file to the new location:

```
C> COPY BEAKENS.VAN A:
```

Above, the file named BEAKENS.VAN is copied to drive A. Now delete the original:

```
C> DEL BEAKENS.VAN
```

The original file is gone, but the copy still exists on drive A. That's moving.

- ✔ For more information on copying files, refer to "Copying a single file" earlier in this chapter.

- ✔ For information on deleting files, refer to "Deleting a file" earlier in this same chapter.

- ✔ Renaming a file is like moving a file in the current directory; you make a duplicate with a new name and delete the original. Refer to "Renaming a file" later in this chapter. Oh. I guess it's next.

Renaming a file

DOS allows you to plaster a new name on a file using the REN command. The file's contents and its location on disk stay the same. Only the name is changed (like they used to do on Dragnet to protect the innocent).

For example, to rename CHAPTER1.WP to CHAPTER01.WP you can use the following:

```
C> REN CHAPTER1.WP CHAP01.WP
```

The old name is specified first, followed by a space, then the new name. No sweat.

If the file isn't in the current directory, you must specify a drive letter or pathname. However, the new filename doesn't need all that extra info:

```
C> REN B:\STUFF\YONDER THITHER
```

Above, the file named YONDER is on the disk in drive B, in the STUFF subdirectory. It's given the new name THITHER by the REN command.

Renaming a group of files is possible — but tricky. No, the REN command cannot rename all files (*.*) individually. It can, however, rename a group of files all at once. For example:

```
C> REN *.OLD *.BAK
```

Above, all files ending in OLD are renamed. They'll keep their original filenames, but each will be given the new second name BAK.

- ✔ REN has a longer version, RENAME. Both are the same command; you can use either, though REN is quicker to type.

- ✔ For information on file naming rules, refer to "Name that file!" in Chapter 14.

- ✔ You can only use wildcards with the REN command when you're renaming a group of matching files. Generally speaking, the same wildcard must be used for both the original filename and the new name. For more information on wildcards, refer to "Wildcards (or, poker was never this much fun)" in Chapter 14.

- ✔ Information about accessing other disks and pathnames is covered in Chapter 13.

Printing a text file

DOS has a command named PRINT, but that command is just way too weird to cover in this book. Instead, you can print any text file using the COPY command. Yeah, it sounds odd — but it works. First a few rules:

1. Try the TYPE command on the file first. If you can read it, then it will print okay. If you can't read the file (it looks "Greek"), then the same garbage you see on your screen will be sent to your printer. That's probably not what you want.

2. Before printing the file, make sure your printer is connected, "on-line," and ready to print. Refer to "Going on-line" in Chapter 9 if you need help.

3. Use the COPY command to copy the file from your disk to the printer:

```
C> COPY PRINTME PRN
```

PRN is the name of your printer. After pressing Enter, DOS will make a copy of the file PRINTME (above) on your printer.

4. If a full page doesn't print, you'll need to eject it from your printer. This is done by typing the following command:

```
C> ECHO ^L > PRN
```

That's the ECHO command, followed by a space and then the Ctrl-L character. Produce that character by holding down the Ctrl (control) key and typing an L — do not type in "^L" (the hat and L characters). Then type a space, the greater-than symbol (>), another space, and then PRN. Press Enter and a sheet of paper will magically eject from your printer. Neat-o.

✔ Text files typically have a name that ends in TXT. The most common text file is named READ.ME or README. Some files ending in DOC are text files, but that's not always the case; type the file first to be sure.

✔ It's usually best to print a file using the application that created it. DOS can only print text files.

✔ For more information on the TYPE command and looking at files, refer to "Looking at files" in Chapter 1.

✔ General information about using a printer with your computer is covered in Chapter 9.

Cosmic drivel about ECHO ^L > PRN

The ECHO command is DOS's "display me" command. Anything you type after ECHO is echoed to the screen. This command is primarily used in batch files, which are quasi-programs written by advanced DOS users who think they're really cool.

Ctrl-L is a special control character, actually a single character you produce by pressing the Ctrl-L key combination. On the screen, this character may look like the ankh symbol, but every computer printer sees this as the direct command to toss out a sheet of paper. For laser printers, that's often the only way you can see your work.

The cryptic (and very cryptic) > PRN is what's called I/O redirection, and it's leagues beyond what's in this book. Basically, the greater-than sign tells DOS to send its output, the Ctrl-L in this case, to another device, something other than the screen.

The named device is PRN, the printer. In the end, the eject-page command (Ctrl-L) is sent to the printer (> PRN) via the ECHO command. And they all live happily ever after.

Chapter 4
Easier DOS:
The DOS 5 Shell

. . . .

In this chapter...

▶ How to start the DOS shell.

▶ How to quit the DOS shell.

▶ How to change the display in DOS shell.

▶ How to move between different parts of the shell.

▶ How to copy files in the shell.

▶ How to delete files in the shell.

▶ How to move files in the shell.

▶ How to rename files in the shell.

▶ How to find a lost file using the shell.

▶ How to change from one drive to another.

▶ How to change from one directory to another.

▶ How to run programs in the shell.

. . . .

*D*OS versions 4.0 and later come with an easy-to-use (yeah, right) *shell program*. The word shell means that the program insulates you from the cold prickly DOS, keeping you in a warm fuzzy graphic environment, supposedly making life easier on you. Inside the shell you can do all of the things you could do outside the shell, though everything's easier thanks to the pretty graphics and fun shell-like ways of doing things. Okay, so it may not be that easy, but it's free with DOS, so who's complaining?

Remember that all of these functions are particular to the DOS shell program, specifically the one that comes with DOS version 5.0 and later. Refer to the other chapters mentioned for information on using plain old DOS to do similar chores.

Starting the DOS shell

To start the DOS shell you type its name at the DOS prompt:

```
C> DOSSHELL
```

Press Enter, and in a few moments you'll see the DOS shell program on your screen.

The DOS shell was installed when your computer was first set up for DOS. If you see a "Bad command or file name" error, then your system was probably set up without the shell. Refer to your system administrator or favorite DOS guru if you would like the DOS shell installed on your PC.

Do you have a mouse?

Let's be serious here: You can only get the most from the DOS shell program if you have a mouse. Things can be done without a mouse, but the shell was really designed with a mouse in mind.

- If you don't have a mouse, buy one. If you can't afford that, force someone else to buy a mouse for you.

- This same, flawless logic also holds true for Windows; you need a mouse to run Windows.

Quitting the DOS shell

To quit the DOS shell and return back to plain old command-line DOS, press the F3 key.

You can also press the Alt-F4 key to quit the shell.

If you have a mouse (and you should), you can click on the File menu, then select the Exit menu item.

If you don't have a mouse, but would like to use the menus, press Alt-F to "drop down" the File menu, then type an X to quit the shell.

Figure 4-1:
Clicking the
"Display . . ."
item in the
Options menu
gives you the
Screen
Display Mode
from which
you can
choose the
type of screen
display for the
DOS shell.

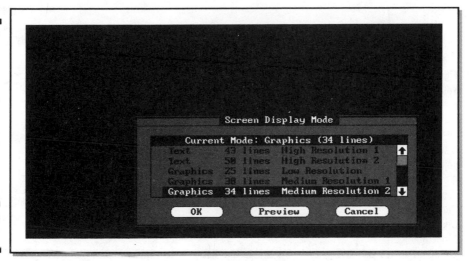

✔ The F3 key is compatible with the DOS shell program offered with DOS
version 4.0, and with an older shell program called the Microsoft Manager.
The Alt-F4 key is compatible with Microsoft's Windows, used there to close
a Window or to quit the Windows environment.

✔ Refer to Chapter 8, "Keyboard and Mouse (or, Where is the "Any" Key?)"
for more information on using a mouse and mouse terminology.

Changing the display in the DOS shell

You can look at the DOS shell in a number of ways, all depending on the
horsepower of your computer's graphics. (Refer to Chapter 7 for more information on graphics and the PC's screen.)

Use the mouse to select the Options menu by clicking on it. Then click on the
item titled "Display . . ." If you don't have a mouse, pres Alt-O, then type a D.
What you see will be the Screen Display Mode dialog box, as shown in Figure
4-1. Use the arrow keys to select a type of display, either text or graphics, or
based on the number of lines of information on the screen. Click on the OK
button or press Enter to see your new screen (see Figures 4-2 and 4-3).

Another way to change the way the shell looks is to change its layout. This is
done with the View menu. You activate the View menu by clicking on it with
the mouse, or by pressing Alt-V. Then you can select from five views (see
Figure 4-4).

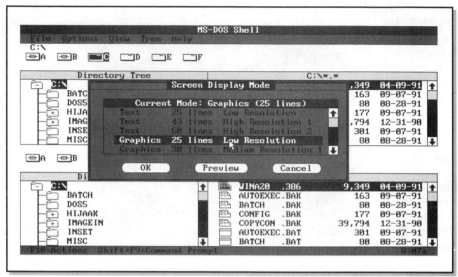

Figure 4-2:
You can change your screen to a 25-line display by selecting that option in the Screen Display Mode dialog box.

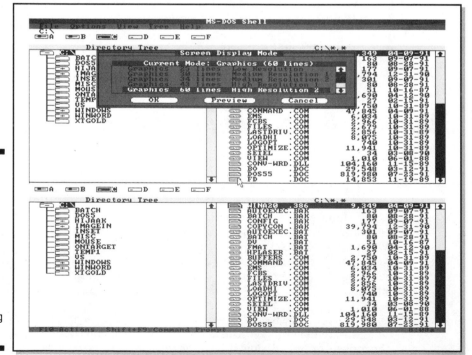

Figure 4-3:
Example of what a 60-line display looks like when that option is selected in the Screen Display Mode dialog box.

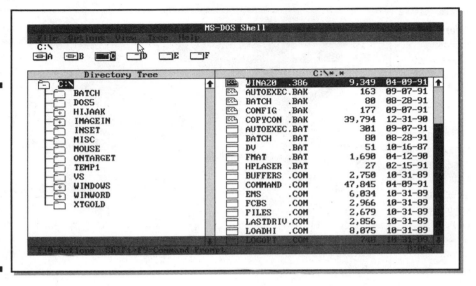

Figure 4-4:
What the
screen
looks like in
Single File
List view
where only
files and
directories
are
displayed.

✔ Single File List: shows only files and directories.

✔ Dual File Lists: shows two sets of files and directories (good for copying and comparing information; see Figure 4-5).

✔ All Files: shows only files (good for locating lost files).

✔ Program/File Lists: shows files, directories, and a list of programs to run.

✔ Program List: shows only programs to run.

Moving between the different parts of the shell

You only work in one area of the shell at a time, which can be frustrating because your eyeballs may be trained on one part of the screen and yet the computer is "using" another part. Major pain.

To move between each of the different *panels* in the shell, click the mouse in the appropriate one, or press the Tab key until that area's panel is highlighted.

Figure 4-5:
You can
change the
layout of the
shell by
clicking on the
view menu and
selecting from
5 views. In this
case, Dual File
Lists has been
selected,
which displays
two sets of
files and
directories.

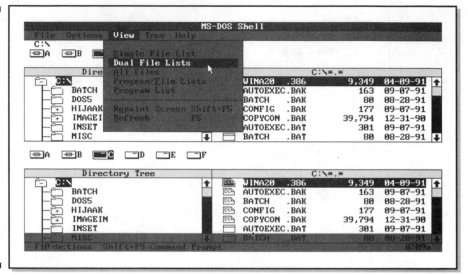

Working with files

To work with a file using the shell you must first select the file. This is done by clicking on the file's name using the mouse. That highlights the file's name, letting you know that it's selected.

Copying files

To copy a file using the mouse, first select it by clicking on it. Next, hold down the Ctrl key and drag the file to the proper subdirectory or disk drive as shown on the screen. A confirmation dialog box will appear; click in the Yes button's area.

To copy a file using the keyboard, highlight it by pressing the spacebar. Press the F8 key to copy the file. The Copy File dialog box will appear; enter the subdirectory destination for the file.

✔ Remember that to copy files using the mouse, you must first press the Ctrl key. If you forget to do this, the file is moved and the original file will be deleted.

✔ Copying files in DOS is covered in Chapter 3, "File Fitness (Stuff You Do with Files)."

Deleting files

To delete a file, highlight it and then press the Del (delete) key. A dialog box appears, asking if you really want to delete the file. Select the Yes button if so, otherwise press Esc.

Deleting files using DOS is covered in Chapter 3, "File Fitness (Stuff You Do with Files)."

Moving files

To move a file, highlight it, then drag the file to the destination directory or drive on the screen. A confirmation dialog box will appear, asking if you want to move the file. Click in the "Yes" area if so, otherwise press the Esc key to cancel.

If you lack a mouse, then you can copy a file by first selecting it and then pressing the F7 key. Type in a new destination for the file, then press Enter.

Moving a file using the DOS command line is covered in Chapter 3, "File Fitness (Stuff You Do with Files)."

Renaming a file

To rename a file, highlight it, then select the File menu's Rename item: Click on the File menu using the mouse, then click on the Rename item. Or if you only have a keyboard, press Alt-F, then N.

A dialog box appears, giving you the file's original name, plus a cute little box in which to type the new name.

✔ Refer to "Name that file!" in Chapter 14 for more information on renaming a file; Chapter 3 has a section titled "Renaming a file" for the basic information on using the REN (rename) command.

✔ You can also use the shell to rename a subdirectory — which is something you cannot do at the DOS prompt. Simply highlight the directory name, then choose Rename from the File menu just as described above. Note that the same rules for renaming a file apply to a subdirectory.

Finding a lost file

Finding a lost file in the shell is a snap — far easier than any other way of finding a lost file. Here's what you do:

Click on the File menu using the mouse, then select the Search item. If you don't have a mouse, press Alt-F, then H.

Type in the name of the file you want to find. Press Enter. After a moment, the search results will be displayed. The file will be listed using its full pathname, which will show you where on the disk it's located. Press Esc to return to the shell.

✔ If the file isn't found, then you'll see the message "No files match file specifier." Odds are pretty good that the file isn't on that drive. Consider trying another drive; refer to "Changing from one drive to another" below for details, then try the file search again.

✔ Refer to "Finding a lost file" in Chapter 14 for methods of locating lost files without using the DOS shell.

Changing from one drive to another

The shell shows you a list of disk drives near the top of the screen. Floppy drive A (and B, if you have it) is listed first, followed by drive C and any other hard drives attached to your PC.

To change, or *log* from one drive to another, press the Ctrl key plus the letter of that drive. For example, to log to drive D, type CTRL-D; to log to drive C, type CTRL-C.

✔ You can also log to another drive by double-clicking on it with the mouse.

✔ Refer to the section, "Changing drives" in Chapter 1 for basic information on logging to another disk drive.

Changing from one directory to another

To switch directories, you must make sure the Directory Tree panel is active. Click in that panel using the mouse, or press the Tab key until that area's title is highlighted.

You select a directory by using the cursor keys, or by clicking once on a directory's name using the mouse. Any files in that directory are shown in the File panel to the right of the Directory Tree panel.

If the directory has a plus by it, then it has subdirectories. Click on the directory using the mouse or press the Plus (+) key to open up the directory and list its subdirectories.

> ✔ Refer to "Changing directories" in Chapter 1 for some basic information on changing directories; Chapter 13 has lots of information on why and how directories are used.

Running programs in the shell

There are three ways to run a program in the DOS shell. The first is to locate the COM or EXE program file in the list of files, highlight that file, then press the Enter key to run the program.

The second way is to select the Run menu item in the File menu. Click on the word File then select Run using the mouse, or press Alt-F and then type R to select the Run item. Then type the name of the program to run in the box provided.

The third way is possible only if someone has configured the shell to show a list of programs at the bottom of the screen in the Main panel. Click in that area using the mouse or press the Tab key until that area is highlighted. Then highlight the name of a program to run and press the Enter key.

> ✔ You may need someone else to set up the shell to contain a list of programs to run on your computer. This is one of those things beyond the scope of what you need to know, so bug your computer manager or a friend into doing it for you. It really does make running things convenient.

> ✔ Refer to Chapter 21 for some other programs that will make life easier for people who hate DOS. Not all of them are free, like the DOS shell. But many of them are easier to use.

Section Two
The Non-Nerd's Guide to PC Hardware

The 5th Wave   **By Rich Tennant**

ITS NOT THAT IT DOESN'T WORK AS A COMPUTER, IT JUST WORKS BETTER AS A PAPERWEIGHT.

In this section...

This is the kind of hardware you won't find in your True Value store. Nope, it's floppy drives, CPUs, EPROMS, cables, and really nerdy stuff. The sad part is, you just can't use a computer without encountering hardware. And you need to know the terminology so when the manual says "Plug this into your mouse port," you will know not to take it personally.

There's no need to go into a technical description of the hardware in your PC. But as a human being, you'll very often have to touch that hardware, frequently at the bequest of some manual or a loftier human who knows such things. This part of the book describes the various hardware goodies associated with a PC, the terms you encounter, and how everything fits into the "big picture."

As a general definition before getting started, you should know that PC hardware is anything you can touch in a computer system, the physical part. Or to put it another way, when you drop hardware on your foot, you will doubtless say "ouch."

Chapter 5
Your Basic Hardware — What it Is and Why

· ·

In this chapter...

► Definitions and explanations of the various parts of a computer system.

► How a microprocessor fits into the "big picture."

► What a math coprocessor is and what it can do for you.

► Where your disk drives are located and what they're called.

► How a port is used to connect interesting external devices to your PC.

► How a printer port works.

► How a serial port works.

► What a modem is and what it can do for you.

► How your PC keeps track of the date and time.

· ·

Human languages offer interesting insight into the thought process. For example, in German it's entirely possible to construct a single, albeit long, verb that means (roughly) please don't spit on the floor. It can be very precise. On the other hand, though Arabic is a highly poetic language, it lacks facilities for technical descriptions; describing a disk drive is basically "the machine inside the machine." I like that, myself.

This chapter defines a few common, German-like things associated with your computer. It describes them using an Arabic-like poetry, without the complex geometric math required to understand the German-like definitions.

The nerd's eye view

Time for the big picture. Note the items listed in the table in Figure 5-1 and their locations. Further, make sure you can identify each on your PC.

Item to Find	Typical nerd description
Monitor	Video display, or CRT (Cathode Ray Tube)
Keyboard	Manually dexterous input mechanism, or "101 Enhanced"
Computer box	System unit, or combative FFC Class B approved anti-EMF regulated shield with titanium white finish
Floppy drive A	Primary disk-based I/O storage device with removable media, or floppy drive A
Floppy drive B	Secondary disk-based I/O storage device with removable media, or floppy drive B (if present)
Hard drive(s) C	Primary fixed disk, non-removable, high-speed, maximum-capacity, hermetically sealed ESDI 960 Mach 3 whopper
Printer	Dot matrix, thermal, impact, or (preferably) laser

Figure 5-1:
Basic hardware components of a computer system.

Inside the computer box are various other items: Stuff you can't see because, well, it's inside the box. Figure 5-2 lists the items you may be able to locate there if, like Superman, you had X-ray vision.

TIP

✔ Generally speaking, the first floppy drive (A) will be on top, and drive B will be on the bottom. But this isn't always so; some systems may have A on the bottom. My advice is to label each drive using a sticker or one of those letter-puncher devices. Don't just label them "A" and "B" either, label them "Drive A" and "Drive B" or, better still, "A:" and "B:" (which is how DOS refers to them). You might also want to label their capacity: 360K, 720K, 1.2MB, or 1.4MB.

✔ For more information on computer memory, refer to Chapter 6.

✔ The back of your PC contains lots of connections for various devices and other goodies you can hook up to a PC. For example, both the printer and your monitor hook up to your PC's rump. For information on other things you can plug in back there, refer to "What are ports?" later in this chapter.

The microprocessor

The computer's brain is called a microprocessor. Like most highways, a computer's microprocessor is named after famous numbers. There's the 8088/8086, 80286, 80386, and 80486. Generally, the bigger the number, the faster and more powerful your computer (and the more you paid for it).

Item inside	Typical nerd description
Memory	RAM, or memory chips or banks, or SIMMS's
Main circuitry board	The motherboard, system board
The computer's brain	The microprocessor, or the Central Processing Unit (C.P.U.), or by its number/name
Expansion cards	ISA bus expansion daughterboards
Power supply	210 Watt, U/L listed, AC/DC power converter
Other stuff	Other stuff

Figure 5-2:
The stuff you can't see inside the computer box.

Telling whether or not you have one microprocessor or another inside your computer box is a job best left up to the gods. The only time this should be a concern of yours is when some piece of software requires one microprocessor and you have another. You'll know this, of course, because the program won't run.

Another issue directly dependant on the type of microprocessor you have is memory, specifically extra memory in your PC. There are two types of extra memory, *extended* and *expanded* memory. Refer to "Expanded memory" and "Extended memory" in Chapter 6 for more information.

✔ You can buy software programs that will tell you the kind of microprocessor you have in your computer, as well as what type of video display you have and other information that's not apparent to most people. Such programs include Quarterdeck's Manifest, Ashton-Tate's Control Room, Norton's SysInfo, and PC Tool's SI (System Information) program.

✔ For all intents and purposes, the i486 systems are identical to the 80386 systems. Any PC software you buy for the 386 won't know the difference if you're using an i486. Okay, there may be the rare i486-only software out there, but chances are it works in such a cryptic capacity that using it would make your head explode.

The differences between an 80386, 80386DX, and 386SX

There is actually a '386 family of microprocessors. The big chip, the one with all the options and extras, is the 80386DX, which can just be called an 80386 or 386. Its little brother is the 80386SX or 386SX (its nickname). The 386SX is a cheaper alternative to the full-on DX chip, offering all the performance but only about half the power (and half the calories of the bigger chip). It's like the equivalent of a four cylinder model of a V8 car; it will get you there, but not as fast and it won't cost as much money.

The math coprocessor

A computer's microprocessor is really nothing more than a very fast calculator. For major mathematical calculations, the typical PC microprocessor can be a real slug. A companion chip is available, however, which is the electronic equivalent of giving your microprocessor its own adding machine. The chip is called a math *coprocessor*.

The math coprocessor just does math. Figuratively speaking, software can detect the presence of a math coprocessor and send off all the complex mathematics to that chip, relieving the main microprocessor of the tedious arithmetic tasks. The software still works without the math coprocessor, but it will run much slower.

✔ Math coprocessors have numbers, just like microprocessors. The difference is that while microprocessor numbers typically end in 6, the math coprocessor will be the same number, but end in 7. (It's the union that makes up those rules.)

✔ Not every application can use a math coprocessor. Typically, spreadsheets and graphic design packages are the only types of programs that will run faster with a coprocessor installed. Refer to your software package to see if it minds a math coprocessor.

✔ Math coprocessors are expensive, so only buy them if you painfully need them. Then force someone else to install it for you.

✔ The 80486, or i486 chip, has a built-in math coprocessor. There is no companion 80487 chip.

Disk drives

Disk drives are storage devices. There are two types: floppy drives, which use removable floppy disks for storage, and hard drives, which typically store information on nonremovable disks. The information stored on a disk are the files you see with the DIR command (refer to "The DIR command" in Chapter 1).

Under DOS, your beloved disk operating system, disk drives are referred to by letters. The first floppy drive on all PCs is called drive A, or the A drive. The second floppy drive, whether or not you have one, is drive B. The first hard drive in any computer system is almost always drive C, with additional drives given letters of the alphabet from D on up through drive Z.

For the floppy drives, there are two popular sizes. These sizes refer to the dimensions of the disks you slide into the floppy drives: 5 ¼-inch for the 5 ¼-inch square disks; and 3 ½-inch for the 3 ½-inch square hard-shelled disks.

Hard drives are internal mechanisms. On most PCs you cannot see the hard drive. If you can see it, it looks like a floppy drive but with tiny air holes instead of a disk slit.

On each disk drive is a *drive light*. The light is on only when DOS is accessing the disk, either reading or writing information. It's important that you do not remove a floppy disk while that light is on.

   ✔ Refer to "Changing disks" in Chapter 1 for instructions on removing and ejecting disks from floppy drives.

   ✔ Most of today's PCs come with both 5 ¼-inch and 3 ½-inch sized drives. Drive A is typically the 5 ¼-inch drive, but that's not always the case.

What are ports?

The term port refers to a "hole" in the back of the computer, or an inexpensive table wine. You can plug one of a variety of external devices with which the computer can communicate into a port.

Presently there are two popular kinds of ports in a PC: The *printer* port and the *serial* port.

   ✔ Other external devices, such as the keyboard and monitor, are each connected via their own special ports. Sometimes external disk drives are added, again via some form of unique port.

   ✔ A special type of port is available on some PCs. Technically, this port is the *analog-to-digital*, or A-to-D, port. A variety of scientific and "real-world" monitoring devices and such can be plugged into that port. However, most people refer to this port by the device hooked up to it 99 times out of 100: the joystick port.

✓ There is no visual clue to determine which port is which. (Well, what did you expect?) Even the experts have to struggle through trial and error sometimes; ports on a PC do look similar. If you ever find out for sure, label them.

The printer port

Mysteriously enough, the printer port is where you plug in your printer. The printer cable has one connector that plugs into the printer and a second that plugs into the computer. Both connectors are different, so it's impossible to plug in a printer backward.

✓ For more information on printers, refer to Chapter 9.

✓ Printer ports are also called *parallel* ports or (to old-time nerds) *Centronics* ports. People who refer to ports in this manner should be slapped.

✓ Other devices can be connected to a printer port, though typically the only one you'll have is the printer. Examples of other devices are voice synthesizers, network connections, external hard drives, extra keyboards, and choo-choo train sets.

The serial port

The serial port is far more flexible than the printer port; it supports a variety of interesting items, which is why it's generically called a serial port instead of a this- or that-port.

Port deciphering hints you may skip

Ports connect to external devices by means of cables. These cables have connectors on both ends that are shaped like the letter "D." From this we get the term "D-shell" connectors.

Your typical monitor port has a 15-line D-shell connector, whereas your typical serial port has a 9-line D-shell connector. This isn't worth mentioning, save for the fact that both D-shell connectors are the same size and could be easily confused.

The parallel port uses a 25-line D-shell connector. On some older systems, the serial port uses the same 25-line D-shell connector. This was done purely for spite, and it caused many PC owners countless hours of agony discovering which port was which.

You'll most often plug the following items into a serial port: a modem; serial printer; scanner or other input device; or just about anything that requires two-way communications. Serial ports are far more flexible than printer ports, which is why most computers come with two of them.

- ✔ A serial port can also be called a modem port.

- ✔ Serial ports are also called RS-232 ports. No, that's not a Radio Shack part number. Instead, it refers to Recommended Standard 232, which I assume is the 232nd standard The Committee came up with that year. Busy guys.

- ✔ You can plug a computer mouse into a serial port. In that case, the mouse is called a *serial mouse*. The mouse can also be plugged into its own port, called — shockingly enough — a *mouse port*. (Refer to your local pet store for more information on mice, or turn to Chapter 8.)

Definitely skip over this stuff

Serial ports are complex in that you must configure them. Printer ports are set up to work in a specific manner and require no configuration. But with a serial port, you must configure both the port on your computer as well as the device with which you're communicating.

There are four items you need to configure on a serial port: the *speed* at which the port operates; the *data word format*, or the size of the bytes you're sending; the number of *stop bits*; and the *parity*. This is only a real hassle when you need to connect a serial printer (refer to "The serial connection" in Chapter 9). To get everything working right you must occasionally make a full moon sacrifice to the Unix god, or sing *Zippity Doo Da* while holding your nose and hopping on one foot.

Modems

The most common device to plug into a serial port is a *modem*. A modem is a device which takes the digital information from your computer and translates it into audio signals that can be sent over common phone lines. Using the modem, you can send information to another computer by calling its modem on the phone.

You run a modem with communications software. It controls the modem, dials up other computers, sends information, and does just about everything in a complex and confusing manner. (Seriously, communications software is perhaps the most consistently cryptic of any application.)

There are two types of modems: internal and external. The internal modems sit inside your computer, snugly wedged into an expansion slot. External modems sit outside the computer and must be connected via a serial port.

Definitions to ignore

Modem is a contraction of the words modulator-demodulator. Also, there are more modem jokes in the computer world than anything else, typically "How many modem do you want?"

The speed of a modem is measured in *bits per second,* or BPS. It's often referred to as *baud,* though that term is technically incorrect. There's no reason to bring this up, other than I'm granting you license to correct anyone who refers to BPS as a "baud rate."

The date and time

Most computers come with an internal clock. The clock is battery operated, which allows it to keep track of the time day or night whether or not the PC is plugged in.

To check or change the current time, use the TIME command. Type the word TIME at the DOS prompt and DOS responds with what it thinks is the current time. For example:

```
C> TIME
Current time is 11:13:55.92
Enter new time:
```

Type in the new time using the hour:minutes format; there's no need to enter seconds or hundredths of a second. (And if you work for the government, there's no need to enter the minutes value either.) If the given time shown is close to correct, just press Enter to keep it. Don't worry — you won't reset the clock to 12:00 a.m. if you do this.

The DATE command is used to view or change the current date. It works like the TIME command:

```
C> DATE
Current date is Mon 8-05-1991
Enter new date (mm-dd-yy):
```

Type in the new date using the format indicated.

The date and time you enter is used by DOS when it creates or updates a file. The date and time is then seen in the directory listing along with each file. If you just want to see the current date or time, press Enter when you're asked to enter the new date or time. Pressing Enter doesn't alter the date or time. (Refer to "The DIR command" in Chapter 1 for more information on the directory listing.)

✔ If the clock's battery goes dead, you'll need to replace it. For an AT-type of computer system, when the clock dies your computer may not start. Before you become incensed, refer to "The computer has lost track of the time!" in Chapter 15.

✔ If you have an earlier 8088/8086 system, it may have a different type of clock/timer installed. You may need to run a special utility program to permanently change or set the date and time. The DOS DATE and TIME commands won't affect your internal clock.

✔ The format for the date and time varies depending on how your computer is set up. DOS uses a date and time format based upon your country or region. This book assumes the typical (and I'll agree, backwards) USA method of listing the date.

✔ Who cares if the computer knows what day it is? Well, since your files are time- and date-stamped, you can figure things out, like which is a later version of two similar files or two files with the same name on different disks. Kind of vague, aren't I? Well, your tech support person can use the info to save your skin sometimes, how's that? It's worth keeping your PC abreast of the times.

Chapter 6
RAM
(or, Memory, the Way We Were)

• •

In this chapter...

▶ What memory does and how it fits into your computer system.

▶ How much memory you need to run your programs.

▶ Which terms are used to describe various amounts of memory.

▶ How conventional memory is used.

▶ What the 640K "barrier" is and why it's so annoying.

▶ How upper memory is used.

▶ How expanded memory is used.

▶ How extended memory is used.

▶ How to upgrade memory on your PC.

• •

In the PC land of Oz, the Scarecrow would be singing, "If I only had some RAM...." Memory, or random access memory (RAM), is a storage place in a computer, just like disk space. Unlike disk storage, memory is the only place inside the computer where the real work gets done. Obviously, the more memory you have the more work you can do. But not only that, having more memory means the computer is capable of grander tasks, such as working with graphics, animation, sound, and music, and your PC will remember everyone it meets without ever having to look twice at their name tag.

This chapter is about memory inside your computer — RAM, as it's called in the nerdier circles. Every computer needs memory, but sadly, life just isn't that simple. There are different kinds of memory — different flavors, different fashions for the different seasons. This chapter goes into all that.

Don't forget memory

All computers need memory. That's where the work gets done. The microprocessor is capable of storing information inside itself, but only so much. The excess is stored in memory. For example, when you create a document using your word processor, each character you type is placed into a specific location in memory. Once there, the microprocessor doesn't need to access it again unless you're editing, searching or replacing, or doing something active to the text.

Once something is created in memory — a document, spreadsheet, or graphic picture — it's *saved* to disk. Your disk drives provide long-term storage for information. Then, when you need to access the information again, you *load* it back into memory from disk. Once it's there, the microprocessor can again work on that information.

The only nasty thing about memory is that it's volatile. When you turn off the power, the contents of memory go poof! This is okay if you've saved to disk, but if you haven't, everything is lost. Even a reset will zap the contents of memory. So always save (if you can) before you reset or turn off your PC.

How much memory you need

The amount of memory you need depends on two things. The first, and most important, is the memory requirement of your software. Some programs, such as spreadsheets and graphics applications, require lots of memory. For example, Borland International's Quattro Pro says — right on the box — that it needs 512K of RAM plus it can use up to 8MB of extra memory, just because!

The second, and more limiting, factor is cost. Memory costs money. It's not as expensive as it was back in the old stone tablet days of computing, but it still costs a lot. That 8MB of extra memory that Quattro Pro would like could cost you as much as $500. (That's almost $3,500 in dog dollars!)

Generally speaking, all computers should have at least 640K of *conventional* or *DOS* memory. This memory is the most important.

Any extra memory you have in your computer is a bonus. Extra memory comes in the form of *expanded* or *extended* memory. You may need to buy a special piece of hardware to get this extra memory into your PC.

- For more information on memory terms, refer to the next section; for information on expanded or extended memory, refer to those sections later in this chapter.

- If your applications need more memory, you'll have to buy it. The programs just won't run without it (or will run sluggishly). Refer to "Upgrading memory" later in this chapter.

Term	Abbr	About	Actual
Byte		1 byte	1 byte
Kilobyte	K or KB	1,000 bytes	1,024 bytes
Megabyte	M or MB	1,000,000 bytes	1,048,576 bytes
Gigabyte	G or GB	1,000,000,000 bytes	1,073,741,824 bytes

Figure 6-1:
How memory quantities measure up.

> ✔ If a program keeps flashing that red "MEM" at you, pull out a large caliber sidearm and shoot the computer. Or refer to "Upgrading memory" in this chapter.

Memory terms to ignore

Many interesting terms orbit the memory planet. The most basic of these terms refer to the quantity of memory (see Figure 6-1).

Memory is measured by the *byte*. Think of a byte as a single character, a letter in the middle of a word. For example, the word "spatula" is seven bytes long.

A whole page of text is about 1,000 bytes. To make this a handy figure to know, computer nerds refer to 1,000 bytes as a *kilobyte*, or one K or KB. (Actually, 1K is equal to 1,024 bytes, probably because 1,024 is two to the tenth power. Computers love the number two.)

The term *megabyte* refers to 1,000K, or one million bytes. The character M (or MB) is used to indicate megabyte, so 8M means eight megabytes of memory. (Actually, one megabyte is 1,024K, which equals somewhat over one million bytes of information; the actual amount is mind boggling.)

Further than the megabyte is the *gigabyte*. As you can guess, this is one billion bytes or about 1,000 megabytes. The *terabyte* is one trillion bytes, or enough RAM to bring down the power on your block when you boot the PC.

Just in case you didn't know, RAM stands for random access memory. It doesn't mean anything useful.

A specific location in memory is called an *address*.

Bytes are composed of eight *bits*. The word "bit" is a contraction of *binary digit*. Binary is base two, or a counting system where only ones and zeros are used. Computers count in binary and we group their bits into clusters of eight for convenient consumption as bytes.

The term *giga* is actually Greek and it means "giant."

There is no reason to worry about how much ROM (read-only memory) you have in your computer.

Conventional memory

Normally, any computer would just have "memory." But under DOS, there are different terms to apply to different types of memory. The memory where DOS runs programs is called *conventional memory*. (It may also be called *DOS memory* or *low DOS memory*.)

When a program says it needs 512K or 384K of "memory" in order to run, what it refers to is conventional memory.

Your PC can have up to 640K of conventional memory installed. So the maximum amount means you can run almost any program.

Any extra memory, memory beyond the basic 640K of conventional memory, is either extended or expanded memory. These subjects are covered later in this chapter.

To see how much memory you have in your computer, you can use the MEM command if you're using DOS 4 or 5. (All other versions of DOS use the CHKDSK command.) After typing MEM at the DOS prompt, you'll see a summary of all the memory in your computer. For example:

```
C> MEM
  655360 bytes total conventional memory
  655360 bytes available to MS-DOS
  637984 largest executable program size

3588096 bytes total EMS memory
2260992 bytes free EMS memory

3407872 bytes total contiguous extended memory
0 bytes available contiguous extended memory
12288 bytes available XMS memory
MS-DOS resident in High Memory Area
```

Your output may be different. But note the three categories. First comes conventional memory. The total installed in this system (above) is 655,360 bytes. Divide that by 1,024K and you get 640K. The "largest executable program size" value indicates how much memory is "free" or available for use by DOS and your programs.

The next section summarizes EMS memory in your system, in case you have any installed. EMS memory is the same thing as expanded memory.

The final section summarizes extended memory.

> ✔ If your PC has less than 640K of RAM, you can add memory to boost your total. Refer to "Upgrading memory" later in this chapter.

> ✔ If you don't have DOS 4.0 or later, you can use the CHKDSK program to check your conventional memory. Type CHKDSK at the DOS prompt. The final values displayed indicate the total amount of conventional memory installed and how much is free or available.

The 640K "barrier"

Conventional memory is limited to 640K. That's all the memory DOS has for running programs. Even if you have megabytes of RAM installed in your computer, you only have 640K in which to run programs. Thus, it's called the 640K barrier.

This is kind of dumb, of course; powerful PCs don't need artificial limitations set on them. I mean, they can tear down the Berlin Wall and eliminate communism, but the smartest engineers in all the land can't pass the 640K DOS barrier. Well actually, they did figure out how to pole vault over the 640K barrier. It's complicated and involves installing extra memory.

The solutions for skirting around the DOS barrier involve adding more memory to your system. This is provided in the form of either extended or expanded memory, which are both covered in the following sections.

Most programs can work fine in 640K, though for many newer programs it's a tight fit.

> ✔ The reason for the barrier in the first place is how DOS was designed. Way back in 1982, 640K seemed like plenty. Since programs use memory through DOS as the intermediary, DOS's limits effect everybody.

Upper memory

There is a region of memory just above the 640K barrier. This is called *reserved memory*, though starting with DOS version 5.0, it's become known as *upper memory*.

Upper memory is only used for special advanced computer operations that "load high." If you have an 80386 computer or some type of third-party memory management software, you can take advantage of upper memory. Otherwise, it's a complex subject not worthy of this book.

Expanded memory

Expanded memory is extra memory in a PC. It's not ordinary-conventional memory beyond the 640K barrier, and you must specifically add expanded memory to your system; no computer comes with it automatically.

What's nice about expanded memory is that lots of DOS programs can use it. Graphics programs like it for storing huge, multi-megabyte images. Spreadsheets, such as Quattro Pro, can use up to 8MB of expanded memory to store large spreadsheets.

Since expanded memory isn't a normal part of your computer, it must be added via a special hardware *expansion card*. Further, you'll need to install a special device driver into your CONFIG.SYS file. That device driver provides the link between your software and the expanded memory. (Refer to Chapter 12 for more information on updating CONFIG.SYS.)

✔ If you have an 8088/8086 or 80286 AT-type of computer, you must add a special expanded memory expansion card to your system. That card contains the expanded memory and a disk contains software that you can use to add the memory to your computer.

✔ If you buy an expanded memory card, make sure it's LIM 4.0 "hardware" compatible. That will give you up to 32MB of really useful memory on your system, opening the doors to interesting applications and other fun stuff.

✔ If you have a '386 or greater system, you can convert that computer's extended memory into expanded using special software drivers. The gory details of doing this are best left to the experts.

Trivial technical details

Expanded memory adheres to the Expanded Memory Specification (EMS) as defined by the Lotus-Intel-Microsoft (LIM) standard. If you really want to babble out the acronyms (impress your friends), this is known as the *LIM 4.0 EMS*.

The expanded memory driver you install into your CONFIG.SYS file is typically named EMM.SYS. EMM stands for expanded memory manager.

Extended memory

Extended memory is any memory beyond 640K in an 80286, AT, '386, or later PC. Unlike expanded memory, this memory is simply memory added to those systems; add two megabytes to your AT clone and you have two megabytes of extended memory.

The problem with extended memory is that it cannot be used by DOS, not directly at least. In some instances it can be used for storage, but programs cannot readily access that memory (not like expanded memory). Basically, extended memory remains a white elephant under DOS. At least it's easy to add.

✔ If you have a '386 computer, it's possible to convert extended memory into the more useful expanded memory. This is a technical feat achieved only by the most brave of PC wizards.

✔ If you have a '286 system, any extra memory you have in your computer is all extended. Unlike a '386, you cannot convert it directly into expanded memory. Instead, you must buy an expanded memory card and add memory that way. (Sorry, but I didn't make up these rules.)

✔ If your computer runs an operating system other than DOS (which would make it silly for you to buy this book), then that operating system may use extended memory.

More trivial, extended memory stuff

Extended memory is handled under DOS using an extended memory manager, XMS. It's a standard, like the EMS is for expanded memory. If you see a line in your CONFIG.SYS file that contains the filename HIMEM.SYS, then that's your XMS device driver.

Upgrading memory

Adding memory to your computer is Lego-block simple. The only problem is that the typical Lego block set, say the cool Space Station or Rescue Helicopter set, costs $27. Your computer, on the other hand, may cost one hundred times that much. This is not something to be taken lightly.

STEPS: Upgrading memory involves five complex and boring steps

Step 1. Figure out how much memory you need to add. For example, if you only have 512K in your system, then you need another 128K to give yourself the full 640K of conventional memory. If you need expanded memory, you'll need to buy an expanded memory card for your system — plus memory to put on the card. If you have a '386 system, then all you need is extra memory.

Step 2. Figure out how much memory you can install. This is a technical step. It involves knowing how memory is added to your computer and in what increments. You should simply tell the shop or your favorite technical guru how much you think you need, and they'll tell you how much you can actually have.

Step 3. Buy something. In this case, you buy the memory chips themselves, or you buy the expansion card into which the memory chips are installed.

Step 4. Pay someone else to plug in the chips and do the upgrade. Oh, you can do it yourself, but I'd pay someone else to do it.

Step 5. Gloat. Once you have the memory, brag to your friends about it. Heck, it used to be impressive to say you had the full 640K of RAM. Then came the "I have four megabytes of memory in my '386" round of impressiveness. But today? Anything less than eight megabytes and your kids will roll their eyes at you.

Remember that the primary reason for upgrading memory is to allow programs to run more efficiently on your system. In light of that, only upgrade when your software requires it or won't otherwise run.

✔ If you want to try it yourself, go ahead. Plenty of easy books on the subject of upgrading memory are available, as well as how-to articles in some of the popular magazines. I'd recommend having someone else do it, however.

✔ More information on these memory terms is covered throughout the first part of this chapter.

Chapter 7
The Video Display
(That's the Computer Screen)

● ●

In this chapter...

▶ How color and monochrome monitors are different (beyond the obvious).

▶ How to tell which type of monitor you have.

▶ How to decipher MDA, CGA, EGA, and VGA.

▶ What graphics resolution is and why you should care.

▶ How to change the number of characters DOS displays on the screen.

▶ The reasons why a game may not show up on your screen.

▶ Why the graphics look great in the store, but are sooo boring at home.

● ●

*P*erhaps the most important part of any computer is the screen, or what a nerd would call the video display monitor, or even CRT (cathode ray tube). In the old days, the wrong type of display could really fry your eyeballs. I remember riding down the elevator with bug-eyed people desperately searching for Visine. Today's computer screens are easier to look at, can produce much more stunning displays, and Visine sales are down considerably.

This chapter is about the video display, computer screen, monitor, or the thing you look at when you use a computer. There's really not much to do with the display as far as DOS is concerned, but there are some terms you'll encounter that will bug you to no end. In fact, there's more acronyms associated with the computer screen than anything else (save the government).

Color and mono

There are two types of computer screens. You can have a color display, which is noted for its colorful text and fantastic color graphics, or you can have a monochrome (mono) display, which is noted for its text. Yes, like a black-and-white TV set, monochrome computer screens are fairly dull, even when they're orange or green.

Most programs display only text, which makes a monochrome display an inexpensive — and the best — alternative for some systems. Why pay for color? But if your applications require color, or offer any color features (such as graphics), then a color monitor is an excellent tool.

Whether you have color or mono, you should know that your PC's video system is composed of two different things. There's the monitor, which sits on top or alongside of your computer. That's the obvious part. But lurking inside your PC is the second, more important part. That's the *graphics adapter*. It's the video circuitry that sits inside the computer on an expansion card. That card plugs into your monitor, which gives you the complete video system.

✔ The whole graphics system, both the monitor and graphics adapter, are referred to collectively, usually by the name of the graphics adapter: MDA, CGA, EGA, or VGA.

✔ If you have a monochrome system, it's possible to swap it out for a color system. It's also possible to have both a color and monochrome display in the same PC, though few programs take advantage of this and watching both screens at the same time will make you cross-eyed.

"Which do I have?"

Since this isn't a buyer's guide, there's no reason to babble on about the advantages of color verses monochrome. Your only concern is which you have. Yeah, it's an interesting question, but one that has a definite answer.

To see if you have a color system, type the following command at the DOS prompt:

```
C> MODE 40
```

That's MODE , a space, and the number 40. If after pressing enter the characters on the screen appear twice as wide, then you have color. If the characters on the display don't change, then you have a monochrome display.

To change the characters back to normal, type the following DOS command:

```
C> MODE 80
```

Graph-a-bits soup

The world of PC graphics involves a lot of TLAs, three letter acronyms. These TLAs refer to the history and abilities of the various types of video displays you can have lashed to your PC (see the table in Figure 7-1). The names actually refer to the graphics adapter located inside your computer. But they're used in general to refer to the complete video system.

Other, future standards may come along. But get this: It takes the software developers literally years to come up with programs that take advantage of the new graphics adapter's features. Sure, there's flash in having a fancy graphics display, but why pay the cash when you won't be using that extra hardware?

✔ Each of these color graphics adapters (CGA, EGA, and VGA) are compatible with their predecessors. They are not compatible with their offspring; so you cannot run VGA graphics on your EGA video system, although you can run EGA on VGA.

✔ Yes, there are other unconventional adapters out there. The four listed here are the most popular. But that doesn't rule out some specific stuff or oddball entries.

Figure 7-1:
The various types of video displays and what they can do for you.

MDA	MDA stands for monochrome display adapter. It's the original monochrome display setup used by the first PCs. This type of display offered no graphics, only text. A clone of the MDA, the Hercules or "monographics" adapter, offered graphics. Today, most monochrome systems are Hercules or compatible.
CGA	CGA stands for color graphics adapter. When the PC first appeared, the CGA was the only way you could see color text or have graphics. But the text quality stank. The CGA could really frost over your contacts, so most people opted for MDA or Hercules.
EGA	EGA stands for enhanced graphics adapter. It was a solution that offered crisper text than the CGA plus many more colors. But it was soon overshadowed by the now-popular VGA.
VGA	In its constant effort to keep everyone off their guard, IBM introduced the VGA standard and told the world that it stands for video graphics array. (Not video graphics adapter, as some are prone to call it.) VGA offers superior colors, high resolution graphics, and nice, readable text. A variation on VGA is the SuperVGA, which I recommend as the graphics standard for all DOS computers.

> ✔ Some high resolution graphics systems are only applicable to certain types of software. Computer graphics, CAD, and animation and design are all areas where paying top dollar for your display is worth it. If you're only using basic applications, such as a word processor, you don't need it.

Funky displays

The standard *resolution* for text on your computer's display is 25 rows of 80 columns of text. That gives you about half a page of written text or, if you're looking at a graphics image, from the top of someone's head to just above their navel.

All color displays have the ability to switch between 80 columns and 40 columns. The text gets twice as wide ("fat text," I call it). To make the text 40 columns wide you can use this command:

```
C> MODE 40
```

That's "40" as in 40 columns wide. To switch the display back to 80 columns, you use this command:

```
C> MODE 80
```

What makes a graphics adapter (stuff to skip)

What you get when you pay for a major graphics adapter are more colors and higher resolution. Colors simply refer to the number of colors that can be displayed on the screen at once. For example, the VGA display can show up to 256 different colors, which makes a very vivid — almost photographic — picture.

Resolution refers to the number of dots, or *pixels*, on the screen. The more pixels, the higher the resolution and the finer the image.

With resolution and color there is a trade-off; you can only have more of one or the other, not both. A high resolution display will give you few colors. A lot of colors gives you low resolution. This works, however, because the many colors fool the eye into thinking you have more resolution. (The typical TV has a low resolution but a nearly infinite amount of colors.)

For the text screen, the resolution is measured by the number of characters horizontally (columns) and vertically (rows). The typical color display shows 80 characters across by 25 characters down.

The text colors for all the color adapters remain the same: You can have up to 16 different foreground text colors and eight different background colors. The text on a VGA display is, however, much easier on the eye than the EGA display.

Again, it's "80" for 80 columns wide. That's about it for the width of your screen under DOS. For the number of rows, you have several choices, depending on the kind of display you have. The best way to see if they work is to try them out.

```
C> MODE CON: LINES=43
```

That's the MODE command, a space, then CON and a colon, a space, and finally the word LINES, an equal sign, and 43 — the number of lines you want to display. Press Enter. Type the DIR command a few times to prove to yourself that you now have 43 lines of text on the screen.

```
C> MODE CON: LINES=50
```

This is the same MODE command as above, but the number of lines is increased to 50. This produces a readable display, but the characters are really scrunchy.

To return the display to normal, type:

```
C> MODE CON: LINES=25
```

✔ DOS only supports screen modes for 25, 43, and 50 lines.

✔ If these screen modes don't work, then you may need to install the ANSI.SYS device driver into your CONFIG.SYS file. If you feel the trouble is worth it, have someone else do it, though you can refer to Chapter 2 in this book if you want to take a stab at it yourself.

✔ If it still doesn't work, then you probably don't have a VGA or EGA display in your system.

✔ Some programs can take advantage of the smaller, more compact text. WordPerfect Corp.'s WordPerfect supports several of the text modes, as does Lotus's 1-2-3. You'll need to refer to your applications' manual for the details. (But only if this really intrigues you.)

✔ Most graphics adapters come with special programs that offer additional, way-out modes. The adapter in my PC allows for a display of 132 columns by 43 rows! Even WordPerfect supports it. But the text is very small and hard to read.

"Why doesn't my game work?"

Of all the graphics-related questions I've ever been asked, this is the most popular: "I tried to run a game on my PC and the screen went blank." The reason is usually that you have a monochrome system. It cannot run color games.

Even if you have a color system, some games are designed specifically for EGA or VGA systems. If you don't have one, then the game won't work.

This seems like a trivial subject, but it's really serious. If you want to play games on your computer (and everyone does), then you'll need a color graphics system. Monochrome just doesn't cut it. In the end, you'll probably be happier with your color system anyway.

Other popular questions you don't have to read

What are the other questions I'm asked? Here's a list along with my answers.

"Should I buy the newest graphics adapter?" Nope. It takes years for the software to catch up with the new adapter. Chances are, at this stage in the game, that any new adapter will only have goodies to offer demanding graphics users. You probably aren't one of them.

"Which graphics adapter is best?" For now, I suggest the VGA or SuperVGA. The uppermost resolution of the card is unimportant, since few applications support it. However, I recommend buying a card with all the memory installed. Don't save money by planning to "upgrade later."

"Can I pick up a used display screen?" Bad idea.

Really skippable stuff

The MODE command can change both the width and depth of the screen in one swift stroke. The format is:

MODE CON: COLS=x LINES=y

For X (above) you can specify "40" or "80" for a 40 or 80 column display. The value of Y is equal to 25, 43, or 50 rows of text on the screen. The following command is the weirdest:

C> MODE CON: COLS=40 LINES=50

Typing in MODE 80 returns the display to normal.

A CON job

The word "CON:" in the MODE command refers to the *console device*, which is a fancy term for your keyboard and display. Above, MODE referred to "MODE:" as the display. COLS sets the number of columns and LINES sets the rows. But you must specify MODE: to make the command apply to the display. (Since MODE also controls the printer in the same manner, it needs to know which device to reconfigure.)

"What about that SIMCGA program that lets me run color graphics on my Hercules monochrome screen?" It stinks. If you want to play games, then buy a color system — or just stock up on quarters and visit your local video arcade once a week.

"The graphics looked great in the store"

They always do, don't they? Graphics sell computers. In the old days, what most people really needed was monochrome. Heck, I had a nice monochrome display on my system for years. But color costs more money and provides a higher sales margin for the computer store. So they push color and you'll always see a lot of color graphics in any computer store.

Since the late '80s, more and more applications have taken advantage of color text. Things just looked gross in monochrome! With color text you could get more information on the screen and a prettier display. For the most part, however, nifty graphics like you see in a computer store just don't find themselves in every computer application. Word processors can have pictures in the text, but you can only see the graphics in a special "preview" mode; spreadsheets have charts and graphs, but again only in preview modes. That picture of the gorilla, parrot, or naked lady you saw in the computer store was only for show.

And, after all, you did buy your computer to do work — didn't you?

TECHNICAL STUFF

A bothersome explanation of what's going on

The MODE command is used to change the modes of a variety of computer devices. In fact, the MODE command is so confusing it's listed seven times in the DOS 5 manual — eleven times in the DOS 3 manual!

The MODE 80 command is used to set the color monitor to a width of 80 columns. The number of rows on the screen remains at 25.

The MODE 40 command is used to set a color monitor to a width of 40 columns, which appear twice as fat as they would on the standard display. The number of rows stays at 25.

The MODE mono command is used to activate a monochrome monitor. If you have both a color and monochrome monitor, this command makes the monochrome one the main screen; typing MODE 80 (or MODE 40) activates the color display. Don't type MODE MONO if you don't have a monochrome display attached to your computer.

Chapter 8
Keyboard and Mouse
(or, Where is the "Any" Key?)

● ●

In this chapter...

▶ How to find special keys on the keyboard.

▶ How to press the "any" key.

▶ How the CapsLock, NumLock, and ScrollLock keys work.

▶ What the difference is between the slash and backslash keys.

▶ Whether to press Enter or Return.

▶ How to press the Alt-S key.

▶ How to pause a long text display using the keyboard.

▶ How to curse at the WordStar cursor key diamond.

▶ How to make the keyboard more (or less) responsive.

▶ How to deal with a keyboard that beeps at you.

▶ How a mouse fits into the big picture.

▶ How to use a mouse.

▶ What all the mouse terms mean.

▶ How to deal with a mouse that leaves a trail of itself on the screen.

● ●

I may be weird, but I think a good keyboard can make a good computer. Nothing beats the full responsiveness of a real keyboard; the keys punch down evenly and are light to the touch. Some keyboards have a built-in click, others may have some pressure point or feel-only click. These features give you the impression that the computer's designers wanted you to feel like you're in control while you use the machine. Who cares if you're typing out mysterious DOS commands when the keyboard feels so good?

This chapter is about the computer keyboard and all the fun things you can do with it. Your keyboard is the direct line of communication between you and the computer. There are subtle ways to use the keyboard and special keys you

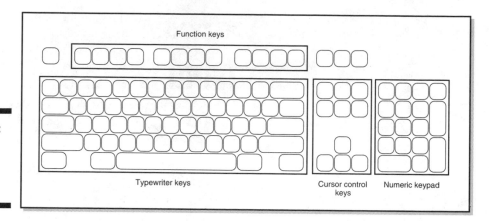

Figure 8-1:
The enhanced 101 keyboard.

can type. Knowing how to use them is like making funny or rude noises with your mouth; they may be socially unacceptable, but in the right situations they offer a unique form of payoff.

Oh, and this chapter also describes the most common of computer rodents, the mouse.

Keyboard layout

The typical keyboard supplied with most of today's computers is referred to as the enhanced 101 keyboard. Yes, it actually has 101 keys on it. You can count them on your own, and you can examine each key individually. In Figure 8-1 you should note the various areas mapped out on the keyboard. There are four main areas:

1. **The function keys, labeled F1 through F12.** These keys perform various functions depending on the application. (And no two applications use the same function keys for the same function — which you should be expecting by now.)

2. **The typewriter keys.** These keys are laid out like the standard typewriter keyboard. All the alphanumeric keys are there, plus a handful of special computer keys and symbols.

3. **The cursor control keys.** The cursor keys, also called arrow keys, are used to move the cursor on the screen. There are four directional keys in an inverted T pattern, then six specialized keys above them. These keys are used most often in text editing.

4. **The numeric keypad.** The keypad contains the numbers 0 through 9, plus the period, an Enter key, and various mathematic symbols. The keypad can be used for fast numeric entry, but it also serves a second function as a backup cursor keypad. Refer to "The keys of state" later in this chapter for more information.

✔ Some older keyboards lack the F11 and F12 keys, as well as the separate cursor control keys. They may also have their function keys in two columns to the left of the typewriter keys.

✔ Important keys to look for are the Esc (Escape) and backslash (\) keys. These keys are used quite often, and over the history of the PC keyboard they've been quite migratory. The only reason for pointing this out is that the Esc key used to be next to the Backspace key. Confusing the two was painful; Esc erased the entire line whereas Backspace erased only one character.

✔ Computers use the following symbols for mathematic operations: + is for addition; - is for subtraction; * is for multiplication; and / is for division. The only important special symbol here is the asterisk for multiplication — not the little *x*. This is universal in all areas of computerdom.

So where is the "any" key?

Nothing is more frustrating than hunting down that elusive *any* key. After all, the manual says, "Press any key to continue." So where is it?

"Any key" refers to, literally, any key on your keyboard. But let's be specific: When it says to press the "any" key, press the spacebar. If you can't find the spacebar, or you think it's a place where you'd order drinks on the Starship Enterprise, then try pressing your Enter key. Enter key = any key.

You can press almost any key on the keyboard for the "any" key. The problem is that some keys don't respond and are ill-suited as "any" keys. These include the shift keys, CapsLock, Pause, the 5 key on the numeric keypad, and other "dead" keys. You can pound away on them all you like and the program will never continue.

So why do they say "Press any key" instead of saying "Press Enter to continue?" I guess it's because they want to make things easy for you by giving you the whole keyboard to choose from. And if that's really the case, why not just break down and say "Slap your keyboard a few times with your open palms to continue...."

The keys of state

There are three keys that affect the way the keyboard behaves. I call them the keys of state. They are the CapsLock, NumLock, and ScrollLock keys.

The CapsLock key works like the ShiftLock key on a typewriter. Press the CapsLock key once to turn it on. After doing so, all the alphabet keys on the keyboard (26 of them at last count) will produce uppercase letters. Press the CapsLock key again to turn it off. Note that unlike a typewriter, CapsLock only shifts the letter keys; all the other keys on the keyboard will remain the same.

The NumLock key controls the numeric keypad. Press NumLock once to turn it on. When it's on, the numeric keypad produces numbers (like you suppose it would). Press NumLock again to turn it off. When NumLock is off, the numeric keypad doubles as a cursor keypad. The arrow keys, Home, PgUp, and so forth, will take precedence. (This is the way most DOS users prefer to use the numeric pad, as a cursor keypad.)

The ScrollLock key is vaguely defined and doesn't do anything under DOS. In some spreadsheets, ScrollLock has the effect of "locking" the cursor keys. So instead of pressing an arrow key to move the cell selector to another cell in the spreadsheet, with ScrollLock, on the whole spreadsheet moves in the direction of the arrow key. Other applications may use the ScrollLock key differently, but under DOS it serves no direct function. (Press it a few times on someone else's computer to irritate a friend.)

The positions of the CapsLock, NumLock, and ScrollLock keys vary. Figure 8-2 shows the locations on an enhanced 101 keyboard. Other keys that are not key of state, like the Shift keys, are where you'd expect them to be on any typewriter; two Ctrl keys are on the outside edges of the typewriter area, in lower corners; and the two Alt keys are inside, on either end of the spacebar. Laptop keyboards and older PC keyboards have these keys in different locations, but they're still labeled Shift, Ctrl, and Alt.

- ✔ If your keyboard has a CapsLock, NumLock, or ScrollLock light, it will be on when the corresponding state key is on.

- ✔ If your CapsLock key is backwards (sometimes it gets that way), then the only way to fix this is to reset. For example, if the CapsLock light is on yet you aren't getting uppercase letters, then reset to remedy the situation. (Exit your applications first!)

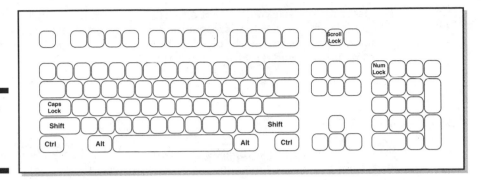

Figure 8-2:
State and
shift key
locations.

Interesting, yet skippable information on reverse state keys

When CapsLock is on, the Shift key can be used to reverse the case of a letter. When CapsLock is off, you press the Shift key plus a letter to get a capital letter. But with CapsLock on, pressing the Shift key plus a letter produces a lowercase letter.

The same weirdness affects the numeric keypad and the NumLock key. With NumLock on, pressing a key on the numeric keypad produces a number key. Yet, pressing the Shift key and a number key will produce the corresponding arrow key, for example, pressing Shift-4 on the keypad with NumLock on gives you the left arrow key. When NumLock is off, pressing Shift plus a key will give you the corresponding number key.

Yeah, this is confusing. If you play around with the keyboard, CapsLock, NumLock, and Shift keys, you'll see what's going on. But why fill your head with such trivial matters?

Slash and backslash

There are two slash keys under DOS. The first is the forward slash (/), the most common of the two. This slash leans forward, like it's falling to the right. On most computers, it's used to denote division, such as 52/13 (52 divided by 13). In English, it's used to divide various words or, most often, as an incorrect replacement for a hyphen.

The backslash is a backwards slanting slash (\), that leans to the left. This character is used in DOS to represent the root directory. It also appears in pathnames to separate the various directory names. For more information on the root directory and directory names, refer to Chapter 13.

Enter or Return?

Nearly all PC computer keyboards have two keys labeled Enter. Both keys work identically, with the second Enter key placed by the numeric keypad to facilitate rapid entry of numbers.

The Enter key is used to end a line of text. After entering the text, you press Enter and the information is "locked in." After pressing Enter at the DOS prompt, the command you typed is sent off to DOS for scrutiny. However, in a word processor you use the Enter key to end a paragraph. (The words "wrap" automatically at the end of a line, meaning you don't have to press Enter to end a paragraph.)

So what is the Return key? Many early computers sported a Return key. Essentially it's the same thing as the Enter key. In fact, some computers had both an Enter and a Return key.

The difference between Enter and Return is only semantic. Enter has its roots in the electronic calculator industry. You pressed Enter to enter numbers or a formula. Return, on the other hand, comes from the electronic typewriter. Pressing the Return key on a typewriter caused the carriage to return to the left margin. It also advanced the paper one line in the machine.

You may freely skip over this trivia

When you press the Enter key, the computer generates two different characters. The first is the *carriage return* character. This has the effect of moving the cursor to the left-most column on the screen, just as a carriage return on a manual typewriter would do so. (Remember whacking the carriage return bar?)

The second character produced is the *line feed*. This character moves the cursor down to the next line on the screen. Again, in the ancient days of typewriting, the line feed advanced the paper in the machine. In fact, the carriage return/line-feed was usually performed by whacking the same lever.

In computer speak, you'll often encounter the terms *carriage return/line feed* or the abbreviation CRLF. (Am I the only person who pronounces that "Crullif?") This simply means you press the Enter key, or it refers to the two secret characters that end a line of text.

The Tab key is also used in some applications (mainly databases) to end entry of information into a *field*. Like on a typewriter, pressing Tab will also move the cursor over eight spaces or to the next *tab stop*, though on some computers pressing Tab causes the computer to produce a can of a refreshing diet beverage.

Alt-S means what?

Alt-S could mean anything, actually. (It's up to each application to assign meanings to certain keys.) But what's more important is when you see Alt-S, or even Alt+S, what should you do?

The Alt key works like the Shift key on the keyboard. In fact, there are three types of shift keys on the keyboard: Shift, Alt, and Ctrl. This baffles most people, since the typewriter only has one shift key, the Shift key.

The positions of the Alt, Ctrl, and Shift keys on the enhanced 101 keyboard are shown in Figure 8-2.

You use the Alt, Ctrl, or Shift keys in the same manner: Press and hold that key and then type another key on the keyboard, usually a letter of the alphabet though function keys are commonly paired with the Shift keys.

Producing an uppercase S is done by pressing Shift-S, though no one needs to say "press Shift-S" because most typewriter-using people know that it works that way. But with three shift keys on a computer, you need to specify things. Pressing Alt-S is done by pressing and holding the Alt key and then typing an *s*. No character will appear on the screen; instead, the program may do something, such as save a file to disk.

The Ctrl key works the same way. When you read "press Ctrl-C," you press and hold the Ctrl (control) key and type a *c*, then release both keys.

✔ Even though you may see Ctrl-S or Alt-S with a capital S, this doesn't mean you must type Ctrl-Shift-S or Alt-Shift-S. In fact, the Ctrl and Alt keys can be used with or without the Shift key, so most users skip it.

✔ The functions of all the Alt and Ctrl keys differ from application to application.

✔ Keep in mind that Alt, Ctrl, and Shift can be used with the function keys. In fact, WordPerfect users will recognize 40 function key combinations using these Shift keys plus ten function keys.

> ✔ The Ctrl key combinations have an abbreviation: The caret or hat character (^) is used to denote control. When you see "^C" it means the keystroke Ctrl-C or the Control-C character.

Ctrl-S and the Pause key

In DOS, several control-key combinations can be used to give you more power over the PC. The two most common are Ctrl-S and Ctrl-C.

Ctrl-C is the universal DOS cancel key. It stops any DOS command and cancels just about anything you're typing — a good thing to know. For more information refer to "Canceling a DOS command" in Chapter 2.

The Ctrl-S key is used to freeze information, suspending it as it's displayed on the screen. This allows you to read rapidly scrolling text by pressing Ctrl-S in a panic-driven frenzy and then . . . the screen stops, dead in its tracks. Press another Ctrl-S (or any other key) and the display scrolls again. This all happens until all the information is displayed, or until you press Ctrl-S again to stop.

To test Ctrl-S, you'll need to display a long document. Typically this is done with the TYPE command. For example:

```
C> TYPE LONGJOHN
```

As the file LONGJOHN (above) is displayed, it scrolls wildly up the screen. But a touch of the Ctrl-S key and it stops. This allows you to read a bit. When you're ready to see more text, press Ctrl-S, Enter, or the spacebar. To freeze the screen again, press Ctrl-S.

The Pause key on some keyboards has the same effect as Ctrl-S, and it's only one key to press. However, unlike Ctrl-S, you must press any other key but Pause to get things rolling again. For me, I prefer pressing Enter as my "any" key.

> ✔ The Pause key may also be labeled "Hold."

> ✔ You can always cancel any long display by pressing Ctrl-C.

> ✔ For more information on the TYPE command, refer to "Looking at files" in Chapter 1.

> ✔ The Ctrl-P key switch is another handy DOS control-key function. Refer to "Printing DOS" in Chapter 9.

Wordstar command	Common key command	Function
Ctrl-E	Up arrow	Move the cursor up one line
Ctrl-X	Down arrow	Move the cursor down one line
Ctrl-S	Left arrow	Move the cursor left (back) one character
Ctrl-D	Right arrow	Move the cursor right (forward) one character
Ctrl-R	PgUp	Move up to the previous page (screen)
Ctrl-C	PgDn	Move down to the next page (screen)
Ctrl-A	Ctrl-Left	Move left one word
Ctrl-F	Ctrl-Right	Move right one word
Ctrl-W	Ctrl-Up	Scroll the screen up one line
Ctrl-Z	Ctrl-Down	Scroll the screen down one line
Ctrl-G	Delete	Delete current character
Ctrl-T	Ctrl-Backspace	Delete current word (or Ctrl-Del)
Ctrl-H	Backspace	Delete previous character

Figure 8-3:
The WordStar cursor key diamond and control-key commands.

The WordStar cursor and cursed-at key diamond

WordStar was the first popular and most widely-used word processor for the personal computer. Not just DOS computers, but the Apple II, a slew of CP/M "boxes," and the old TRS-80 could run WordStar. Back then it was the Cadillac of word processors. Sheesh, it even had *block* commands and featured *word wrap*. How could anyone compete? It showed you where the page ended — right there on the screen!

Since most keyboards at the time lacked cursor key pads, the folks who made WordStar came up with an interesting alternative for moving the cursor around. They came up with the WordStar cursor *key diamond*. This is a set of control-key combinations on the keyboard that represent pressing certain arrow keys, whether or not your computer already has enough arrow keys.

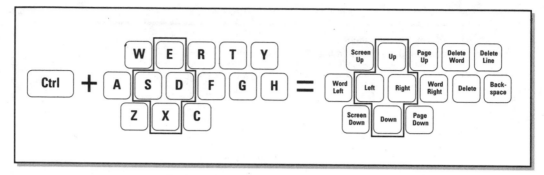

Figure 8-4: The WordStar cursor key diamond diagram.

I'm bringing all this up because many popular programs still offer the WordStar cursor key diamond and control-key commands. Generally, the application will also support the standard cursor key commands. But if not, the table in Figure 8-3 lists all the key commands. Figure 8-4 shows the WordStar cursor key diamond as mapped out on your keyboard.

✔ There is no need to memorize the table in Figure 8-3; though after a while, using these key commands may seem logical to you.

✔ Different applications use different key commands to do similar things. The only way to be certain is to refer to the manual, although the basic cursor keys plus the control keys listed above are usually common in all DOS programs.

Controlling the keyboard

You can use the MODE command to control two aspects of the keyboard: how long you have to wait after pressing a key for more characters to appear, and how fast those characters repeat.

The PC keyboard sports a feature IBM dubbed the *typematic*. This means that if you press and hold any key, it will repeat. Press and hold the I key and soon you have a dozen or so I's all across the screen. That's the typematic at work.

The initial delay before the key repeats is referred to as *delay*. It can be set to any time interval from ¼ to a full second. The rate at which the key repeats (once it starts repeating) is the *rate*. Keys can repeat at any rate from 2 to 30

characters per second. Both the *rate* and *delay* are set using the MODE command in the following format:

```
C> MODE CON: RATE=20 DELAY=2
```

Above, the MODE command sets the computer to the standard typematic repeat and delay: MODE is followed by a space and then CON: (which somehow means the keyboard). Then the word RATE is followed by an equals sign and 20 for a 20-character-per-second repeat rate, and DELAY is followed by an equals sign and 2, which means $^2/_4$ or $^1/_2$ seconds after the key is held down it starts to repeat.

Now, suppose you're a heavy handed typist. To avoid having keys repeat on you all the time, you could enter the following:

```
C> MODE CON: RATE=20 DELAY=4
```

This command sets the delay to $^4/_4$'s of a second, or one second even. That should eliminate the repeating keys you see all the time. (You must list both the *rate* and *delay* words after the command.)

If you want your keyboard to be slippery slick, enter this command:

```
C> MODE CON: RATE=32 DELAY=1
```

Press Enter and you'll get an idea of how annoying an overly responsive keyboard can be. Enter the first command (listed above) to restore your computer — or just whack the Reset switch (Ctrl-Alt-Del) if it severely annoys you.

The MODE command in this capacity only works with certain keyboards. If you have an older PC, you may not be able to change the delay and repeat rates.

"My keyboard beeps at me!"

On the typical computer, you can type "ahead" up to 16 characters. A word processor is usually able to eat those characters as fast as you type them. But sometimes, say when you're accessing a disk or the computer is out doing something, you can still type. Apparently, the keyboard will remember up to the last 16 keys you typed, and then . . . it will start beeping at you, once for each key beyond the 16 you've already typed. Those extra keys, typed as you hear the beeps, won't be displayed. Essentially, your keyboard is "full."

There's nothing you can do about this. Some special programs, utilities, or keyboard enhancers, may give you more than 16 characters to type ahead. But generally speaking, when the keyboard starts beeping, just stop typing and wait a few moments. Then wait a few minutes more — I had a program that took two minutes to come back to life!

If the keyboard continues to beep, then you've locked it up! The only way to escape this peril is to reset: Ctrl-Alt-Del.

Having a mouse

The computer mouse is a handy pointing device used primarily in graphics programs. It comes in two parts: the mouse-like, hand-held device, usually as big as a fat deck of cards that can fit in the palm of your hand; and the software that tells DOS and all your programs that you have a mouse.

The mouse faces towards you with it's tail going back to the computer's rump. There it plugs into either a serial port or a special mouse port. The mouse will usually have one or more buttons on top, which you press with your index finger.

The mouse software is installed in your system configuration file, CONFIG.SYS. You should have someone else do this, preferably at or near the time when they attach the mouse to your computer. (If you want to dabble with editing your CONFIG.SYS file yourself, refer to Chapter 12.)

The mouse works by rolling it around on the desktop. To use a mouse you'll need a comparatively wide area of space on your desktop. Look around your desktop. Do you see an open flat area about 8 by 12 inches in size? I didn't think so. To use a mouse you'll have to give it some room. On my desk I get by with about a four-by-four square for the mouse.

You might want to invest in a mouse pad, a handy device upon which to roll the mouse. It gives the mouse's little ball-foot more traction than your typical formica pressboard computer desk.

For more information on the serial port, refer to "The serial port" in Chapter 5.

Using a mouse

The mouse just doesn't become immediately useful; you must have software that takes advantage of it. Fortunately, there is a standard method for using the mouse which makes it a rather painless part of PC computing.

The mouse controls a *pointer* or *mouse cursor* on the screen. This may be the same as the text cursor, the one you see all the time at the DOS prompt, or it may be its own unique cursor, pointer, or square block. Sometimes the mouse cursor is just anyone who barges into the room and starts yelling at the furless little guy.

When you move the mouse around, rolling it on your desktop, the pointer on the screen moves in a similar manner. Roll the mouse left and the pointer moves left; roll it in circles and the pointer mimics that action; drop the mouse off the table and your DOS prompt changes to read "Ouch!" (Just kidding.)

There may be one or more buttons on the mouse. You press them with your index finger while keeping the mouse in the palm of your hand. You use the button(s) to manipulate various items on the computer screen. It goes like this: You move the mouse which moves the cursor on the screen over to something interesting. You click the mouse button and something even more interesting happens.

What happens, of course, depends on the software you use. And if the mouse has more than one button, then each button may perform different functions. It's all up to the application; like everything else in DOS, there are no standards, no rules, no guidelines . . . it's personal computing run amok!

Mouse terminology

Associated with using a mouse are various mouse terms. It really pays to have a mouse and an application that supports the mouse to appreciate these terms. In case you don't, I've defined them here anyway.

Button

The button is the button on top of the mouse. Pressing the button is referred to as "clicking," though clicking has another definition (covered below).

Pointer or cursor

The thing the mouse moves around on the screen is called the mouse pointer. I call it the pointer. Some applications call it the cursor, which is easily confused with the true cursor God created, the DOS text cursor.

Click

A click is a press of the mouse button. Often you'll read "click the mouse on the NO button." This means there's a graphic something-or-other on the screen with the word "NO" on it. Using the mouse, you hover the pointer over the word

NO. Then, with your index finger, click the mouse button. This is referred to as "clicking the mouse" on something, usually something on the screen. (Though you could roll the mouse around on your forehead and click it if you like — just make sure no one's looking.)

Double-click

A double-click is like a click-click, two rapid clicks in a row. This is done in many applications to quickly select some item. (The time between clicks varies, but it doesn't have to be that quick.)

Drag

A drag happens when you press and hold the mouse button down, then move the mouse around. On the screen, this has the effect of grabbing something (pressing the button) and then moving it about on the screen (dragging it). When you release the mouse button, you "let go" of whatever it was you were dragging.

Select

Selecting is the process of highlighting something, making it the "target" for whatever future plans you have. For example, you select a box by clicking on that box. You select text by dragging the cursor over the text you want; that highlights the text, similar to marking a block of text.

These terms are quite simple and, thanks to millions of dollars of research by Apple Computer, Inc., they make sense! Only by practicing using your mouse will they become obvious to you.

Mouse droppings

As with everything else in a PC, occasionally the mouse will screw up. It does so by producing a trail on the screen, commonly called *mouse droppings.* This occurs when you move the mouse around yet still see the cursor scattered all over the screen, typically more than one cursor that traces the pattern in which you're moving the mouse.

When you see mouse droppings it usually means one thing: The computer screwed up. Whichever program you were running just forgot to turn the mouse off, and you're faced with the ugly consequences.

There is one solution to mouse droppings: Reset (Ctrl-Alt-Del). You might consider telling one of the loftier PC users about it. They love to hear about computer bugs.

Chapter 9
The Printer
(Making the Right Impression)

• •

In this chapter...

▶ How to hook up a printer to your computer.

▶ How to connect a serial printer, both hardware and software.

▶ How to unjam a printer.

▶ How to set a printer "on-line" and get ready to print.

▶ How to eject a page from a printer.

▶ How to see what you've printed on your laser printer.

▶ How to solve the annoying double-spaced problem.

▶ How to print what you see on the screen (a screen snapshot).

▶ How to deal with screen snapshot problems.

▶ How to send DOS commands to the printer.

▶ How to print a directory listing.

▶ How to fix funny-looking printouts.

▶ How to cure odd-looking characters at the top of the page.

• •

Your PC needs a printer to get that all-important hard copy — a permanent record of your work, output, efforts, what-have-you. Without a printer, you'd have to lug the PC around everywhere and show people your stuff on the monitor. That's tacky.

There are lots of printers out there. The problem is that there are few standards. There is no CGA-EGA-VGA type of compatibility with printers like you have with the computer's monitor. This isn't a problem as long as you stick to the major brands. But when you don't, it's time to rev up that chain saw . . .

This chapter is about using a printer with your computer. By themselves, printers are harmless enough. But umbilically connect one to the evil PC — nay, the child of Satan himself! — and you're bound for trouble. Here is where you'll learn how to get out of trouble and put your firm thumb of control over the printer.

Getting connected

Every PC should have at least one printer attached. It's connected via a separate cable; one end of the cable connects to the PC, the other to the printer. It's fairly obvious which end goes where, though on your PC's rump you may confuse the printer port for a serial port.

You can have up to four printers connected to your computer. This all depends on how many printer ports your PC has. The typical PC has two printer ports, numbered one and two (low-end PC's only have one). If you only have one printer attached, make sure it's connected to port number one, which the dweebs call "LPT1".

Once the printer is properly connected, you can test it by printing something. There are examples of printing under DOS later in this chapter. But I recommend diving into some application, then test printing in there.

✔ It's also possible to have a serial printer installed on your computer. This printer connects to the PC via a serial port — not a parallel port. Refer to the next section for more information.

✔ If you're plugging in cables on the back of your PC — and this can be any cable from the printer cable to a keyboard cable — make sure your PC is off. Having a PC on while you plug something in can lead to some rather nasty results.

✔ If the printer doesn't work, you may have it connected to the wrong port. Try plugging the cable into another, similar connector on the rear of your PC.

✔ For more information on ports, refer to "What are ports?" in Chapter 5.

DOS's forgettable printer names

DOS refers to everything it controls by a *device name*. The name for the printer is PRN, a nice handy three-letter word (without vowels) that means "printer." So far so good.

DOS can control up to three printers for each PC. The device name PRN actually only refers to the first printer, the main printer. The real, secret names for the three possible printers are LPT1, LPT2, and LPT3. LPT stands for line printer. It's probably one of those massive, 1940s type of computer devices.

I bring this up because, well, I'm a nerd. Beyond that, you may occasionally see these names used and confused. For example, you may be asked, "Is your laser printer connected to LPT1?" As far as I can translate this, it means "Is your printer hooked up to the first printer port?" Beware of such deceptive terms that weave their way into computer manuals and books.

The serial connection

Out of the 1,700 or so printer makes and models available for the PC, you'll find a handful that operate out of a serial port — not the almost-sane printer port, which you would expect. These are usually older printers, or printers designed for use on non-IBM-type computers.

Nothing is bad about owning a serial printer. They work just fine, and connecting them to your computer is as easy as plugging in the special serial printer cable. That's the easy part. The hard part comes with setting up the computer and telling DOS about it.

The first part is to set up the printer to a specific speed or "baud" and a *data word format*. This is done by holding the manual in one hand and setting these minute switches on the printer with the other. I really have no idea how your particular printer does it, but what you want to set it to is either:

```
9600, 8, N, 1
```

This is the fast setting. Or:

```
2400, 8, N, 1
```

This is a slower setting. Refer to the manual for the proper settings, or something that looks similar to the above.

On the DOS side, before you can use the serial printer you must give DOS the following two commands. The first is used to set up the serial port in the exact same manner as you've set up the printer:

```
C> MODE COM1:9600,N,8,1
```

Above, the MODE command is followed by a space. Then comes COM1 and a colon, which represents your first serial port. That's followed by the speed, 9600 above, then N, 8, and 1 to match the 8, N, and 1 you set your printer to. If you specified a different speed (say 2400), substitute it for 9600 above.

The second step is to tell DOS that its printer device, called PRN, is now on the serial port instead of the printer port. That's done with the following command:

```
C> MODE LPT1=COM1
```

Ugh. Real Greek, no less. Basically, this is the MODE command, a space, the hieroglyph LPT1 (meaning DOS's primary printer) and then COM1 (which means the first serial port to which your printer is attached).

After entering those two commands you can use your printer under DOS — even in applications, as you would a parallel printer.

These commands are confusing. Trust me on this: No one I know has memorized them. Even I had to look them up to write them down here. You're forgiven if you repeatedly have to refer to this section to start your computer each day.

✔ If these commands are something you'll be typing every day when you start your computer, then why not make them a part of your AUTOEXEC.BAT automatic startup file? Refer to Chapter 2 for the details.

✔ Note that the serial printer cable is a special type of cable, usually labeled as a "serial printer cable." You cannot use the same serial cable as you would to, say, connect a modem; it won't work.

✔ For more information on the parallel and serial ports, refer to "What are ports?" in Chapter 5; for information on setting up a serial port, refer to "The serial port," also in Chapter 5.

Going on-line

Before a printer can print, three things must happen: the printer must be connected to the computer; you must have paper in the printer; and the printer must be *on-line* or *selected*.

Somewhere on your printer is a button. That button may be labeled *on-line* or *select*. Pressing it puts the printer into the "ready" mode, making it ready to print. If the printer is off-line or deselected, it's still on but not ready to print. Usually you take a printer off-line to advance paper, change a font, or unjam it. But you can only print again by putting the printer back on-line or selecting it.

✔ Most on-line, select, or ready buttons have a corresponding light. When the light is on, the printer is ready to print.

✔ If the printer lacks an on-line, select, or ready button, then it's probably ready for printing all the time.

Form feeding

The act of ejecting a sheet of paper from the printer is referred to as a *form feed*. There's a button for this purpose on most printers. It's called, remarkably enough, "Form feed" though sometimes the label "Eject" is used. To eject a page of paper from the printer, you first take the printer off-line by pressing the "On-line" or "Select" button, then press the "Form feed" or "Eject" button. Zwoop! Out flies a sheet of paper.

This button seems rather silly . . . until you need a full sheet of paper to shoot out of the printer. Even more important, a laser printer won't spit out a sheet of paper until it has printed the whole thing. So if you want to see what you've printed and you haven't printed a full page, you must take the printer off-line and press the "Form feed" or "Eject" button. Press "Select" or "On-line" to turn off the little light.

✔ For more information about the on-line or select buttons, refer to the previous section.

✔ Most nonlaser printers also have a *line feed* button. This button simply advances the paper one line of text each time you press it. Like "Form feed," you must have the printer off-line or deselected to use the "Line feed" button.

Force a page out

There is a special character called the *form feed*. It's the Ctrl-L character, often shown as "^L." When this character is sent to the printer — any printer — it's an immediate instruction to the printer to eject a page. But while typing Ctrl-L produces the form feed character, sending it to the printer isn't obvious.

To send the Ctrl-L keystroke to the printer, type the following DOS command:

```
C> ECHO ^L > PRN
```

That's the ECHO command, a space, then the form feed character produced by pressing Ctrl-L. (That's not the caret and L characters.) This is followed by a space, the greater-than symbol (>), another space, and then the letters PRN (for printer). Press Enter and the printer spits up a page.

"The page didn't come out of my laser printer!"

Laser printers are unlike their more primitive dot-matrix printer cousins. With a dot-matrix printer, aside from getting mediocre text quality, you get to see what you print as it's printed (even hear it, too!). Laser printers are quiet. But they don't print until one of two circumstances are met:

1. The laser printer will print if you've printed a whole page full of text, not before. Unlike the dot-matrix printer, nothing is really put down on paper until you fill up a sheet.

2. You can always force a laser printer to print what's been sent to it so far by giving it a form feed. You can do this by pressing a special button on the printer or by using a secret DOS command. Both of these are covered in the previous section, "Force a page out."

In a jam?

Paper flows through your printer like film through a projector; each sheet is magically ejected from a laser printer like the wind blowing leaves on an autumn day. Poppycock! Paper likes to weave its way through the inner guts of your printer like a four year-old poking his fingers into your VCR. When this happens, your printer can become jammed.

For dot-matrix printers, you can un-jam most paper by rewinding the knob. But turn off the printer first! This disengages the advancing mechanism's death grip on the paper platten, which means it makes it easier to back out the jammed paper. If the paper is really in there tight, you may need to remove the platten. When that happens, you need to take the printer apart to get at the problem; call someone else for help unless you want to take it apart yourself.

For laser printers, a light will flash on the printer when the paper gets jammed. If the printer has a message read-out, you may see the message "Paper jam" displayed in any of a variety of languages and sub-tongues. Make your first attempt at unjamming by removing the paper tray. If you see the end of the paper sticking out, grab it and firmly pull toward you. The paper should slip right out. If you can't see the paper, then pop open the printer's lid and look for the jammed sheet. Carefully pull it out either forward or backward. You don't have to turn the printer off first, but watch out for hot parts.

Sometimes printers jam because the paper you're using is too thick. If that's the case, removing the paper and trying it again probably won't help; use thinner paper. Otherwise, paper jams for a number of reasons, so just try again and it will work.

Printing on one line or massive double spacing

Two common printer flubs are the "Everything is printing on one line!" expression of panic, then the "Why the heck is everything double spaced all the time?" annoying interrogation. Both problems are related though solving them doesn't involve laying on a couch and talking about your mother.

Somewhere on your printer is a series of tiny switches. The computer weenies call them *DIP switches*. Flipping one of those tiny switches will solve your problem, whether everything is printing on one line or you're seeing all your text double spaced. (They're both actually the same problem, which is covered in the information below that you can ignore.)

The switch will be identified in your manual. It has the name "Add linefeed" or "Automatic linefeed" or "LF after CR" or something along those lines. To fix your problem, flip the switch. It's a tiny switch, so you may have to mutilate a paper clip to reach in and flip it (turn off the printer first).

✔ If flipping this switch is something you don't feel like doing, then have someone else do it.

✔ If you cannot locate the switch on the back of your printer, it may be inside, under the printing mechanism. If so, turn the printer off when you're in there fumbling around.

✔ If this doesn't fix the problem right away, turn the printer off, wait, then turn it back on again.

Printing the screen

There is a special button on your keyboard — a feature — that will cause all the text you see on the screen to be printed. It's called the Print Screen key, though that particular key may be labeled "Print Scrn" or "Prt Scn" or something even more cryptic.

The technical term for printing the screen is a *screen dump*. Normally I wouldn't mention that here, but I personally find it hilarious: "Excuse me, dear, I've got to take a screen dump." Riotous stuff!

To practice, make sure your printer is on-line and ready to print. Then press the Print Screen key. Zip-zip-zip. A few minutes later, you'll see a copy of your screen on the printer. (If you have a laser printer, you'll have to eject the page; refer to "Form feeding" earlier in this chapter.)

✔ For more information about the keyboard, refer to Chapter 8.

✔ If the printer isn't on and you hit Print Screen, one of two things may happen. The first, and hopefully what happens all the time when you accidentally press Print Screen, is that nothing happens. Whew! The second thing that happens is that the computer waits for the printer so it can print your screen. And it waits. And waits. Turn the printer on and watch it print; there's no way to cancel out of this with Ctrl-C.

Printing problems explained, which you can ignore

Each line sent to the printer ends in two special codes: The *carriage return* and *line feed*. The carriage return tells the printer to start printing on column one again — on the left side of the page. The line feed, following the carriage return, tells the printer to print down on the next line on the page. Simple enough.

The problem is that not every computer sends the printer a carriage return/line feed combination. Some computers only send a carriage return. When that happens, no line feed takes place and all your text is printed on one ugly, ink-stained line.

To solve the problem of printing on one line, the printer can be told (via a switch) to supply its own line feed automatically after each carriage return received. That way, if your computer is dumb enough to only send the carriage return to end a line, the printer supplies the line feed and everything prints as you've intended.

The problem of double spacing happens when that same add-a-line-feed switch is on and the computer is already sending a carriage return/line feed combo. In that case, at the end of the line the printer adds its own line feed, giving a double-spaced effect. Turning the tiny switch off fixes that problem.

Print Screen woes

The Print Screen key isn't the miracle most people suppose it is. For example, if your screen shows lines and boxes along with text, you may not see those characters printed. In fact, you may see lots of *m*'s or colons or other odd characters or even italic text.

The reason for the Print Screen garbage is that your printer isn't capable of printing the IBM *graphics set*. If your printer can somehow wiggle itself into an IBM-compatible mode, then you'll see the characters just fine. Otherwise, you'll have to live with all the *m*'s and whatnot.

Another Print Screen woe is that the *screen dump* only copies text. If you're using a graphics program and are looking at a picture of Michelle Pfeiffer or Tom Cruise seductively biting their lower lip — and, by God, you want a hard copy of this to tape up by your pillow — then pressing the Print Screen key won't help you. Unfortunately, Print Screen only copies text and any attempt to "dump" a graphics image (no matter how badly you crave it) results in garbled output...and emotional disappointment.

✔ If you're running Windows, then pressing the Print Screen key "captures" the current screen or window. That image is stored in the Clipboard, and you can paste it elsewhere for editing or printing.

✔ Some programs are available that will replace DOS's lame Print Screen key with a smarter program, one that will print graphics. Refer to your local software-o-rama for the particulars.

✔ If you hit Print Screen and your printer is turned off (or disconnected) the computer will sit there and wait for it — forever if need be. Turn the printer on — or reboot.

Printing DOS

The normal way you use DOS is to type in a command and expect (hopefully) that DOS will display something that pleases you on the screen. In fact, all of your interaction with DOS is shown on the screen which, I'll admit, comes in handy. Even more handy is to sometimes have a *hard copy* of all DOS's output — a transcript of your DOS session, but without sending the $2 to "Transcripts," at some P.O. Box in Jersey. This is done using the DOS print switch, which is actually a keyboard command.

If your printer is on and ready to print, you can press Ctrl-P to activate DOS's printing function. After pressing Ctrl-P, DOS sends all output to both the screen and the printer. Everything is output, even embarrassing errors, but more importantly you'll see vital information such as file listings, displays, and other trivia.

To turn off DOS's printing function, press Ctrl-P again.

- ✔ If you just want to print a single file, refer to "Printing a text file" in Chapter 3.

- ✔ If you just want to print a directory listing (the output of the DIR command), refer to "Printing a directory" in the next section.

- ✔ Laser printers won't print anything until a full page is generated. To see what you've printed before then, refer to "Form feeding" earlier in this chapter.

- ✔ The only way to be sure you've turned off DOS's printing function is to press Enter a few times. If the DOS prompt doesn't appear on your printer, then the printing is off. If it does, try Ctrl-P again.

- ✔ Ctrl-P is what computer wizards call a *toggle*. Like a toggle switch, it's a single command that turns something both on and off, going either way each time you use the command.

Printing a directory

The handiest thing to print is a list of files on disk. Under DOS, you see a list of files using the DIR command. But that only spits out the file information to the screen. To send the information to a printer, first make sure the printer is on and ready to print, then type the following command:

```
C> DIR > PRN
```

That's the DIR command, followed by a space, the greater-than symbol (>), another space, and then PRN (which means "Printer" in the Land of No Vowels).

- ✔ If you want to use any of the DIR command's options, then sandwich them between DIR and the greater-than symbol (>). Note that the /P (pause) option would be rather silly at this point.

- ✔ If you print a directory to a laser printer, you may need to eject the paper from the printer to see the output; refer to "Form feeding" earlier in this chapter.

> ✔ You won't see the directory on the screen when you use this command. If you want to see the directory on the screen, then use the DOS printing function, as discussed in the previous section.

"Why does it look funny?"

Printing anything from DOS has its consequences: If your printer cannot display the IBM graphics characters, then they'll appear as other, odd characters on your hard copy. Seriously, the best place to print anything is from an application. But even then you may not get what you want from your printer.

The answer lies in a piece of software called a *printer driver*. Like a slave driver, the printer driver utterly controls the printer, telling it to do exactly what the application wants. Why can't the application do this itself? Because there is no standard DOS printer. There are hundreds of printers, any one of which you may have attached to your PC. To tell your application which printer you have, you must set up the printer by directing the application to talk to it via a printer driver.

Installing a printer driver is usually done when you first set up an application (which is covered in Chapter 11). You select your printer's name and model number from the list and then your application and your printer can work in sweet harmony. But this isn't always the case.

Sometimes, someone (maybe you) will select the wrong printer driver. Or worse, the application may not support your printer. As an example, WordPerfect has printer drivers for more than 1,000 different printers. My mailing label program (which I won't name because I'm sorry I bought it) only supports five printers — and I don't have any of them. Needless to say, the output from that program looks terrible (but, what-the-hey, only the post office has to read the labels).

Each application lets you set up your printer differently, so it would be impossible to mention all the possibilities here. If you cannot find the proper driver or locate your printer by name, you can always opt for the "Dumb printer" option. This is where the program will control your printer in a text-only mode. It may not be the miracle of computers you dreamed of, but it works.

Those funny characters at the top of the first page

Occasionally you may see some odd characters at the top of every page or just the first page you print. For example, you may see a ^ or &0 or E@, or any of a number of ugly looking characters that you didn't want there and that don't show up on your screen. It requires a major "Hmmm."

Hmmm.

Those characters are actually secret printer control codes. Normally the characters are swallowed by the printer as it prepares itself to print. The problem is that the software on the computer is sending your printer the wrong codes. Since your printer doesn't understand the codes, it just prints them as is. Hence, you see ugly characters.

The solution is to select the proper printer driver for your software. You want a printer driver that knows your printer and how to send it the proper codes. This is stuff that's best done by the person who (supposedly) installed your software on the computer. It can be changed in most cases. But better make someone else do that for you.

Chapter 10
All You (Don't) Want to Know About Disks

• •

In this chapter...

▶ Why disks are really "hardware."

▶ How to buy disks.

▶ How to prepare a disk for use by DOS (formatting).

▶ How to format different size disks.

▶ What not to do with disks, the no-no's.

▶ How to tell which type of disk is which.

▶ How to change a volume label.

▶ How to write-protect a disk.

▶ How to reformat an already-formatted disk.

▶ How to duplicate disks.

• •

*B*oth computers and humans have two types of long-term storage. The internal storage in a human is provided by a wet slimy thing called a brain. It's fast on the uptake and can store volumes of information, but is sluggish on the retrieval. Inside a computer, the hard drive provides fast but limited storage, and retrieves quickly.

Humans supplement their brain-storage device with storage media, such as scraps of paper with things written down upon them. Computers use floppy disks, upon which information can be written and removed from the computer, taken elsewhere, or just stored. Both systems have their pluses and minuses.

This chapter is about using floppy disks, the removable long-term storage devices used by computers. You use floppy disks to make safety copies of your important files, move files between computers, back up information from the hard disk, or play a limited-distance version of Frisbee. Floppies can be frustrating or fun, but above all they must be formatted (see "Formatting a disk" in this chapter).

Figure 10-1:
When buying disks, it's important to match their size to the capacity of your floppy drive.

Floppy drive size and capacity	Buy these disks
5 ¼-inch, Low	Low capacity, 360K, or DS/DD
5 ¼-inch, High	High capacity, high-density, 1.2MB, or DS/HD
3 ½-inch, Low	Low capacity, 720K, or DS/DD
3 ½-inch, High	High capacity, high-density (HD), 1.4MB, or DS/HD
3 ½-inch, Extended	Extended capacity, 2.8MB, or DS/ED

Why are disks hardware?

A common misconception among computer users is that a floppy disk is actually software. This is not so. Floppy disks are hardware. Keep in mind that hardware is something you can touch or drop on your foot. (Though the floppy disk doesn't hurt as much as dropping a monitor on your foot, it is still hardware.)

The confusion comes about because floppy disks store software. The software is on the disk, magnetically encoded. So just as you wouldn't call a compact disc "music," don't confuse the floppy disk with the software that's recorded on it.

Buying disks

You should always buy disks that match the size and capacity of your floppy drives. Buying high-capacity disks may be expensive, but the cost works itself out over the long run because they store more data per disk. And forget about buying cheap low-capacity disks and trying to format them to high-capacity; it just doesn't work.

There are two sizes of disks: 5 ¼-inch and 3 ½-inch. These values refer to the length of the disk's edge (since all disks are square).

The capacity of the disk refers to how much information it can hold. There are two capacities: low-capacity and high-capacity. For 3 ½-inch disks, a very high or *extended* capacity also exists.

The object is to buy disks to match the size and capacity of your floppy drive. See the table in Figure 10-1 for details on what disks to buy.

✔ If you have a high-capacity, 1.2MB, 5¼-inch drive, or the 1.4MB or 2.8MB, 3½-inch drive, then you buy the corresponding disks. You can, if you like, buy the low-capacity disks, but you can only format them at their lower capacity. Refer to "Formatting a low-capacity disk in a high-capacity drive" later in this chapter.

✔ If you only have a low-capacity drive, then buy the low-capacity, DS/DD disks. You cannot use the high-capacity disks and you shouldn't even buy them.

✔ There is nothing wrong with buying discount disks in bulk. I do this all the time, though I prefer to buy brand name and guaranteed disks for backups and serious work.

✔ Do not buy so-called "quad density" disks. These disks are for an older PC disk format that no longer exists.

✔ Do not format high-capacity disks to a low-capacity. Refer to "Formatting a low-capacity disk in a high-capacity drive" in this chapter for more information.

Skippable background info on DS/DD

Often when you buy a box of disks you'll see DS/DD (it stands for double sided/double density). This is an ancient relic from the days when floppy drives were of limited ability and mankind had dozens of confusing disk formats to choose from.

The first type of disk drive only wrote on one side of the disk. This was referred to as the single-sided floppy drive — like a record player. (Actually it was just a disk drive since double-sided drives didn't yet exist.)

Through the miracle of technology, the wizards were able to store more information on this single-sided floppy. This type of storage was called _double density_ because it put almost twice as much information on the disk. So there were two different types of disks you could by: SS/DD, for single sided/double density; and SS/SD, for single sided/single density.

When mankind figured out how to write information on both sides of a disk in a single drive, the _double-sided_ disks emerged. Two new flavors of disks could be bought: DS/DD, for double sided/double density; and DS/SD, for double sided/single density. Madness ensued.

For a while there was also a _quad density_ format, then came the _high-density_ or _high-capacity_ formats. Today, there are four basic disk formats and four types of disks you should buy. These are all listed in the table in Figure 10-1.

The newest format is the _extended-density_ disk, which stores eight times as much as a double-density disk. This brings to light the utter silliness of referring to a disk by its density. (Actually, they're called "Ed" disks, after the famous horse.) So what will the next density be? Maybe "super density." And then what's next? The "super dooper density" disk.

> ✔ If you're thinking about buying a low-capacity disk and magically making it into a high-capacity disk, *don't!* Refer to "Why can't I 'notch' a disk to make it high-capacity?" later in this chapter.

Formatting a disk

Before you can use a disk it must be formatted. All disks come "naked" out of the box. (A few are preformatted, but you pay extra for it.) This is because you can use floppy disks on a variety of computers, not always DOS computers. For DOS to use the disk and store information on it, you must format that disk the way DOS likes. This is done with the FORMAT command.

To format a disk, first place it label side up and toward you into your A floppy drive. Close the drive's door latch after inserting a 5¼-inch disk. Type the following:

```
C> FORMAT A:
```

After pressing Enter, you'll be asked to insert the disk. That's already done, so press Enter again and the disk begins formatting.

After formatting is complete, you'll be asked to enter a *volume label* for the disk. Press Enter (unless you want to type a label name; it's optional). If you want to format another disk, press Y when it asks you, then remove the first disk and replace it with another.

You can also format disks in drive B. Here is the command you use:

```
C> FORMAT B:
```

Follow the same steps as listed for drive A above.

> ✔ Never format any drive other than A or B; you should always use the two FORMAT commands listed above when formatting disks.

> ✔ The disk you format must be the same size and capacity of the drive you're using: High-capacity disks for high-capacity drives; low-capacity disks for low-capacity drives.

> ✔ If you see the message "Track 0 bad" or "Disk unusable," refer to Chapter 17.

> ✔ You can format a low–capacity disk in a high-capacity drive; refer to the next section.

Formatting a low-capacity disk in a high-capacity drive

It's possible to format a disk of lower capacity in a high-capacity drive. You would do this to be compatible with computers that only have the lower capacity drives or if you're using cheaper, low-density disks. If that's never your situation, then there's no need to do this.

To format a low-capacity disk in a high-capacity drive, you must first get the low-capacity disk. Never format a high-capacity disk to a lower format. (It renders the disk useless.)

Insert the low-capacity disk into your high-capacity drive, label up and toward you. For a 5¼-inch drive, latch the drive's door shut after you've inserted the disk.

If you're formatting a low-capacity (360K) disk in a high-capacity 5¼-inch drive, type the following FORMAT command:

```
C> FORMAT A: /F:360
```

That's FORMAT, followed by a space, "A:" meaning drive A, a space, /F and a colon, then the number 360. Press Enter and follow the instructions on the screen. Keep in mind that if you answer Y when asked to "Format another?" you will still be formatting the low-capacity disks.

If you're formatting a low-capacity (720K) disk in a high-capacity 3½-inch drive, type this FORMAT command:

```
C> FORMAT A: /F:720
```

This is the same FORMAT command as listed above, save for typing the number 720 instead of 360. Follow the same instructions listed under the first FORMAT command listed above. Remember that any additional disks you format by answering Y will be formatted at 720K.

If you have an extended-density (2.8MB) drive, you can use the above FORMAT command to format a 720K disk, or you can use the following FORMAT command to format a 1.4MB high-capacity disk:

```
C> FORMAT A: /F:1440
```

Follow the instructions on the screen. (Technically this is formatting a high-capacity disk in a higher capacity drive. Silly? Yeah, I know.)

▶ If you want to format the low-capacity disk in drive B, substitute B: for A: in either of the above commands.

▶ If the FORMAT command refuses to format the disk for any reason, you can force it to format by adding the /U option. Here are the modified commands:

```
C> FORMAT A: /F:360 /U
C> FORMAT A: /F:720 /U
C> FORMAT A: /F:1440 /U
```

Again, *do not* use these commands to force-format a high-capacity disk to a lower capacity. Always use low-capacity disks when you're formatting low-capacity.

"Why can't I 'notch' a disk to make it high-capacity?"

One of the worst "tricks" you can pull with disks is to format a low-capacity disk to a higher capacity. It sounds simple, and it even works for a time. But will you trust your valuable data to it, especially when you're only saving a few cents on the dollar?

It goes like this: When the high-capacity 3½-inch disks came out, most people noticed that the disks were identical in every way to the low-capacity disks, save for two things. First, the high-capacity disks had an extra hole in them. And second, the high-capacity disks cost more than the low capacities. This lead many misguided souls to believe that you could magically make a low-capacity disk into a high-capacity one simply by punching a hole in it. They even justified this by saying that both the disks "looked alike." This is as silly as it sounds.

True, if you mutilate a low-capacity disk you can format the disk at the higher capacity. You can even use the disk for a time with no ill effects. This is how the charlatans were able to dupe so many people; their demonstration disks worked flawlessly back at the store. But once you tried to use those disks two or three times, they became riddled with errors.

Eventually, the modified disks would become worthless. Forget about getting your data back! In fact, you couldn't even reformat the disks to a lower capacity. By punching a hole in a 3½-inch disk you're taking a losing gamble. Don't do it no matter what you hear.

How low-density disks are different than high-density disks

Though all disks look alike, the magnetic recording material on the disk has differences the eye cannot see. I like to make the comparison between a disk's surface and a sandbox (minus the kids and Tonka trucks).

A low-density disk is like a sandbox filled with coarse sand. Using a rake, you can draw lines in that sand. This works because the lines the rake makes are fairly far apart. If they aren't, the sand will fall back in on itself; it won't hold the grooves made by the rake because the sand is so coarse.

If the sandbox is filled with fine sand, then you can use a finer rake and make many more grooves in it. Because of the fine sand, the grooves hold their pattern. This is essentially the difference between a low-capacity and high-capacity disk. A high-capacity disk has "finer" magnetic material and can hold many more *tracks* (where information on the disk is stored) than a low-capacity disk.

When you format a low-capacity disk to a high-capacity, typically by fooling it with a hole punch, it's like making fine grooves in coarse sand. This may hold for a while. But since the sand isn't fine, eventually the grooves (tracks on a disk) disappear. The same thing happens on the disk. Since the information you write to the disk clings to these tracks, when they go so does your data.

Which disk is this?

Ever pick up a disk and wonder silently to yourself, "Where the heck did this disk come from?" If you do it a lot, then I have one maxim for you:

Label your disks!

Every box of disks — even the cheapies — comes with several sticky labels. Here's how you use them:

1. Write information on the sticky label using a pen. Describe the disk's contents or give it a general name: "Files for home" or "Backup stuff" or "Emergency disk" or...you get the idea.

2. Peel the label off and gently apply it to the disk.

There. That's easy. With all your disks labeled, you'll never worry about wondering what's on them. And you'll be able to find commonly-used disks quicker.

- ✔ If you don't label a disk, you can use the DIR command to find out what's on it. Refer to "The DIR command" in Chapter 1.

- ✔ As a suggestion, label disks right after you format them. That way, all formatted disks will have labels. If you find a disk without a label, that tells you it's probably unformatted. (But check it with the DIR command first to be certain.)

- ✔ You may also want to write the capacity of the disk, say 1.2MB or 360K, on the label. This will help out in situations where you have many computers with different types of drives in them.

- ✔ You can write on the labels after they're on the disk. Use a felt tip pen and don't press too hard. If you use a ball point pen or pencil you may dimple the disk inside and ruin any data there.

- ✔ You can peel and remove a label from a disk if you want to change it.

- ✔ Don't write on the disk's sleeve instead of the label. Disks can change sleeves.

- ✔ Programs are available that allow you to custom label disks, even putting filenames and the disk's contents on a nifty little sticky label.

- ✔ Don't confuse the sticky label with the *volume label*. The volume label is an electronic name you attach to a disk when it's formatted. Refer to "Changing the volume label" later in this chapter.

- ✔ Don't use Post-Its as disk labels. They fall off when you're not looking.

What kind of disk is this?

Even if a disk is labeled, sometimes it's hard to tell if it's a low-capacity or high-capacity model. The following tips should clue you in to which disk is which:

If the disk is a 360K, 5¼-inch floppy:

It may have a label that contains one of the following: DS/DD; double sided/Double Density; 40 TPI or 40 Tracks Per Inch.

As a visual clue, if you remove the disk and look at its center hole, you'll see a reinforcing *hub ring*. The 1.2MB disks typically lack this feature.

If the disk is a 1.2MB, 5¼-inch floppy:

One of the following clues may be written on the label: the letters HD or the term High-density; double sided/High-density; Double Track; 96 TPI or 96 Tracks Per Inch.

The visual clue is the absence of a reinforcing hub ring typically found on most 360K floppies.

If the disk is a 720K, 3½-inch floppy:

It may have one of the following clues written on its label: DS/DD; double sided/ Double Density; DD; Double Track; 135 TPI or 135 Tracks Per Inch.

The primary visual clue is that the disk is missing a hole in the lower right corner as you insert the disk into the drive. (This hole is opposite from the write-protection hole.)

If the disk is a 1.4MB, 3½-inch floppy:

The 1.4MB disk may have one of the following clues on its label: DS/HD; double sided/High-density; the interesting graphic (double line) letters HD. (The "HD" is usually your best clue; all the manufactures use it.)

The key visual clue is the extra, see-through hole in the lower-right corner of the disks. The lower capacity disks lack this hole.

If the disk is a 2.8MB, 3½-inch floppy:

Extended density, 2.8MB disks have one of the following clues on their label: DS/ED; double sided/Extended Density; or the best clue, a large graphic "ED" on the disk.

The key visual clue is the extra, see-through hole on the corner of the disks, which the 720K disks lack. Note that this hole is not even (horizontally) with the write-protect hole; it's a bit lower, which is how you can tell the difference between a 2.8MB and a 1.4MB disk.

These tips are provided primarily for unformatted disks. If a disk is formatted, you can use the CHKDSK ("check disk") command to determine its size. Refer to "Checking the disk (the CHKDSK command)" in Chapter 13.

Changing the volume label

When you format a disk, the FORMAT command asks you to enter a *volume label*. This is an electronic name encoded on the disk — not the sticky label you should apply later. Giving your disk a volume label can be a good idea, especially if your sticky label falls off the disk. In that case, you could find out the name of your disk electronically using the DIR command. The volume label will appear at the top of the DIR command's output, and you can use the handy VOL command to find a disk's volume label. Type:

```
C> VOL A:
or  VOL B:
```

The VOL command will report back the disk's volume label, or it may tell you that the disk "has no label."

After you've formatted a disk, you can change the volume label using the LABEL command. Type LABEL and then follow the instructions on the screen:

```
C> LABEL
```

After pressing Enter you'll see the current label for the drive, as well as (in some versions of DOS) the cryptic "volume serial number." DOS will ask you to enter a new label up to 11 characters long. The label can contain letters and numbers. If you want a new label, type it in. If you don't want to change the label, don't type anything and press Enter.

If you entered a new label, DOS will change it on the disk. You can use the VOL command again to verify the new label.

If you just pressed Enter, DOS will ask if you want to delete the old label. If so, press Y. Otherwise, press N and you'll keep the original label.

To change the label on a disk in any drive, follow the LABEL command with that drive letter and a colon. For example:

```
C> LABEL A:
```

Above, the label will be examined/changed for drive A. Substitute B: for A: above to replace the label on drive B.

✔ The VOL command can be followed by any drive letter and colon. This is used to see the volume label for any other disk in your system.

✔ Remember to insert a floppy disk in drive A or B before using the LABEL or VOL commands on those drives.

Write-protecting disks

You can protect floppy disks in such a way as to prevent yourself or anyone else from modifying or deleting anything on the disk.

To write-protect a 5¼-inch disk, go grab one of those tiny, Velamint-sized tabs that came with the disk in the box. Peel the tab and place it over the notch in the disk, which should be on the lower-left side as you insert the disk into the drive. With that notch covered, the disk is write-protected.

To write-protect a 3½-inch disk, locate the little sliding tile on the lower-left side of the disk as you slide it into the drive. If the tile covers the hole, then the disk can be written to. If you slide the tile off of the hole (so you can see through it), then the disk is write-protected.

When a disk is write-protected you cannot alter, modify, change, or delete anything on that disk. And you cannot accidentally reformat it. You can read from the disk and copy files from it. But changing the disk — forget it!

To unwrite-protect a 5¼-inch disk, peel off the little tab. This renders the disk sticky, but it's a livable problem. The 3½-inch disks are unwrite-protected by sliding the tile over the hole.

Reformatting disks

Disks must be formatted before DOS can use them. But once formatted, it's possible to reformat them. This can be done under two circumstances: when you want to totally erase the disk and all its data, or accidentally.

Obviously, you shouldn't erase a disk that you don't want to erase. All the data on the disk goes bye-bye. The only way to avoid this is to be careful: Check the disk with the DIR command first. Make sure it's a disk you want to reformat.

Personally, I erase disks all the time. I have stacks of old disks that I can reformat and use. The data on them is old or duplicated elsewhere. So reusing the disk is no problem. Here's the FORMAT command you want to use:

```
C> FORMAT A: /Q
```

That's the FORMAT command, a space, then A and a colon, which directs the FORMAT command to format a disk in drive A. That's followed by another space and a slash-Q. This tells DOS to "QuickFormat" the disk. It's very fast.

If DOS refuses to QuickFormat the disk, then try the following FORMAT command:

```
C> FORMAT A: /U
```

This is the same command as above, but with a slash-U instead of a slash-Q. This tells DOS to *unconditionally* format the disk. It takes longer than the QuickFormat, but it generally works.

- ✔ If you want to reformat a disk in drive B, then substitute B: for A: above.

- ✔ Note that you cannot QuickFormat a disk to a different size. In fact, you shouldn't be reformatting disks to a different size anyway. But if you must, then use the /U option as shown above.

- ✔ Accidentally reformatted disks can be recovered using DOS (version 4 and 5 only). Refer to "I just reformatted my disk!" in Chapter 16.

Duplicating disks (the DISKCOPY command)

To make a duplicate of a file on disk you use the COPY command. (Refer to "Duplicating a file" in Chapter 3.) To make a duplicate of a floppy disk, you use the DISKCOPY command. DISKCOPY takes one floppy and makes an exact duplicate of it, even formatting a new disk if it was previously unformatted.

There are two things you cannot do with the DISKCOPY command:

- ✔ You cannot DISKCOPY two disks of different size or capacity.

- ✔ You cannot use DISKCOPY with a hard disk or a RAM drive. (If you don't know what a RAM drive is, go to the refrigerator and reward yourself with a cool, carbonated beverage.)

When you copy disks, DOS refers to the original disk as the *source*. The disk to which you're copying is the *target*.

To make a copy of a disk, first write-protect the original, the source. (Refer to the section "Write-protecting disks" earlier in this chapter.) Type the following command at the DOS prompt:

```
C> DISKCOPY A: A:
```

That's DISKCOPY, a space, then A: meaning drive A mentioned twice and separated by a space. Press Enter and DOS asks you to insert the source disk. Put your write-protected original into drive A. Close the drive's door latch for a 5 ¼-inch disk.

The drive will churn away for a few moments. Then you'll be asked to insert the target. Remove the source disk and insert your duplicate disk. Close the door latch if you have a 5 ¼-inch disk.

If you're lucky, that will be it. In most cases, however, DOS may ask you to swap the disks a few more times. Always keep track of the source and target. Nothing will screw up as long as you've write-protected the original.

When the operation is complete, DOS asks if you want to do another DISKCOPY . Press Y if you do, N to return to DOS.

✔ You can do a DISKCOPY in your B drive by substituting B: for A: in the above command.

✔ If and only if your drive A and B are of the same size and capacity, you can use the following DISKCOPY command:

```
C> DISKCOPY A: B:
```

This command is faster since you don't have to sit there and wait to swap disks.

✔ If the target disk is unformatted, DISKCOPY will format it. If it's already formatted, DISKCOPY will replace the original contents with the copy.

✔ The DISKCOPY command is the only accurate way to duplicate a disk. Even the COPY command cannot always make a full copy of all the files on a disk.

Section Three
The Non-Nerd's Guide to PC Software

The 5th Wave   **By Rich Tennant**

In this section...

Essentially, software is what makes the hardware go; the computer is the orchestra and software is the music. (Software is to the computer nerd what sheet music is to the conductor.)

Software is the reason you bought your computer. Forget brand names and speed and power and pretty cases. What makes a computer work is software, and software is what makes your work on the computer productive.

Chapter 11
Basic
Software Setup

● ●

In this chapter...

▶ How to locate software that will work on your computer.

▶ How to install software (generally speaking).

▶ How to operate your new program and perform basic functions.

▶ The best way to learn a new program.

▶ How to update software.

▶ How to read a "command format."

● ●

*H*opefully, if you play your cards right, you'll never have to install any software on your PC. Someone else, someone who loves to do such things, will install the software for you. To install a program, you have to learn steps that are required only once. So making someone else do it for you can be a blessing.

This chapter is about using software for the first time. It also includes information on selecting and installing a program, which can be pretty involved. There is also a strategy covered here on learning and using software for the first time — not that you'd want to become an expert or anything.

Finding compatible software

The proud new computer owner — and enthusiast — finds it hard not to gravitate to the local software store. They come, they drool, they buy. For everyone else, the software store is like the fourth ring of hell — or an eight mile square auto parts store. But armed with the proper knowledge, you may be able to find what you want, or at least someone to help you.

STEPS: Finding the software that's right for you

Step 1. Know what you want to get done. Software does the work, so finding software means you need to first know what kind of work you need to do. For example, will you be writing? Then you need a tool to help you write, a word processor. There are dozens of them out there — an overwhelming number. But at least you've taken the first step by narrowing down what you need. (Even if you think it's a category that doesn't exist, ask someone. There may be a software package just for you.)

Step 2. Find compatible software. At this point, you know you have a DOS computer. Therefore, you can only buy DOS software. There are lots of technical details about software that may limit which computer it runs on. For example, some software require fancy graphics hardware, some require a lot of memory. If you know these details, then you can compare what your computer has to the software's requirements, usually listed on the side of the box.

If you don't know what you have, then ask the salesperson. Tell them you're not sure of your system and that you don't want to buy something that requires too much horsepower. (Besides, that stuff is expensive.)

Step 3. Try that software. Pick a few different packages to try out. At most software stores they'll let you try before you buy. Let the salesperson set you up. Then play. Since you know what you want to do, this step will show you how easy some of the software is, and how difficult it can be. Check for the level of so-called "help" offered in each package. Maybe one out there is just for you!

You should also find out what kind of support is available for the software. Does the company have a support line? Is it toll free? These are vital questions and the answers may tell you to choose one package over another. You should also check the software store's return policy.

Step 4. Maybe shop around. If you don't like one store, go to another. If there's something in particular you don't like, be sure to be nasty and tell the store's manager. Also tell them where you're headed. You can price shop if you want, but most software stores offer great discounts anyway. However, if you find a store where the salesperson really knows the package you're interested in, it may be a good idea to buy it there. Nothing beats someone to call on the phone for help.

Step 5. Buy it. Slap down your VISA card and buy the software! But don't buy too much at once. A common mistake is to overwhelm yourself with too much software. Often some packages will gather dust while you concentrate on others. So work on the issue at hand, solve one problem at a time, and don't over do it.

Installation

No one really likes to install software. Well, I do (but I'm a nerd). I love the smell of a new software package. And, like everyone else I know who owns a computer, I take pride in trying to set the thing up without first reading the manuals. Of course, I don't think you're this crazy.

Installation means copying the program you've just bought from floppy disks to your computer's hard drive. It also means more, typically configuring or setting up the program to work with your particular PC, printer, and the rest of that stuff. This is why installation is best left up to your local computer guru. If not, you can follow the outline given here. Since each computer program installs itself differently, this material is covered in a broad sense. But it will give you a general idea of the task you're about to undertake.

Read me first!

Computer manuals and those national sweepstakes with you-know-who's picture on the envelope, both have something in common: There are lots of little pieces of paper and instructions for the interesting things you must do. But computer manuals are easier to deal with. Seriously. There's no need to hunt through everything, fill out various forms, or paste Uncle Ed's picture in the TV set. Just look for a sheet of paper somewhere that says *Read me first!* Read it and you're on your way.

The installation program

You install the program by sticking "Disk 1" into your PC's first floppy drive (drive A), and then running the installation program. If the disk doesn't fit into drive A, stick the disk into drive B and substitute B for A in the following instructions. The name of the installation program is usually INSTALL, though SETUP is also popular. There are two steps here. The first is *logging to drive A*. This is covered in the section, "Changing drives" in Chapter 1. Basically, after sticking Disk 1 into floppy drive A (and closing the drive door latch for a 5 ¼-inch disk), you type in the following:

```
C> A:
```

Typing A and a colon logs you to drive A. Press Enter.

Next you enter the name of the installation program. This is probably listed on the *Read me first!* sheet of paper, or that paper will tell you where to find these instructions. Be wary! Even though installing the program is the first thing you'll ever do with it, it's rarely the first chapter in the manual. (I've always wondered why that's the case.)

For example, if the name of the installation program is INSTALL, you type:

```
A> INSTALL
```

Press Enter.

Don't forget to *read the information on the screen!* It's important. In fact, many "experts" usually screw up software installation by not reading the screens. Follow the instructions closely.

The location

The first thing the installation program will ask you is "where do you want to put me?" Dumb question. You want to put the program in your computer.

The application needs its own workspace on your hard drive. This is referred to as a *subdirectory*. Only advanced users may have some special scheme or plan in this instance. You should accept whatever suggestion the installation program makes — it's probably a good one.

Configuring a computer application

Configuration is the stupidest part of setting up a computer application. This is where the program asks you information about your own computer: What kind of printer do you have? What kind of display or monitor is attached? How much memory do you have? Do you have a mouse? These questions are ridiculous! After all, the computer program is asking you those questions and it's already inside the computer where it can look around more easily than you can.

Still, you may have to tell the computer what it has (which, again, is like asking other people how old you are at your next birthday party). These questions can be difficult. If you don't know the answers, grab someone who does. Otherwise, guess. The "default" or "automatic selection" options tell the program to guess on its own, so if they're available, select them.

An important item to select is a *printer driver*, which is a fancy way of telling the application which printer you have manacled to your PC. Look for your printer's name and model number listed. If it's not there, select "Dumb" or "Line" printer (then go to your dealer and beat up the guy who sold you the printer).

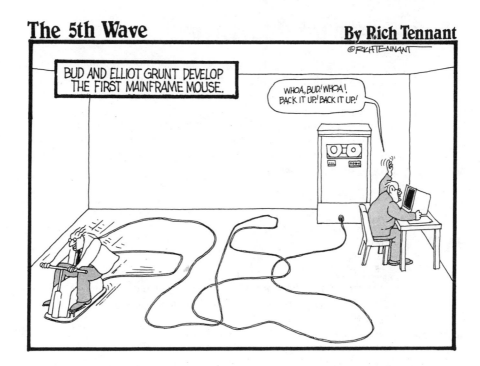

The 5th Wave — By Rich Tennant

The READ.ME file

Finally, there are last minute instructions or information offered in a special file on disk. It's given the name README, READ.ME, README.TXT, or README.DOC. Good installation programs will ask you if you want to view this file. Say "Yes." Look through the file for any information that applies to your situation.

There is usually a utility offered with the program to provide automatic viewing of the READ.ME file. If not, you can view it using the following DOS command:

```
C> MORE < READ.ME
```

That's the MORE command, a space, a less-than sign (<), another space, and the name of the READ.ME file. If the file is named just README, type it in without a period in the middle.

✔ For information on pathnames and directories, refer to Chapter 13.

✔ For information on the TYPE command for viewing files, refer to "Looking at files" in Chapter 1.

Using your new software

After running the install or setup program comes using your new software. As a suggestion, after installing any new software, reset your computer. Press Ctrl-Alt-Del or punch your Reset button.

To use the new program, you type its name at the DOS prompt. A list of popular program names is provided in Chapter 1. If your program isn't on the list, type the name mentioned in the manual. (If nothing happens, refer to "Where is my program?" in Chapter 16.)

You're doing this step just to make sure that the program works as advertised. If something doesn't work, don't be too quick to blame yourself. Programs have bugs. Keep in mind that the features of a new program aren't immediately obvious.

If anything out of the ordinary happens, do the following: Check with your computer supervisor or local computer guru. Check with the software developer (their help number should be listed somewhere in the manual or material that came with it). Finally, you can check with your dealer. Dealers try to be helpful, but it would be impossible for them to know the details of every piece of software they sell. They can, however, replace defective disks for you.

> ✔ For information on resetting, refer to "Resetting" in Chapter 1.

> ✔ Running programs in a general sense is covered in "Running a program" in Chapter 1.

Learning and using

Using software to get work done is why, unfortunately, we need computers. But using software involves learning its quirks. That takes time. So my first suggestion to learning any new software is to give yourself plenty of time.

Sadly, in today's rush-rush method of doing everything, time isn't that easy to come by. It's a big pain when the boss sends you down to the software store and expects you to come back and create something wonderful before the end of the day. In the real world, that's just not possible (not even if you're an "expert").

Most software comes with a workbook or a tutorial for you to follow. This is a series of self-guided lessons on how to use the product. It also tells you about the program's basic features and how they work.

I highly recommend going through the tutorials. Follow the directions on the screen. If you notice anything interesting, write it down in the tutorial booklet and flag that page.

Some tutorials are really dumb, granted. Don't hesitate to bail out of one if you're bored or confused. You can also take classes on using software, though they may bore you as well. Most people do, however, understand the program much better after the tutorial.

After doing the tutorial, play with the software. Make something. Try saving something to disk. Try printing. Then quit. Those are the basic few steps you'll take when using any software program. Get to know them, then expand your knowledge from there as required.

If you feel bold, you can take a look at the manual. Who am I fooling? Computer manuals are awful. Sometimes they'll help, especially if the manual is a reference, allowing you to quickly thumb to what you want, read it, then get right back out (like this book). But never read the manual all the way through.

✔ Some offices may have their own training classes that show you the basics of using the in-house software. Take copious notes. Keep a little book for yourself with instructions for how to do what. Take notes whenever someone shows you something. Don't try to learn anything, just note what they do so you won't have to call them should the situation arise again.

✔ If your computer is set up using a menu system, then your program will probably be added into the menu. Further, there may be additional automation offered in the form of *macros* or *templates*. These will simplify the operation of the program and make your life a heck of a lot easier (see "Black box program rules," in Chapter 21).

Updating your software

Occasionally your computer or your software may be updated. For computer updates, you may have to make modifications to your program, telling it about the new hardware just installed.

For example, if they change printers, add a network, or new monitor, give you a mouse, or change anything else on your computer, you should ask your favorite computer wizard if any of your software needs to be alerted to the modifications. Then let them make those changes.

Computer software is also updated on a frequent basis. New *versions* come out all the time. If you fill in your registration card, you'll be alerted to the new version and what it has to offer. Then, for a nominal or outrageous fee, you can order the new version. My advice: Only order the update if it has features or makes modifications you desperately need. Otherwise, if the current version is doing the job, don't bother.

- ✔ If you notice nothing different after changing hardware (all your programs run), then there's no need to update anything. Just keep on (ugh) working.

- ✔ If you "don't bother" updating your software for several years, you may miss out on something. After a time, software developers stop supporting older versions of their programs, books on the subject go out of print, and it gets harder to find help. When that happens, you'll need to buy the new version.

About the darn command formats

Whenever you see a DOS command listed in a book or manual, you'll often see its *command format*. This is perhaps the most cryptic part about using DOS. The command format tells you what to type, what's optional, what's either-or-ish, and what everything does. If street signs were like this, people would ignore them.

The command format has three parts, though they're not separate:

- ✔ Requirements

- ✔ Options

- ✔ Switches

The requirements are items that you must type at the command line. Take the FORMAT command. Here is what its command format may look like:

    FORMAT *drive*

FORMAT is the name of the command. It's required. *drive* is also required, but it's in italics. This means that you must type something there — something that means "drive" — but what you type is up to you. Here, *drive* means to put a drive letter (and colon) there. This would be explained in the command's description: *drive* is required and indicates a disk drive letter. For *drive* you would substitute A: or B:.

The following command contains an option:

    VOL [*drive*]

The VOL command is required. But anytime you see square brackets, it means what comes between them is optional. Above, *drive* appears in brackets, meaning that a drive letter (and colon) is optional after the VOL command. Again, this would be explained in the definition that follows the command format. It will also explain what happens if you don't specify the option.

Note that you do not specify the brackets when you type the command at the DOS prompt. Brackets are only a visual clue in the command format. For example:

```
VOL B:
```

Above, the volume label of the disk in drive B will be displayed. B: is the optional [*drive*] part of the command, specified above (and without the brackets).

Here is the command format for the DEL command, which deletes files:

```
DEL filename [/P]
```

Above, DEL and *filename* are both required. *filename* indicates the name of the file you want to delete, which can be any file on your disk. The /P (slash-P) is a *switch*, and it's optional, appearing in brackets. What /P does and why you would want to list it would be listed in the instructions that follow.

All switches start with either a slash or a dash and most of them are optional. The typical switch is a single letter, and it can be either upper- or lowercase. Some switches are more than one letter long, and some have options. For example:

```
[/D=drive]
```

That whole whatchamacallit above is optional. The switch (/D) is followed by an equal sign and *drive*, which indicates that you must specify a disk drive letter (and colon) in that spot. So /D is optional, but if you use it you have to fill in a disk drive letter.

Finally, there are optional either-or situations. These are options where you must specify either one switch or the other. This is written out as follows:

```
[ON|OFF]
```

Above, this item is optional since it's in brackets. If you specify it, you must either use ON or OFF , not both. The vertical bar or pipe character (|) tells you to pick one or the other if you want this option.

> ✔ The *pièce de résistance* for this notation is your friendly DOS manual. But don't stare at it too long or you'll turn to silicon.

Chapter 12
"It Tells Me to Edit My CONFIG.SYS or AUTOEXEC.BAT File!"

. . . .

In this chapter...

▶ How to edit your CONFIG.SYS and AUTOEXEC.BAT files.

▶ How to locate the CONFIG.SYS and AUTOEXEC.BAT files.

▶ How to use the DOS 5 Editor.

▶ How to use the EDLIN Editor for other versions of DOS.

▶ How to reset your computer to see the edits you've made to the files.

▶ Where to put the new lines you're adding to the CONFIG.SYS or AUTOEXEC.BAT files.

. . . .

*O*ne of the most puzzling redundancies for the DOS dummy happens when a program says "Put the following into your CONFIG.SYS file" or "Edit your AUTOEXEC.BAT file and add the following." To carry out these instructions, you're told to refer to your DOS manual. The DOS manual, on the other hand, says to refer to your application's manual. Herein we have the rumblings of any great bureaucracy: confusion and consistency in equal amounts.

This chapter contains information on editing your CONFIG.SYS and AUTOEXEC.BAT files. What these two files do is important, yet how they do it isn't crucial knowledge. How to edit the files, specifically the instructions for inserting special text, is described here in a — yes, I'll admit it — tutorial fashion. You don't need to know why you're doing this; you don't even need to know what you're doing. But when it tells you to edit your CONFIG.SYS or AUTOEXEC.BAT file, these are the instructions you need.

Before diving into this, you should know two things: First, you should always know what it is you're adding to CONFIG.SYS or AUTOEXEC.BAT. The exact line of text you need to add should be specified somewhere. Never edit these files without a purpose.

Secondly, use this tutorial only as a last resort or when no other help is around. Especially in a business situation, someone should be in charge of the computers and they should be updating these two important files. If you're at home, or there isn't anyone else around to help, then this is where you turn. But beware: This is funky.

Hunting down the files

To get at CONFIG.SYS or AUTOEXEC.BAT, you must log to the root directory of your hard drive. Type the following two commands:

```
C> C:
```

Press Enter. You're logging to drive C. Now type:

```
C> CD \
```

That's CD, followed by a space and the backslash character — not the forward slash.

The two commands you used above will ensure that you're logged to the root directory of drive C, your boot disk. You're now ready to edit either CONFIG.SYS or AUTOEXEC.BAT. The next step is to determine which *text editor* you have.

- ✔ If you want to make a duplicate "safety" copy of the file you're editing, refer to "Duplicating a file" in Chapter 3.

- ✔ For more information on "logging," refer to "Changing drives" and "Changing directories," both in Chapter 1.

- ✔ The CD command is covered in "Finding the current directory" and "Changing directories," both in Chapter 13.

Using the DOS 5 editor

If you have DOS 5.0 or later, these instructions here are specific to its editor, EDIT. If you have an older version of DOS, you'll need to suffer through something called EDLIN; jump forward to the section titled "Using EDLIN."

You can discover which version of DOS you're using with the VER command. Refer to "Names and versions" in Chapter 2.

Editing the file

If the instructions told you to "edit your CONFIG.SYS file," then type the following:

```
C:\> EDIT CONFIG.SYS
```

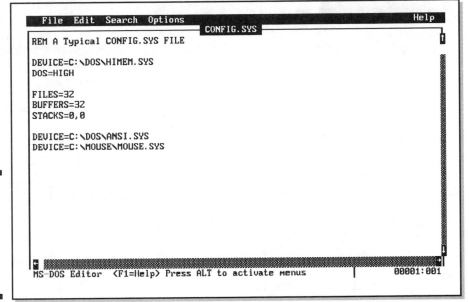

```
   File  Edit  Search  Options                              Help
                               CONFIG.SYS
 REM A Typical CONFIG.SYS FILE

 DEVICE=C:\DOS\HIMEM.SYS
 DOS=HIGH

 FILES=32
 BUFFERS=32
 STACKS=0,0

 DEVICE=C:\DOS\ANSI.SYS
 DEVICE=C:\MOUSE\MOUSE.SYS




 MS-DOS Editor   <F1=Help> Press ALT to activate menus        00001:001
```

Figure 12-1: Here is the MS-DOS Editor with someone's CONFIG.SYS file in it.

Above, EDIT is the name of the DOS 5 editor — the program that edits files on disk. It's followed by a space, then CONFIG.SYS, the name of the file you want to edit.

If you're told to "edit your AUTOEXEC.BAT file," then substitute AUTOEXEC.BAT for CONFIG.SYS as follows:

```
C:\> EDIT AUTOEXEC.BAT
```

After pressing Enter, you'll see the MS-DOS Editor appear on your screen. It will look something like Figure 12-1.

✔ If you see a box or window on the screen asking if you want to use the "Survival Guide," press the Esc (Escape) key.

✔ If you don't see the MS-DOS Editor, or you get a "bad command or file name" error, then it's time to contact someone else for help. Double check the instructions here first. Also, make sure to tell the person that you've already tried to do it yourself. Even the most surly of computer wizards appreciate effort.

✔ You can always use EDLIN if the EDIT program appears uncooperative. Refer to the section "Using EDLIN" later in this chapter.

Adding the new line

Since we're not going to make any assumptions here, put the new line at the end of the document, way down toward its bottom. If your instructions explicitly tell you where to put the new line, then follow them as best you can.

Press and hold down the Ctrl (control) key, then press the End key. Release both keys. This moves you to the last line in the file.

Press the Enter key.

Now type the line you need to add. For example, if you were adding the PROMPT command to AUTOEXEC.BAT, you would type in that command. If you were adding a command to CONFIG.SYS, type that command in as well.

After you enter the exact text of the command, double check your work. Make sure you typed in exactly what you should. Once that's done, press Enter.

✔ The Ctrl and End key combination is often written Ctrl-End. Refer to "Alt-S means what?" in Chapter 8 for more information about key combinations.

✔ If you make a mistake while you type, use the backspace key to back up and erase.

✔ Sometimes commands in CONFIG.SYS require a full pathname in order for them to work properly. Refer to "What is a pathname?" in Chapter 13 for information on pathnames.

Saving the file

After double checking your work, you need to save the file back to disk.

Press and release the Alt key, then press the F key. This "drops down" the File menu at the top of the screen.

Press S to save the file.

Information about the editor not worth reading

The editor uses drop down menus to contain its commands. You activate the menu by pressing the Alt key, then the first letter of the menu you want to use. You can also press both the Alt key and the letter key at the same time; Alt-F drops down the File menu.

Each menu contains menu items, all of which pertain somehow to the title of the menu, for example, the File menu contains file commands. These commands are selected by typing the highlighted letter in their name.

If you have a mouse, you can select menu items with it. This involves using a whole lot of mousey terms, which I don't really care to get into at this point in the book (but do get into in Chapter 8).

Quitting

The file has now been updated and saved. All you need to do is quit the editor and return to DOS.

Press and release the Alt key, then press the F key. Again, this drops down the File menu.

Press X to exit the Editor and return to DOS.

> ✔ If you haven't saved at this point, a box or window appears asking if you want to save. Press Y in that instance.

> ✔ Please skip forward to the section titled "Reset."

Using EDLIN

Boy, do I feel sorry for you. EDLIN is just the worst example of a text editor in the history of DOS. This program was originally written in 1981 — back when the only people using computers were puffy and pale Neanderthal nerds, just rising from the mud swamps of the slide-rule age. It makes me shudder.

Editing the file

When you're told to "edit your CONFIG.SYS file," type in the following command:

```
C:\> EDLIN CONFIG.SYS
```

Above, EDLIN is the name of the primitive and hasty DOS editor. It's followed by a space, then CONFIG.SYS, the name of the file you'll be editing.

To "edit your AUTOEXEC.BAT file," substitute AUTOEXEC.BAT for CONFIG.SYS as follows:

```
C:\> EDLIN AUTOEXEC.BAT
```

After pressing Enter, you'll see the following:

```
End of input file *
```

Yikes! I shudder to think of the user hostility this program harbors. You see "End of input file," which means God-knows-what, then an asterisk on the next line. Is this like shaking hands with a snake or what?

> ✔ If you don't see the above message, or you get a "Bad command or file name" error, then it's time to contact someone else for help. Double check these instructions first. Also, tell the computer guru in charge that you've already given it your best shot.

Painful background information about EDLIN

EDLIN is the same program it was originally in 1981, on the first version of DOS ever made. It's an enigmatic text editor, which means that you only edit one line of text at a time and you generally can't see what it is you're "editing." This program really reeks!

Quite a few books offer tutorials on EDLIN. An educational book I wrote once lacked such a tutorial — much to the chagrin of the blockheaded educators who reviewed my text. I told them EDLIN stinks, but they insisted I include it because "it's taught at the college level." Poor kids, I thought.

Adding the new line

The new line you're adding will be placed at the end of the file. This is usually the safest bet.

To add your new line at the end of the file, you use the #I command. At the asterisk prompt, type a pound sign (#) and the letter I (no spaces!):

```
*#I
```

Press Enter. You'll see something like the following displayed:

```
13:*
```

There will be a number, a colon, and an asterisk. The number is a line number, the last line in the file. The asterisk is EDLIN's friendly prompt.

Type the line you need to add. For example, if you were adding the PROMPT command to AUTOEXEC.BAT, you would type in that command.

If you were adding a command to CONFIG.SYS, you would type it in as well.

After you enter the exact text of the command, double check your work.

Once you've made sure that everything has been typed correctly, press Enter. You'll see something like the following:

```
14:*
```

The number will be one higher than the new line you entered. At this prompt, type a Ctrl-C: Press and hold the Ctrl (control) key and, with that key down, type a C. Release both keys. You'll see "^C" displayed and then the main asterisk prompt two lines down:

```
14:*^C
```

(Isn't this painful? Imagine if you had to write everything in EDLIN! People have had massive brain seizures doing just that.)

✔ If you make a mistake while you type, use the backspace key to back up and erase.

✔ Sometimes commands in CONFIG.SYS require a full pathname in order for them to work properly. Refer to "What is a pathname?" in Chapter 13 for information on pathnames.

Saving the file and quitting

You now need to save the file back to disk. In EDLIN you do this by quitting the program with the E command, which stands for Exit back to DOS. (Though I prefer it standing for Enough!)

Press E, then Enter. Soon you'll see the happy DOS prompt displayed.

✔ Note that EDLIN automatically makes a backup file: CONFIG.BAK for CONFIG.SYS or AUTOEXEC.BAK for AUTOEXEC.BAT. These files contain the original text you edited.

✔ If you've totally screwed up, then you can quit EDLIN using the Q command. EDLIN will ask if you want to "Abort edit?" Press Y to return to DOS.

Reset

You're back at the DOS prompt, ready to continue working. Congratulations, your CONFIG.SYS or AUTOEXEC.BAT file has been updated. Whew! But now comes the scary part.

You must reset your computer to see the results of any changes you've made to these files. This is only true for AUTOEXEC.BAT and CONFIG.SYS; any other file you edit or program you run doesn't require a reset. (I told you this would be funky.)

- You reset by pressing Ctrl-Alt-Del, or by punching that big red button on your PC. Refer to "Resetting" in Chapter 1 if you feel anxious about doing this.

- If you see any errors when the computer restarts, that means you may have typed something incorrectly. Go through these steps again and re-check your work. Make sure that what you typed is exactly what was required. Then call for help.

Chapter 13
The Hard Drive: Where You Store Stuff

• •

In this chapter...

▶ How information is stored in separate work areas on the hard drive.

▶ How the root directory fits into the "big picture."

▶ What the "<DIR>" thing in a directory listing means.

▶ How a pathname is created and used.

▶ How to find the current directory.

▶ How to change from one directory to another.

▶ How to see your hard disk's tree structure.

▶ How to use the CHKDSK command.

▶ How to back up.

▶ How to perform a daily backup.

▶ How to perform an incremental backup.

• •

I've always been fascinated by "hard disk management." Why isn't it *easy* disk management? Computers are supposed to make life easier, not harder. Yet the computer nerds are fascinated by hard disk management. They've even come up with a whole row of verbal hurdles to leap over for anyone who attempts to understand hard disk management. Even given that it's a hard disk you're managing, the subject could easily be called hard hard-disk management. Ugh.

All kidding aside, hard disk management is simply using files on a hard drive. This involves some organization, and that's where the funky terms come into play. This chapter describes the ugly terms you'll encounter when you use a hard drive, what they mean, and why the heck you'd ever want to use them. This stuff is really important. If you learn only one thing from this book — how to find your way around a hard disk — it will be worth the inflated price of this book.

What is a subdirectory?

A subdirectory is workspace on-a-disk. It's almost like a disk within a disk. Into a subdirectory or workspace you can copy files and programs, and use DOS commands. The advantage to them is that you can store information in a subdirectory and keep it separate from other files in other subdirectories on the same disk. That keeps the disk from getting file-messy.

Any disk can have subdirectories, though they're used primarily on hard drives to keep files separate and your programs organized. So rather than let you suffer through a hard drive with bazillions of files all in one place, the subdirectories allow you to organize everything by placing information into separate areas.

🖝 Subdirectories should just be called "directories." The prefix sub means "under," just as submarine means any large naval vessel a marine is standing on. All the work spaces on a disk are really directories. However, when you refer to one directory in relationship to another, the term "subdirectory" is used.

🖝 If you want to create a directory to keep some of your files separate from other files, refer to "How to name a directory (the MKDIR command)" in Chapter 14.

🖝 All the directories on your disk create what's called a *tree structure*. For information, refer to "The tree structure" in this chapter.

The root directory

Every disk you use under DOS has one main directory, called the *root directory*. The root directory (often just called "the root") exists on all DOS disks; it happens naturally, created there when you first formatted the disk.

The symbol for the root directory is the single backslash (\). This is an abbreviation — shorthand — which DOS uses in reference to the root directory. It also plays an important role in the *pathname*, which is covered later in this chapter.

Additional directories on a disk are subdirectories *under* the root directory. They branch off of the root like branches of a tree. In fact, if you map out the directories on a disk linking each subdirectory, it looks like a family tree of sorts (see Figure 13-1).

🖝 The FORMAT command is used to prepare disks for use under DOS. It also creates the root directory. For more information, refer to "Formatting a disk" in Chapter 10.

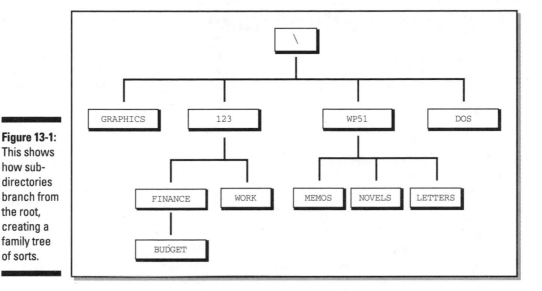

Figure 13-1:
This shows how sub-directories branch from the root, creating a family tree of sorts.

✔ Whenever you're using a disk, you're *logged* to or currently using a directory on that disk. To change to another subdirectory, refer to "Changing directories" later in this chapter; to change to another disk refer to "Changing drives" in Chapter 1. To see which directory you're currently logged to, refer to "Finding the current directory" later in this chapter.

You are not required to know this stuff

Subdirectories are often called "child" directories. And from a subdirectory's point of view, it has a "parent" directory. For example, in Figure 13-1, DOS is a subdirectory of the root directory (\). DOS is the root directory's child directory. The root directory is the parent of the DOS directory.

If you were logged to or using the 123 directory in Figure 13-1, then its parent directory would be the root. The 123 directory also has two child directories — two subdirectories. They are named FINANCE and WORK.

The visual representation shown in Figure 13-1 is only for your head; you'll "see" nothing of the sort as you use your computer. However, it's a good visual representation of the relationships between various directories on a disk. The TREE command, covered later in this chapter, lets you see the representation in a different format.

That funny "<DIR>" thing

To find a subdirectory on a disk, you use the DIR command. Directories are listed there, along with other files. The way you identify a directory name is by the <DIR> thing shown after its name (where other files would have their file size in bytes).

For example, consider the following output from the DIR command:

```
Volume in drive C is DOS 5
Volume Serial Number is 16CE-9B67
Directory of C:\
123          <DIR>                    03-18-91      9:33p
COMM         <DIR>                    08-07-91      9:37p
DOS          <DIR>                    09-20-90     10:52p
GAMES        <DIR>                    09-22-90      5:18p
WP51         <DIR>                    09-21-90      5:12p
AUTOEXEC     BAT           574        08-01-91     10:04a
COMMAND      COM         47845        04-09-91      5:00a
CONFIG       SYS           464        07-25-91     10:20a
WINA20       386          9349        04-09-91      5:00a
             14 file(s)   58232       bytes
                       16345088       bytes free
```

The "files" 123, COMM, DOS, GAMES, and WP51 are actually directories on disk. At the top of the above output, DIRECTORY OF C:\ tells you that you're looking at a directory of drive C (that's the C:), the root directory (shown by the backslash). The <DIR> entries in the listing are all subdirectories of the root directory.

✔ Subdirectories appear in the DIR command's listing because they're part of your disk just like files. In fact, directories are named just like files and can even have an extension like a file. Refer to "How to name a directory" in Chapter 14 for more information (if you're curious).

✔ For more information on the DIR command, refer to "The DIR command" in Chapter 1.

✔ For information on finding a lost directory on disk, refer to "Finding a lost subdirectory" in Chapter 14.

✔ The C:\ is actually a pathname.

What is a pathname?

A pathname is like a long type of filename. But, like a path, it tells you a location or a way to get somewhere. On a disk, a pathname tells you how to get to a specific file or subdirectory — an exact location.

For a directory, the pathname tells you which drive it's on, and all its parent directories on up to the root. For example, consider this pathname:

```
C:\WP51\DATA
```

Above, DATA is a subdirectory of WP51, which is a subdirectory of the root directory. This all sits on drive C, as seen by the C: at the start of the pathname. (Since this pathname contains a drive letter, it's also called a full pathname; pathnames don't always need the drive letter.)

To break this down, you have:

C:	The drive letter; the subdirectory is on drive C
C:\	The root directory of drive C
C:\WP51	The WP51 subdirectory on drive C, a subdirectory of the root
C:\WP51\DATA	The DATA subdirectory under the WP51 directory

Note that the backslash is used both as a symbol for the root directory as well as a separator. A backslash always separates subdirectories from each other. There are no spaces in a pathname.

Dot to dot (and skip this stuff if you wanna)

How many times have you seen something like the following in the DIR command's listing?

```
.     <DIR>   8-24-93  4:44p
..    <DIR>   8-24-93  4:44p
```

Doesn't that just bug you? A single period, or dot, isn't the name of a file, and dot-dot isn't the name of a file either. (Filenames, legal and illegal, are covered in "Use these filenames — go directly to jail!" in Chapter 14.) But from the previous section you know that these are both directories on disk. Where are they? What are they?!

The dot and dot-dot entries are abbreviations. Dot, the first entry above, is an abbreviation for the current directory. Dot-dot refers to the parent directory.

You can use these abbreviations to refer to the current or parent directory in various DOS commands. This, however, is an advanced and secretive subject, best left up to the loftier books on using computers. But if dot and dot-dot ever bugged the heck out of you, now you know what they represent.

A pathname can end with a filename, which tells you exactly where that file is located on which disk. For example, if the file CHAP12.DOC was in the WORK subdirectory on drive C, its pathname would be:

```
C:\WORK\CHAP12.DOC
```

This breaks down as follows:

C:	Drive C
C:\	The root directory
C:\WORK	The WORK subdirectory
C:\WORK\CHAP12.DOC	The file CHAP12.DOC and its full pathname

Again, note how the backslash is used to separate the items in the pathname.

✔ The drive letter is optional in a pathname. However, I recommend using it because it's more specific.

✔ When you use the CD command by itself to locate the current directory, what it returns is a pathname; refer to the next section.

Finding the current directory

To find out which directory you're logged to or currently using, type the CD command:

```
C> CD
```

The directory you're using will be displayed on the following line. (Actually, what you see is a pathname of the current directory.) You can change to any other subdirectory on the same drive by using the CD command followed by that directory's pathname. Refer to the next section for the specifics.

✔ CD has a longer form, CHDIR. Both do the same thing, but CD is quicker to type (and you can say "current directory" in your head instead of "chiddur").

✔ For more information on changing drives, refer to "Changing drives" in Chapter 1.

✔ For more information on pathnames, refer to "What is a pathname?" earlier in this chapter.

✔ The PROMPT command can be used to tell you the current directory at all times. Refer to "Prompt styles of the rich and famous" in Chapter 2.

Technical background junk

Whenever you use a computer, you're using or attached to some specific disk drive. Though your system may have several drives, you're only actually using one of them at a time. That drive is said to be the *currently logged drive*. ("Logged" in computer lingo means "using.") The same holds true with directories on a disk; you can only use — or be logged to — one directory at a time.

When you first use a disk, you're automatically logged to its root directory, the main directory on disk. After you've been using the computer for a while, you'll probably wind up elsewhere on the disk, say in some subdirectory somewhere. To find out the pathname of that subdirectory, use the CD command as described above.

Changing directories

To change to another directory, type the CD (change directory) command followed by the pathname of the directory to which you want to change. In computer jargon, this *logs* you to that new directory.

For example, suppose you want to change to the root directory. Type this in:

```
C> CD \
```

That's the CD command, followed by a space and the root directory's name/ symbol, the backslash.

To change to the \WP51 subdirectory, type:

```
C> CD \WP51
```

Try to type in a full pathname for the directory. Full pathnames start with a backslash, which indicates the root directory. If you know the full pathname of the directory, then type it in. Otherwise, you can refer to "Finding a lost subdirectory" in Chapter 14 for finding lost directories.

You can use the DIR command to find the name of a subdirectory to log to. If you find a name, a full pathname isn't needed. For example, if you use the DIR command and see the DATA directory (marked by <DIR> in the directory listing), then you can log (change) to it by typing:

```
C> CD DATA
```

Since DATA is a subdirectory, or child, of the current directory, there's no need to specify a full pathname.

Another shortcut can be taken to log to the parent directory:

```
C> CD ..
```

The dot-dot is an abbreviation for the parent directory — no matter where you are. This is much quicker than typing out the full pathname for the parent directory.

- ✔ You cannot use the CD command to change to a subdirectory on another drive. You must first log to that drive, then use the CD command. Refer to "Changing drives" in Chapter 1 for logging to another drive.

- ✔ If you see an "Invalid directory" error, then you didn't type in a full pathname or you mistyped something. It could also be that you're not logged to the proper drive. Refer to "Finding a lost subdirectory" in Chapter 14 for finding lost directories.

- ✔ You can also use the CHDIR command, the longer form of the CD command. CHDIR stands for Change Directory, supposedly.

- ✔ Refer to "What is a pathname?" in this chapter for information on pathnames.

The tree structure

All the subdirectories on a disk make for a fairly complex arrangement. I know of no one, nerd or non-nerd alike, who actually knows exactly what's where on their system. So to find out — to get a view of the "big picture," the TREE command is used.

Type the following command:

```
C> TREE C:\
```

That's the TREE command, a space, C, a colon, and a backslash character. The TREE command is followed by a pathname; C:\ means drive C's root directory. Press Enter and the TREE command displays a graphic representation of your tree structure, how your subdirectories are organized for drive C. Early versions of DOS don't have graphic trees; they use a confusing text display instead.

The display scrolls off the screen for a time. If you want to pause the display, press the Ctrl-S key combination; to continue press Ctrl-S again. You can also use the following command:

```
C> TREE C:\ | MORE
```

That's the same command as before, followed by a space, the pipe character (|), another space, and the word MORE. This inserts an automatic "more" prompt at the bottom of each screen. Press the spacebar to look at the next screen.

> ✔ If you want to print a copy of the output, turn on your printer and type in this command:

```
C> TREE C:\ > PRN
```

That's the same TREE command described above, a space, a greater-than symbol (>), another space, and the word PRN. Press Enter. If the printed output looks gross, try this variation of the command:

```
C> TREE C:\ /A > PRN
```

That's a slash-A in the middle of the command, surrounded by a space on each side. (Well, as you make more demands on DOS it gets more cryptic. But at least your printed copy won't look so gross.) For more information on using a printer, refer to Chapter 9.

> ✔ For more information on Ctrl-S, refer to "Ctrl-S and the Pause key" in Chapter 8.

Checking the disk (the CHKDSK command)

The CHKDSK command is known as "check disk," which is kind of what CHKDSK looks like without all the superfluous vowels. Basically, this command reports information about your disk, most of it technical. About the only useful thing you can discover with CHKDSK is how large a hard drive you have and how much space is still available for storing programs and data.

To use CHKDSK, type it in at the DOS prompt, press Enter, and prepare to be overwhelmed:

```
C> CHKDSK
```

After pressing Enter you'll see something like this:

```
Volume DOS 5 created 09-21-1990 1:26p
Volume Serial Number is 16CE-9B67

42366976    bytes total disk space
73728       bytes in 2 hidden files
110592      bytes in 52 directories
25837568    bytes in 879 user files
16345088    bytes available on disk

2048        bytes in each allocation unit
20687       total allocation units on disk
7981        available allocation units on disk

655360      total bytes memory
637984      bytes free
```

There are four chunks of information here. The first is trivia about your disk. The second, with five items, is more important. The first value tells you the size of your disk. It says there are 42,366,976 bytes of "total disk space." That means the drive holds about 40MB of stuff. The last value tells you how much space you have left. That's 16,345,088 bytes "available on disk," which means that drive has about 16MB of unused storage.

The third section is really useless, with "allocation unit" sounding like something the government would say about every 35 billion dollars it spends.

The final section tells you how much memory you have and how much is open for use by programs.

✔ CHKDSK only works on one drive at a time. To use CHKDSK on another drive, first log to that drive, then run CHKDSK. Refer to "Changing drives" in Chapter 1 for information on logging to another drive. You can also use CHKDSK on another drive by typing the following command:

```
C>CHKDSK A:
```

✔ CHKDSK is often thought of as some form of cure-all for disk ailments. It's not. CHKDSK merely reports information that the computer already knows about itself, so if some computer weirdo says "run CHKDSK" to fix the problem, they probably don't know what they're talking about. There is one exception; refer to the next section.

✔ If CHKDSK reports any errors, specifically "Missing files" or "unallocated clusters" or "lost chains" or something along those lines, it will ask you a question. Type N for no, then refer to the following section.

✔ For more information on available memory, refer to Chapter 6.

"CHKDSK says I have lost files in clusters or something"

The CHKDSK command is good at finding lost files on disk. These aren't important files that you may have lost, but rather pieces of files that were blown to bits by DOS. Usually, these files are shattered when you reset in the middle of something or when the computer goes bonkers; there is typically nothing CHKDSK finds that's important, so don't take its message as a bad omen.

When CHKDSK does report something wrong, you should fix it. In order to fix the problem, run CHKDSK a second time with its slash-F option. Type in the following command:

```
C> CHKDSK /F
```

That's the CHKDSK command, a space, then slash-F. Press Enter. CHKDSK will discover the same errors. This time, however, press Y when it asks you the "Convert lost chains to files?" question.

When you use the slash-F and answer "Yes" to the question, CHKDSK will gather up all the pieces of the lost files it finds and place them on your disk. There is really nothing you can do with these files, so delete them. This command does the job:

```
C> DEL \FILE*.CHK
```

That's DEL, a space, a backslash, then FILE, an asterisk, a period, and CHK. This is a filename "wildcard" that matches all the files CHKDSK creates in your root directory.

✔ For more information on deleting files, refer to "Deleting a group of files" in Chapter 3.

✔ For information on filename wildcards, refer to "Wildcards (or, poker was never this much fun)" in Chapter 14.

Backing up

Backing up is making a safety copy of your data, typically the data on your hard drive. You make a copy of all the files on your hard drive to a large stack of floppy drives using the painful and wrongfully ignored DOS BACKUP command.

Few people like to back up. In fact, the thought is almost too ridiculous to bring up in this book. Hopefully, someone will have implemented a backup scheme for you to follow, listing the proper commands for you to type each day. If not, the next few sections offer brief explanations of several popular backup commands.

✔ If you're using a third-party backup program, such as FastBack, Central Point Backup (in PC Tools), or the Norton Backup, then you'll have to look elsewhere for instructions on how they work. Generally, they do the same things the DOS backup (covered here) does, but with more switches and fancy displays.

✔ You always back up from a hard drive to a floppy disk, usually in your A drive, though you can back up to drive B.

✔ If you think backing up is a pain, you're in the majority. No one likes to back up. I'm not going to waggle my finger here, describing the possible perils if you don't back up. I'll leave that for someone closer to you to go over.

Backing up the hard drive using DOS BACKUP

If you don't have a convenient third-party backup program, you can still use DOS's BACKUP command to back up your hard disk. Why not just use COPY? Well, you could — only if you need to back up a few files that change regularly — and if none of the files are bigger than a floppy disk. Backup programs can do what COPY can't: They can break up a file and put half on each of two separate disks.

To back up your entire hard drive using DOS BACKUP, the first thing you'll need is a stack of formatted disks. You should label each disk and sequentially number them one through however many are in your stack. (I have no idea how many disks you'll need. Typically, a 40MB hard drive requires about 40 1.2MB disks; you can do the math for different sized hard drives and larger or smaller disks.) The third-party backup programs usually give you an estimate, but not DOS — oh no, that would be too easy.

Given that you have a stack of formatted and numbered disks nearby, type the following command:

```
C> BACKUP C:\*.* A: /S
```

That's the BACKUP command, a space, then C:*.* which means all files in the root directory of drive C. That's followed by a space, A: for drive A, another

The 5th Wave   By Rich Tennant

"WELL, WE TOOK A POLL AND FOUND THAT WHAT PEOPLE REALLY WANTED WASN'T MORE POWER OR INCREASED APPLICATIONS, BUT JUST REALLY NEAT TAIL FINS."

space, and then a slash-S. Above, C: is the drive you're backing up. If you're backing up another hard drive, substitute its letter for C: above. If your backup is to another floppy drive, put B: in the same spot A: is in above.

Press Enter and follow the instructions on the screen.

✔ If you're using DOS 3.3 or earlier, and you don't have a stack of backup disks, use this version of the BACKUP command instead:

```
C> BACKUP C:\*.* A: /S /F
```

The extra slash-F tells BACKUP to format any blank disks you may insert into the drive.

✔ Refer to "Formatting a disk" in Chapter 10 for more information on formatting.

✔ Refer to "Names and versions" in Chapter 2 to see which version of DOS you have.

Backing up a single file

The BACKUP command can back up a whole hard drive, a subdirectory, or just a single file. Why would any sane person want to do this instead of just using the COPY command? Because BACKUP is the only method you have of copying a very large file to a floppy disk (or more than one floppy disk, as is usually the case). Here is the format:

```
C> BACKUP C:\WORK\LARGE.FAT A:
```

Above, you see the BACKUP command, a space, then the full pathname of the large file you want to back up. That's followed by a space, then the letter of the floppy drive you're backing up to, plus a colon. Press Enter and follow the instructions on the screen.

> ✔ Refer to "What is a pathname?" in this chapter for more information on a file's full pathname.

Backing up today's work

You can back up the stuff you've worked on today, usually in one single subdirectory, using the following BACKUP command:

```
C> BACKUP C:\WORK\STUFF\*.* A:
```

Above, you type the BACKUP command, a space, then the name of the subdirectory (work area) that contains your files — plus a backslash and the star-dot-star wildcard. That's followed by a space, then the drive letter of the floppy drive to which you're backing up, plus the required colon.

Refer to "Using *.* (star-dot-star)" in Chapter 14 for information on that wildcard.

Backing up modified files

A special type of backup command can be done to back up those files that have been changed or modified since the last "real" hard disk backup. This is what's known as an *incremental* backup. The following is the BACKUP command to perform an incremental backup of drive C.

```
C> BACKUP C:\*.* A: /S /M
```

The BACKUP command is followed by C:*.* for all the files on drive C. That's followed by a space and A: meaning that you're backing up to drive A. Then comes a space, slash-S, another space, and finally a slash-M.

> ✔ If you're doing an incremental backup of another hard drive, substitute its letter for C: above.

> ✔ If you're backing up to floppy drive B, substitute B: for A: above.

Chapter 14
Files — Lost and Found

In this chapter...

▶ How to name a file.

▶ What not to name a file.

▶ Which filenames are important.

▶ How to create and name a subdirectory.

▶ How to use the DIR command.

▶ How to display a wide format directory.

▶ How to sort a directory listing.

▶ How to find a lost file.

▶ How to find a lost directory.

▶ How to use wildcards to match groups of files.

Did you know that "file" can by anagrammed into the word *life*? Aside from that, there's really nothing interesting about files. Well, actually only two things: What you can and cannot name a file (which is much akin to getting a 14 letter last name on a vanity license plate) and that files, like certain socks, occasionally get sucked into some parallel universe since the last time you've seen them. It's like the car keys gremlin who goes around snatching up your keys for a few seconds. There's a file gremlin who will steal files — even though you just saved them to disk.

This chapter contains instructions for defeating the file gremlin. Actually, this chapter contains tidbits of information about using files, naming files, and all that file stuff. It doesn't contain information on copying, renaming, or deleting files, which is conveniently stored in Chapter 3.

Name that file!

When you create a file you give it a name. The name should reflect what's in the file or somehow be able to describe the file's contents. After all, it's that name that gives you the clue as to what it is when looking at a directory listing. But rather than grant you poetic license to create highly accurate and descriptive filenames, DOS puts on the binders and gives you only so many letters to use. It's frustrating.

All filenames fit into a specific pattern, called the 8-dot-3 pattern:

```
FILENAME.EXT
```

The first part of the filename can have up to eight characters. This can be followed by an optional dot (period) plus up to three additional characters. This is where they get the 8-dot-3 (which really sounds like Mr. Spock calling out photon torpedo spreads).

The first eight characters of a filename are the descriptive part. These characters can be any number or letter. For example, the following are all okay filenames:

```
TEST
A
80PROOF
HELLO
1040
LETTER
KINGFISH
```

If you wish to add an extension (see below for definition) to a filename, you must specify the dot (or period), then up to three more characters. Here is the same group of rowdy files with extensions added:

```
TEST.OUT
A.1
80PROOF.GIN
HELLO.MOM
1040.X
LETTER.DOC
KINGFISH.ME
```

The extension is normally used to identify file types, for example, whether a file is a word processing document or a spreadsheet. Common file extensions are:

BAK	A copy of a data file as a backup
BAT	A special type of program; a batch file
COM	A command program or command file (program file)
DBF	A database file
DOC	A document or word processing file
EXE	An executable file or another type of program

FON	A font file
GRA	A graphics file
PIC	A picture file
SYS	A system file
TXT	A text file
WKS	A worksheet file
YUK	A collection of jokes

Of course, the list goes on and on. None of this is etched in stone anywhere, so feel free to give a file whatever extension you want — save for the dreaded COM, EXE, or BAT extensions (which are covered in "Significant filenames" below).

✔ Some programs supply their own extensions automatically; you simply type in the first part of the filename and the program will add the rest as it creates or loads the file.

✔ You can enter a filename in upper- or lowercase, DOS doesn't care. The DIR command displays filenames in uppercase.

Use these filenames — go directly to jail!

If you goof when you name a file, you'll usually get some pleasing error message or an idle threat. Generally speaking, as long as you stick to naming a file using letters and numbers, you'll be okay.

You cannot, however, under any circumstance — even if the building were on fire and St. Peter appeared to you, winked, and said it was okay just this once — use the following characters in a filename:

```
. " / \ [ ] : * | < > + = ; , ?
```

The biggest boo-boo most users make is putting a space in a filename. A space! Heavens! Filenames cannot contain spaces.

✔ The period cannot be used, unless it's the separator between the filename and extension.

✔ The special characters asterisk (*) and question mark (?) are actually filename wildcards, covered later in this chapter.

✔ The colon (:) is only used after a letter of the alphabet to identify a disk drive, so it cannot appear in a filename.

✔ The special characters less-than (<), greater-than (>), and the pipe character (|) are all used by DOS for other, confusing purposes.

> ✔ And the rest of the characters have special meaning to DOS as well, so using them will offend your operating system. (Not a nice thing to do to something that holds life-and-death control over your data!)

Significant filenames

Filenames that end with a COM, EXE, or BAT extension are special. Those are actually programs that do things on your computer. As such, please don't name any of your files with those extensions. You can use any other extension or three-letter combination you can dream up. But COM, EXE, and BAT are for programs only.

How to name a directory (the MKDIR command)

Directories are given names just like files. They can contain numbers and letters, and can have up to eight characters, plus an optional period and a three-letter extension. As a rule, however, directories usually lack extensions.

Directories are named as they're created. This is done by the MD command. For example:

```
C> MD DATA
```

The above command is MD, for make directory, followed by a space and the name of the directory to create. In this case, DOS creates a subdirectory named DATA. (For more on subdirectories, refer to Chapter 13.)

Creating directories is a job best left to someone else. However, you can create your own directories to store your favorite files, keeping them together. More information on subdirectories is offered in Chapter 13.

Unlike files, you cannot rename a directory after it's been created. This is usually for the best, since many programs are set up to find certain directory names and changing them makes the computer goofy.

Using the DIR command

The DIR command is used to see a list of files on disk. You just type DIR and press Enter:

```
C> DIR
```

The files are listed in a special format, shown with their size and date and time of creation or last update. But note that the special format separates the filename from the extension, padding the distance between them with spaces. While this lines up the directory listing nice and pretty, it doesn't show you how to accurately type in the filename.

To see a list of files on another drive, use the DIR command with the drive letter and a colon:

```
C> DIR A:
```

Above, you'll see a listing of all files on the disk in drive A. If you want to look at drive B, substitute B: for A: above.

To see a list of files in another directory on the same disk, specify that directory's pathname after the DIR command:

```
C> DIR \WP51\DATA
```

Above, the DIR command lists all the files in the \WP51\DATA subdirectory.

To see a single file's information, just type that file's name after the DIR command:

```
C> DIR BLOOP.NOF
```

Above, the DIR command is followed by the file named BLOOP.NOF. Only that single file (and its associated and miscellaneous information) will be displayed.

To see only a specific group of files, follow the DIR command with the proper, matching wildcard:

```
C> DIR *.COM
```

Above, DIR is followed by a space, an asterisk, a period, then COM. This command displays only those files with the COM extension.

✔ For more information on subdirectories and pathnames, refer to Chapter 13.

✔ For more information on using wildcards, refer to "Wildcards (or, poker was never this much fun)" later in this chapter.

The wide DIR command

When you long for the wide open spaces of the Big Sky country, then you can use the following DIR command:

```
C> DIR /W
```

That's the DIR command, a space, and slash-W. Pressing Enter displays the directory listing in the wide format, with only filenames marching across the screen five abreast.

If you want to display a wide directory of another drive or a subdirectory, sandwich the drive letter or subdirectory pathname between the DIR and the /W above. For example:

```
C> DIR A: /W
```

or:

```
C> DIR \WP51\DATA /W
```

Refer to the previous section for more details.

Making DIR display one screen at a time

When the DIR command scrolls and scrolls, rolling up and up the screen and you cannot find the file, not to mention you've completely forgotten about the Ctrl-S key combination mentioned in Chapter 8, you can use the following DIR command at the next DOS prompt:

```
C> DIR /P
```

That's the DIR command, followed by a space and a slash-P. The P means page or pause, and DOS will insert a friendly "press any key" message after each screen of filenames. Press the spacebar to continue.

✔ To cancel the listing, press Ctrl-C. Refer to "Canceling a DOS command" in Chapter 2.

✔ If you're just hunting down a specific file, then follow the DIR command with that filename. Refer to "Using the DIR command" earlier in this chapter.

✔ If you're looking for a group of files that can be matched with a wildcard, refer to "Wildcards (or, poker was never this much fun)" later in this chapter.

✔ You can use this DIR command to see a directory listing of another drive or subdirectory. Just sandwich that drive letter or subdirectory pathname between DIR and the /P. For example:

```
C> DIR A: /P
```

or:

```
C> DIR \WP51\DATA /P
```

Refer to the section "Using the DIR command" if you care to fondle the DIR command further.

Displaying a sorted directory

Have you ever gotten the impression that DOS could just care less? It's true. When DOS displays a list of files, it shows them to you in any old order. To sort the files in the listing alphabetically, use the following DIR command:

```
C> DIR /O
```

That's the DIR command, a space, then slash-O. The O must stand for "Oh, sort these," or maybe the word "sort" in a foreign language. (It may mean "order" — naaa.)

Finding a lost file

In some cases, losing a file is worse than losing a pet or a small child in the mall. Pets and children have legs and wander off. Files? Where do they go? (And would one expect to find them in the video arcade?)

The first step in locating a lost file is knowing its name. If you wanted to copy said file and are greeted with the happy "File not found" error, then you might have mistyped the name. (It happens.) Check your typing. Further, you may want to check the directory listing to see if the file is there. Type this command:

```
C> DIR /P
```

The slash-P pauses the listing, allowing you to scan each entry. Even the author of this book has transposed filenames as he's saved them. (Here's a hint: The new files are usually listed at the end of the directory, though that's not a hard-and-fast rule.)

If the file still doesn't show up, then use this command:

```
C> DIR \WHERE.AMI /S
```

That's the DIR command, followed by a space, then a backslash and the filename. Above the filename, WHERE.AMI is used. After the filename comes a space, then slash-S.

By pressing Enter, you tell DOS to search the entire hard drive for the file you've specified. If it's found, you'll see it on the screen as follows:

```
Directory of C:\LOST\FOUND
WHERE   AMI    574 08-01-92 10:04a
   1 file(s)    574 bytes
```

Above, DOS has found the lost file in the subdirectory \LOST\FOUND. You then need to use the CD command to move to that subdirectory and from there you can get at the file. (The CD command is covered in "Changing directories" in Chapter 13.)

- ✔ If any additional matching files are found, they'll be listed as well, along with their directory.

- ✔ When you find the lost file, consider copying it to the proper location, or use the REN command to rename the file to the name you originally thought you used. Refer to "Copying a single file" in Chapter 3 for information on the COPY command; refer to "Renaming a file," also in Chapter 3, for information on REN.

- ✔ If the list scrolls off the screen, you can tack on the slash-P option. For example:

```
C> DIR \WHERE.AMI /S /P
```

Everything else in the command remains the same.

✔ If the file still isn't found, it may be on another disk drive. Log to that drive, then type the same DIR command again.

✔ If you still cannot find the file on any drive, then you probably saved it under a different name. Since I don't know what that name is, it's up to you to scour your drive looking for it. Use the CD and DIR commands to move around and find the file.

Finding a lost subdirectory

A lost subdirectory is a bit harder to find than a lost file, especially when you know that it's somewhere on the drive — but where? As with finding a lost file, the first step is to use the DIR command. Look for the telltale <DIR> in the listing. That shows you all the subdirectories.

If you don't find your subdirectory, you can use the DIR command to search for it. Type in the following (this is bizarre, so watch your fingers):

```
C> DIR \*.* /A:D /S | FIND "SUBDIR"
```

That's the DIR command, a space, then a backslash and star-dot-star. That's followed by another space, a slash-A, colon and D, then a space and a slash-S. A space follows slash-S, then the pipe or vertical bar character, another space, the FIND command, a space, and then the name of the subdirectory you're looking for (SUBDIR above). The subdirectory name *must* be in uppercase (all caps) and have a double quote character (") on either side.

Press Enter and DOS scours the drive, looking for your subdirectory. If it's found, it will be displayed as follows:

```
SUBDIR    <DIR>   09-23-92  7:23p

Directory of C:\LOST\SUBDIR
```

The subdirectory's name comes first — as it would in a directory listing. That's followed by the pathname. To change to that subdirectory, you would type in the pathname following the CD command. Above, that would be:

```
C> CD \LOST\SUBDIR
```

✔ If more than one subdirectory appears, then you may have to log or change to each one in turn to find the one you're looking for.

✔ There is a chance that this command may not find your subdirectory. In that case, you can use the TREE command to view your hard disk's *tree structure*. Refer to "The tree structure" in Chapter 13.

✔ Refer to Chapter 13, for more information on the CD command and pathnames.

Wildcards (or, poker was never this much fun)

You can use *wildcards* with some commands. They allow you to manipulate a group of files using a single DOS command. The object here, just like using wildcards in poker, is to specify wildcards in a filename in such as way as to match other files on disk.

For example, if you've named all the chapters in your Great American Novel with the DOC extension, you can treat all of them as a group using a wildcard. If all your special project files start with PROJ, then you can do things to those files en masse — even if the rest of the files are named something completely different.

There are two wildcards DOS uses, the question mark (?) and asterisk (*). These are covered in the following two sections.

✔ Wildcards are generally used with DOS commands. Seldom can they be used inside programs.

✔ Not all DOS commands will swallow wildcards. The TYPE command, for one, must be followed by a single filename. Refer to "Looking at files" in Chapter 1.

Using the ? wildcard

The ? wildcard is used to match any single letter in a filename. It can be used by itself or in multiples of however many characters you want to match. For example:

The wildcard filename T??T matches all filenames starting with T and ending with T, including THIS and THAT.

The wildcard filename CHAP?? matches all files starting with CHAP and having one or two more letters in their name. This includes CHAP00 through CHAP99 and any other combination of characters in those two positions.

You can also use the ? wildcard in the second part of a filename:

The wildcard filename BOOK.D?? matches all filenames starting with BOOK and having D as the first letter of their extension.

You can even mix and match the ? wildcard:

The wildcard filename JULY???.WK? matches all files starting with JULY that have WK as the first two letters of their extension.

All of these wildcard combinations can be used with DOS's file exploitation commands: DIR, DEL, COPY, REN, etc. Refer to Chapter 3 for more information on manipulating groups of files.

Using the * wildcard

The * wildcard is more powerful than the single-character ? wildcard. The asterisk is used to match groups of one or more characters in a filename. For example:

The wildcard filename *.DOC matches all files that have DOC as their second part. The first part of the filename can have any number of characters in it; *.DOC matches them all.

The wildcard filename PROJECT.* matches all files with PROJECT as their first part, with any second part — even if they don't have any second part.

But beware! The * wildcard is rather lame when it comes to being used in the middle of a filename. For example:

The wildcard filename B*ING will match all filenames that start with the letter B. DOS ignores the ING part of the name because it comes *after* the wildcard. I know. It's dumb. But that's the way DOS is.

Quirky, yet easily skippable stuff

If you want to match all filenames that start with B, use this wildcard:

```
B*
```

This matches all files, whether or not they have a second part. True, you could use B*.*, but DOS matches the same files, so why bother with the extra dot-star?

The wildcard *. (star-dot) matches only filenames *without* an extension. This is the only time under DOS that a command could end in a period. For example:

```
C> DIR *.
```

The above DIR command only shows files without any extension (typically only the subdirectories).

*Using *.* (star-dot-star)*

The most popular wildcard is the "Everyone out of the pool!" wildcard, *.*, which is pronounced "star-dot-star." It means everything, all files, no matter what their name (but usually not directories).

Since star-dot-star matches everything, you should be careful when using it. This is that one rare occasion in your life where you can get everyone's attention. It's like: You can't fool all of the files some of the time, but you can fool all of them all of the time with star-dot-star.

- ✔ The COPY *.* command copies all files in the directory. Refer to "Copying a group of files" in Chapter 3.

- ✔ The DEL *.* command is deadly; it ruthlessly destroys all files in the directory; refer to "Deleting a group of files" in Chapter 3.

- ✔ The REN command with *.* is tricky. You must specify a wildcard as the second part of the REN command; you cannot give every file in the directory the same name. For example:

```
C> REN *.DOC *.WP
```

Above, all files with the doc extension are renamed to have a WP extension. That's about the most you can do with the REN command and wildcards.

Section Four
Yikes!
(or, Help Me Out of This One!)

"ALRIGHT, STEADY EVERYONE. MARGO, GO OVER TO TOM'S PC AND PRESS 'ESCAPE',...VERY CAREFULLY."

In this section...

There is a certain level of fear required when using a computer. Don't worry, even the DOS gurus have it. It must come from watching all those Irwin Allen TV shows of the 1960s. They were kind of science fictiony and all had computers — computers that loved to explode and pop sparks whenever they didn't like something. Today's computers are much more powerful and produce much better explosions.

Seriously, computers don't explode. But they will do some unfriendly things that will make your heart drop a few flights. Some of this stuff isn't serious at all, which is what this part of the book tries to explain. But there are times when it pays to call in an expert. This is where you'll learn how to tell the difference between the two situations.

Chapter 15
When it's Time to Toss in the Towel (and Call a DOS Guru)

In this chapter...

▶ How to spot computer problems and narrow down the causes.

▶ How to detect and deal with software problems.

▶ How to fix a broken battery (when the computer forgets the time).

▶ How to locate a lost hard drive.

▶ How to determine when it's time to reset the system.

▶ What you should do after you've reset your computer (in a panic).

▶ How to prepare for getting help.

▶ How to deal with some form of beverage spilt into the keyboard.

Computers, like anything made by the hand of man, aren't perfect. For the most part, they work flawlessly. But, suddenly you feel that something is wrong — like when you're driving your car and it feels a little sluggish. Then you hear "the noise." Computers won't usually make noises when they go south, but they will start behaving oddly. This chapter tells you what you can do in those situations, and will give you an idea of when it's time to yell out for a professional to deal with the situation.

"My computer's down and I can't get it up!"

You have a problem. The computer isn't working the way it should. Something is amiss, definitely.

The first step is to analyze the problem. Break everything down and find out what *is* working. Even if you can't fix the problem, you'll be better prepared to tell an expert about it and have them deal with it.

Check the following items first:

Is the computer plugged in? Seriously, check to see if it is. If the computer is plugged into a power strip, make sure the power strip is plugged in and switched on. Further, you may want to check other items plugged into the same socket. Bad sockets happen. And check the *circuit breaker*.

Is everything else plugged in? Monitors, modems, and printers all need to be plugged in. Are there power cords attached? Are they turned on?

Note that most power cords on your computer have two connections: One end plugs into the wall (or a power strip) and the other plugs into the computer, printer, modem, etc. Believe it or not, *both* ends need to be plugged in for the computer to work. One end is *not* built into the computer the way it would be in an iron or TV set.

Check other connections:

- ✔ Computers have a ganglia of cables attached. There are power supply cables, then there are data cables. A printer has two cables: a power cable and a printer cable. The power cable connects to the wall socket and your electrical company; the printer cable connects to the computer.

- ✔ Modems can have three or four cables attached: power supply; a data line between the modem and the computer's serial port; one phone line from the modem to your telephone; and often a second phone line from your modem to the phone company's wall socket.

- ✔ Make sure all the cables are connected to their proper *ports* on the PC's rump. You may have to trace each cable with your finger, seeing how the back of a PC resembles the tail end of a squid. Also, serial and parallel ports look similar on some PCs. If your modem or printer isn't working, try swapping the plug around a few times (of course, this is assuming that it did work before).

- ✔ Keyboard cables can become loose, especially given the unique design of most PCs where the keyboard is connected on the back (which never made sense). But be careful here: Only plug or unplug the keyboard connector when the computer is off.

Here are some other things to check:

- ✔ Is the computer locked? There's a key on the front of most PCs. It must be turned to the unlocked or open position for you to use the computer.

- ✔ Is the monitor off or dimmed? Monitors have their own on/off switch; make sure it's on. Also, monitors can be dimmed, so check the brightness knob. Further, some computers have *screen dimming* programs. Try pressing the spacebar to see if the monitor comes back on.

✔ Is there a blackout? If so, you won't be able to use the computer. Sorry.

✔ Is there a brownout? A brownout happens when the electrical company isn't sending enough juice through the power lines. A computer won't turn on if there isn't the required number of volts present. If the system is already on, a brownout will force the system to shut itself off. This is unusual because, during a brownout, the lights in the room and all your clocks may continue to work.

These are all general things to look for and quick items to check if you're not a professional computer doctor. They're also all hardware items. If your problem is in software, refer to "It's just acting weird" in this chapter.

✔ If possible, you can further narrow the problem down to a specific part of the computer: the computer box, disk drives, keyboard, monitor, printer, or some other peripheral. If everything works okay save for one part of the computer, then you've narrowed down the problem far enough to tell the repair person about it over the phone.

✔ Fixing this stuff isn't hard. Most repair places or computer consultants will simply replace a defective part with a brand new one. In fact, I would go out on a limb here and say: Never trust anyone who claims to fix what you have without the need to replace anything. I speak from personal experience here. Some bozo claimed he could fix my $4,000 laser printer. After $600 of his attempts, it ended up costing me only (relatively speaking) $1,000 to fully replace the defective part. An expensive lesson, but one worth passing on.

✔ For more information on ports, refer to "What are ports?" in Chapter 5. A general discussion of all types of computer hardware is offered throughout Section Two of this book.

"It's just acting weird"

Computers act weird all the time. Sometimes, however, they act more weird than they usually do. If you've gone through the previous section and have determined that your hardware works fine, then what you may have is a software problem.

The best thing to check for with a software problem is any recent changes made to the system, specifically the CONFIG.SYS and AUTOEXEC.BAT files. Adding new items or deleting old ones can drastically affect how the system works: You can lose disk drives, some programs won't find enough memory, and some applications will refuse to work. To remedy the problem, undo the changes to either file (CONFIG.SYS or AUTOEXEC.BAT), or call someone else for help. For more details on editing CONFIG.SYS and AUTOEXEC.BAT files, see Chapter 12.

Frequently, weirdness can occur after a period of time. The longest I've been able to continuously run WordPerfect (without shutting the computer off) is about three weeks. (Okay, I slept a little every night.) After three weeks, mold must grow on the circuits because the computer suddenly stopped working. The same thing happens to DESQview after about a week and a half, and to Windows after about three days of nonstop performance. Resetting the computer seems to solve the problem.

Be wary of memory-resident programs, (also called TSRs). If you notice your computer locking up tight, the memory-resident program may be to blame. Also, *popping up* a memory-resident program while your computer is in graphics mode may cause the screen to tweak — if not right away, then definitely when you return to your graphics mode.

The mouse has been known to cause many problems, sometimes even with programs that don't use a mouse. If you notice any random characters on your screen, it's probably due to a misbehaving mouse. The only real cure for this is to turn the *mouse driver* off, which should be done by your local computer guru.

✔ Don't be surprised if you suspect a hardware problem and it turns out to be software. For example, losing your hard drive is really a software problem; the physical hard disk hasn't left your computer to go outside and frolic through the garden. Instead, DOS has mislaid it's map of what equipment it's got on board.

✔ Any program you're just learning (including DOS) will act wierd until it's used to you. You'll experience at least three confounding, unreproducible errors that your guru never heard of in the first month you use a program intensively — then they'll never occur again. Try not to get too mad at the machine or the software.

✔ Refer to "Resetting" in Chapter 1 for more information on resetting the computer.

"The computer has lost track of the time"

About 90 percent of the computers sold today have battery-backed-up clocks inside. They keep the time no matter what, even if you unplug the PC. So when you notice that the time isn't correct — or the computer thinks it's January 1, 1980 (and Carter is still in office!), then you need to check your battery.

Replacing a computer's battery is as easy as replacing the battery in a clock or camera. Of course, if you don't particularly think that's easy, then make someone else do it for you.

✔ If you have an AT or later computer, then you'll also need to run your PC's SETUP program to reset the clock. You may further need to reset other information in the SETUP program, which means this operation should be performed by your dealer or a computer "expert."

✔ Every once in a while you should type the word DATE at the DOS prompt just to make sure your PC hasn't drifted. It's annoying to look for files by date only to find your computer has been date-stamping everything for 1951. Type TIME too and see if it thinks it's 1:15 in the morning.

Gulp! The hard drive is gone!

Hard drives do have a tendency to wander. We wouldn't normally care, but hard drives contain all sorts of important information. So concern over their whereabouts is justified.

There are two reasons a hard drive suddenly disappears. The first is related to the computer's battery. In addition to maintaining the current time, the battery keeps a special area of memory active. In that memory, the computer remembers a few things about itself, including whether or not it has a hard drive. When the battery goes, the computer forgets about the hard drive. Oops!

To fix the battery problem, replace the battery. This requires opening up the computer, so it's okay to pay someone else to do this if opening up the computer would make you wince.

After the battery is replaced, you need to run your computer's SETUP program. You'll need to tell the computer all about itself again; give it the current time, tell it about its floppy drives, memory configuration, and what *type* of hard drive is installed. Most hard drives are type 17, though this isn't a hard-and-fast rule. If you're in doubt, make someone else do this.

The second reason a hard drive suddenly disappears is age. The average PC hard drive can run flawlessly for about four years. After that, you're going to start experiencing problems, typically "Access," "Seek," "Read," or "Write" errors in DOS. This is a sign that the hard drive is on its last legs. You should back up all your work and start hunting for a new drive.

Read this if you care about your data

Buy a new drive when the old one starts to go. There are special software utilities that claim to fix these intermittent problems. Look at it this way: An old, failing hard drive is like a bald tire. You need a new tire to replace it — not a toupée.

Keeping the old, worn out hard drive around is a bad idea as well. Even if it's only marginal, there's no sense in keeping it for games or as a "temporary" files disk. That's like keeping your old bald tire as a spare.

A record of your SETUP program

Since your SETUP program's information is so important, run that program right now and jot down this important information. If running SETUP isn't obvious to you, or this seems a little out in left field, then make someone else fill in the blanks below:

Program name to run SETUP: _____

Keys to press to run SETUP: _____

First floppy drive: _____

Second floppy drive: _____

First hard drive (type): _____

Second hard drive (type): _____

Main (motherboard memory): _____

Extra memory: _____

Total memory: _____

Monitor/display: _____

Keyboard: _____

Serial port 1: _____

Serial port 2: _____

Printer port 1: _____

Printer port 2: _____

Math co-processor: _____

Other stuff: _____

Other stuff: _____

Other stuff: _____

Note that not every computer will have all of the above items. If there are any extra items mentioned, write them down in the blank lines provided.

Steps to take for a "locked" computer

The reset button is not a panic button, but it's the next best thing. When your computer is all locked up and the programs appear to have flown to Orlando, try the following steps:

STEPS: Dealing with a computer that is locked up

Step 1. Press the Esc (Escape) key. Or if the program uses a different cancel key and you know what it is, press it. For example, WordPerfect uses the F1 key.

Step 2. Press the Ctrl-C (Control-C) or Ctrl-Break (Control-Break) key combination. This will usually (and safely) cancel any DOS command.

Step 3. In Windows, you can press the Alt-Esc key combination to leave a window and move to the next window. To get rid of a program run amok, you can press Ctrl-Esc to bring up the Task List, then click on the End Task button to close the highlighted task (program).

Step 4. In DESQview, you can press and release the Alt key to pop up the DESQmenu. Select the Close Window item to close a window. Or you can press Ctrl-Alt-Del to close any DESQview session. (Under DESQview, Ctrl-Alt-Del doesn't reset the computer.)

Step 5. If none of these tricks work, try Ctrl-Alt-Del to reset your computer. If that doesn't work, or if your keyboard is beeping at you, then punch your reset button.

Note that you only resort to resetting after trying all the alternatives. Resetting is such a drastic measure that you should really run through your options before trying it. Never act in haste.

- ✔ If your system lacks a reset button and Ctrl-Alt-Del doesn't reset, then you'll have to turn off the PC. Refer to "Turning the computer off" in Chapter 1.

- ✔ Information on using the Ctrl-C cancel key is covered in "Canceling a DOS command" in Chapter 2.

- ✔ What does the reset button do? It interrupts power to the main chip which causes it to restart.

"I had to reset my computer"

Okay. So you had to reset. Further, I'm going to assume that you've reset in the middle of something. Resetting at the DOS prompt is okay, and generally doesn't do anything bad. But resetting in the middle of a program isn't nice. It's not a sin, but it's not nice (see below for why).

After your system comes up again, get to the DOS prompt. This means you should quit any automatic startup program, such as WordPerfect or especially Windows. Then, type the following at the DOS prompt:

```
C> CHKDSK C: /F
```

That's the CHKDSK command, followed by a space and drive C (C and a colon), then another space and a slash-F. Press Enter. If you're asked the question "Convert lost chains into files?" or something similar to that, press Y.

After CHKDSK is done running, you need to delete some "garbage" files it created. Type the following command:

```
C> DEL C:\FILE*.CHK
```

That's the DEL command to delete a file, followed by a space, then C, a colon, a backslash, and the filename wildcard FILE*.CHK. You only need to type this command if you told Check Disk to convert the lost chains into files. Otherwise, you can skip this step.

✔ You may want to repeat this CHKDSK (check disk) procedure for each hard drive in your system. If so, substitute the proper drive letter for C: in the first command listed above. Remember that you only need to use the second DEL command if CHKDSK says it found lost clusters or files.

✔ Refer to "CHKDSK Says I have lost files in clusters or something" in Chapter 13 for additional information about CHKDSK .

Now go back to your program, open the file you were working on, and see how much work you lost. (And they say computers are time-saving devices!)

Freely skip this stuff on why you need to reset

When you reset in the middle of something, you often catch some programs with their pants down, so to speak. These programs may have created temporary files or may have some files that are "half-open" on disk. Resetting leaves the files on disk, but not officially saved in any directory. The result is the "lost chains" or "lost clusters" that the CHKDSK command is designed to look for.

Running CHKDSK with its slash-F option causes the program to scour the drive and put the missing clusters and file fragments into real files on disk. They're named FILE0000.CHK, FILE0001.CHK on up through however many files were found. There's nothing the novice computer user can do with these files, so they're okay to delete.

If you don't delete the files, nothing drastic will happen. However, two negative things will take place after a time: First, the files do occupy space on disk, even though they never appear in any directory. After a time, your disk will be full and you won't figure out why. The second long-term bad thing to happen is that your hard drive will become a real pig — very sluggish. Only by deleting these files will things speed up.

When to scream for help

There comes a time when you must scream for help. When that happens, and when you've exhausted all other options mentioned in this book, be a good computer user and obey the following:

- ✔ First, get mad. Get it out of your system.

- ✔ Know the problem. Be able to offer a full report on what you were doing, what you just did, and what happened. If you've narrowed down the problem, don't be afraid to say what you suspect it is.

- ✔ Be at the computer when you call for help. They'll always ask you questions you can only really answer while at the computer.

- ✔ Tell the person you're begging for help about anything new or changed on your PC. Always let them know if you attempted to modify something yourself or changed something.

- ✔ In order of preference, contact the following people: your office computer specialist or MIS manager; a friend who knows something about computers (and is still willing to help you); your computer dealer; or the manufacturer.

- ✔ If the problem cannot be fixed over the phone, then take the computer in to the shop. If possible, try to back up your data before you do this (refer to "Backing up" in Chapter 13). Remember to bring along cables and any necessary peripherals. Ask the computer fixit person what they'd like you to bring in just to be sure.

✔ Always opt for the diagnostic first. Typical repair places will do a look-see for about $30 to $60. Then they should call you with an estimate. If they fix anything else "voluntarily" (for example, items not mentioned in the estimate or items they have not phoned you about), then it's free. Check with the laws for your state or county, but generally speaking, repairing a computer is covered by the same laws that protect people at car repair places.

✔ It's easier to replace something than to fix it. If possible, try to order a bigger, faster, and better version of the thing you're replacing.

"I just spilled java into the keyboard"

I've added this as a special section because, believe it or not, many people spill things into their keyboards. Maybe not coffee (my personal favorite is lemonade), but something liquid that will make your eyes bulge out for a few comic moments.

Okay. Suppose you've just spilled something into your keyboard. (You'll be reading this fast, so I'll type it in as quickly as I can.)

Just turn the computer off!

Never, under any circumstances, should you unplug the keyboard with the computer light still on!

Depending on the size of the spill, you may be able to save your information and quit the application; it's always better to turn off the PC at the DOS prompt. If not, then it's okay to just flip the power switch.

Let the keyboard dry out. For coffee, this should take about 24 hours. After that time, turn on your PC, and refer to the section above "I had to reset my computer." Everything else should work as before.

If you've spilled something sugary into your keyboard, the dry-out time is still 24 hours. However, sugary stuff tends to create a sticky film. It won't interfere too heavily with the electronics, but it will make your keys stick. I've heard of people giving their keyboards a "bath" in a special solution. However, I recommend taking the keyboard to a pro for cleaning. In fact, this is a good thing to do on a regular basis, given all the cookie crumbs, chip fragments, and hair (ugh!) that ends up in your keyboard.

✔ If you have to unplug your keyboard, do it with the computer turned off.

✔ If you're accident prone and you expect to spill other liquids into your keyboard from time to time, you can buy a clear plastic cover molded to fit the keyboard's contour. You can still type and use the keyboard, but it's sealed.

Chapter 16
After You Panic, Do This

- -

In this chapter...

▶ How to tell where you are when you suddenly find yourself there.

▶ How to return to where you were before.

▶ How to find a lost file.

▶ How to find a lost program.

▶ How to recover from DEL *.*.

▶ How to undelete an entire subdirectory.

▶ How to unformat a disk.

▶ How to restore from a backup disk.

- -

If you're still in a panicky mode, then refer to the previous chapter. That's more of a panic-stricken chapter. This chapter is about what to do after you panic. The situation can always be resolved, no matter what. Even if the system is making popping noises and you see smoke, there's nothing to worry about (unless the drapery catches fire).

"Where am I?"

Has this ever happened to you: You're driving your car and suddenly you realize that you've been under highway hypnosis? What happened the last few miles? Where are you? Well, that's never happened to me. But I do wake up in the middle of the night screaming sometimes (if that makes you feel any better).

Getting lost is part of using a computer. If you ever find yourself lost, try one of the following remedies:

✔ If you were using a familiar program and suddenly find yourself in the unfamiliar — but still in the program — try pressing Esc to "back out" (or press whatever the cancel key is, such as F1 in WordPerfect).

- ✔ If pressing Esc doesn't work, check the keyboard. Type a few keys. If the keyboard starts beeping, then the system is locked. You'll need to reset. Refer to "Resetting" in Chapter 1.

- ✔ If you're suddenly out at the DOS prompt, refer to the next section.

- ✔ If you find yourself lost at the DOS prompt, use the CD command to find out where you are. Typing CD will tell you the current drive and directory, and it may explain why the program you were trying to run doesn't work. Refer to Chapter 13 for more information.

- ✔ If you notice that your DOS commands aren't working, or the display doesn't quite look right, you might want to check the DOS version. Type in the VER command and DOS will dutifully tell you its make and model number. Refer to "Names and versions" in Chapter 2 for more information.

- ✔ Finally, if nothing works at all, try resetting. Computers do, occasionally, pick up and go to Hawaii to watch the surf. Pressing the Reset button or Ctrl-Alt-Del will bring them back to reality.

"How do I get back?"

Sometimes you may find yourself in a different place. Say you were working in 1-2-3 and tried to save a program when suddenly you find yourself at the DOS prompt. What happened? Or maybe you were at the DOS prompt just a moment ago, and now there's a strange program on the screen.

In the case of the latter, you've probably just brought up a *pop-up* program by accident. These programs are triggered by certain key presses and you may have stumbled across them. Press Esc to exit. This should work and return you to the DOS prompt (I've never seen a pop-up program that didn't pop back down after you press Esc.)

If you were just in a program and are now at a DOS prompt, and you know you didn't purposefully quit the program, then look at the screen. Do you see a DOS copyright notice? If so, then type the following:

```
C> EXIT
```

This will return you to your program. (If you're wrong, typing EXIT won't hurt anything.)

If you don't see the copyright notice, then you've probably been dumped out of the program. To re-enter the program, press the F3 key and then Enter. If you press F3 and don't see anything, then try typing MENU or whatever command you normally type to use your computer (or the application you were so rudely ejected from).

Some programs require you to type in two things when the program starts. For example, if you were running an accounting package in Basic, you may have to type:

```
C> BASIC GL
```

dBASE also requires you to type in two things to run a dBASE program. If you know the name of the program to run, put it after DBASE at the DOS prompt:

```
C> DBASE PAYROLL
```

✔ Refer to "The handy F3 key" in Chapter 2 for information on using the F3 key.

✔ The section "Running a program" in Chapter 1 has a list of popular program names and the commands required to run them.

"Where is my file?"

If you just saved a file, or are looking for one you absolutely know exists somewhere, then it may just be out of sight for now. Refer to the section "Finding a lost file" in Chapter 14 for details on getting the file back.

"Where is my program?"

Programs are harder to lose than files, but it happens. The approach to finding a lost program depends on how you run the program.

If you run a program manually then you may just be lost on the disk. The manual way usually involves typing in a CD command, then typing in the name of the program at the next DOS prompt. If you type in your CD command and get an "Invalid directory" error, then you're probably in the wrong place. Type this command:

```
C> CD \
```

This logs you to the root directory. Try running your program again. If it still doesn't work, try logging to the proper drive. For example, to log to drive C, type in the following:

```
D> C:
```

That's C and a colon. To log to any other drive, type its letter and a colon, then type the above CD command. That should get you on the proper footing.

If you normally run your program by typing its name at the prompt, and you get a "Bad command or file name" error, then DOS may not remember where it put your program. This usually happens because, somehow, the *search path* has been changed. Rather than explain how that can be undone here, simply reset your computer to get the proper search path back. Press the reset button or Ctrl-Alt-Del.

✔ If you notice DOS loses your files a lot, yet resetting seems to bring them back, tell someone about it. Let them know that some program on your system is "resetting the search path" and that you aren't particularly fond of that. They should be able to fix the problem for you.

✔ Refer to "I had to reset my computer" in Chapter 15 if you do reset.

✔ Information on the CD command and your disk's directory structure can be found all over Chapter 13.

The perils of DEL *.*

Yeah, deleting all your files can be a drastic thing. The DEL *.* command will raze every file in a directory with abandon. However, there is a warning before this happens. DOS will tell you that all files in the directory are about to be churned to dust. It asks you if this is okay. You must type a Y to go on. Simple enough; you've been warned. Yet too many DOS beginners and experts alike are quick to press the Y key.

Before typing DEL *.* make sure you're in the proper directory. Use the CD command if the prompt doesn't display the current directory. (Refer to "Finding the current directory" in Chapter 13, and to "Prompt styles of the rich and famous" in Chapter 2.) Too many times you mean to delete all the files in one directory, but you happen to be in another directory when that happens.

If the files were accidentally deleted, they can be recovered using the UNDELETE command. As soon as you've recognized your mistake, type in the following command:

```
C> UNDELETE *.* /ALL
```

If you've got the right version of DOS, or a utility that uses this command, that should bring back as many of your files as possible. Note that each may have a funky name, with the # character replacing the first letter. Use the REN command to rename the files back to their original states.

- ✔ Refer to "Undeleting a file" in Chapter 3 for more information on the UNDELETE command; refer to "Renaming a file" in the same chapter for information on REN.

- ✔ If a file cannot be recovered, then it cannot be recovered. DOS knows about these things and won't push the subject any further.

"I just deleted an entire subdirectory!"

Neat. This really requires effort on your behalf. Not only must you delete all files in a subdirectory, but you also have to use the RD (or RMDIR) command to peel off a directory. That isn't even covered in this book! Congratulations.

Now the bad news: You cannot use the UNDELETE command to recover a lost subdirectory. It should, but it doesn't.

The only way to recover a subdirectory is to *restore* it from a recent backup. Depending on how recent your backup is, and how new the files were in the subdirectory, you may or may not get a full recovery.

Suppose, in a massive Freudian slip, you just deleted the C:\FAMILY\FATHER directory. To restore this directory from a recent backup disk set, place the first backup disk into drive A and type the following command:

```
C> RESTORE A: C:\FAMILY\FATHER\*.* /S
```

That's the RESTORE command, a space, then the drive you're restoring from, A, and a colon. That's followed by a space and the name of the subdirectory you deleted — plus a backslash and star-dot-star. Then comes another space and finally a slash-S.

DOS will scan your backup disks, asking you to remove each one and insert the next one in sequence. It will do this until all the files are restored.

If you're using a third-party backup program, such as FastBack, CP Backup or the Norton Backup, the procedure is essentially the same. However, the commands or methods you type to restore the directory are different. You may have to scream for help with this one.

"I just reformatted my disk!"

This is why disks are labeled: so you know what's on them. Before you reformat a disk, check to see that it's empty. Refer to "Reformatting disks" in Chapter 10. But if you do reformat a disk, type the following:

```
C> UNFORMAT A:
```

If you're unformatting a disk in drive B, substitute B: for A: above. Press Enter and follow the instructions on the screen. Be patient: It takes a few minutes to unformat a disk. This only works if you have DOS 5 or later, or a third-party utility.

Your disk may not be in the best of shape after it's unformatted. For example, most of the files in the root directory may be gone. If they're found, they will probably be given generic names, as will any of your subdirectories. On the bright side, the data in your subdirectories, and all the subsubdirectories, will be totally intact.

Unformatting a disk only works if you UNFORMAT the disk before putting any new files on it.

Restoring from a backup

Backing up is something you should do often. Your computer manager probably has you set up on some type of backup schedule or, if you're on your own, you should back up your important stuff every day with a full backup on a weekly or monthly basis, depending on how much you use your computer.

Rarely is the restore part of backup done. It happens only in those few circumstances where something goes wrong with the hard drive, you lose files or a subdirectory, or you need to recall an older version of a program.

If you need to restore a single file, then use the following command:

```
C> RESTORE A: C:\WORK\PROJECT\FILE1.DAT
```

Above, A: is the drive containing your backup disk(s). You can use B: if the backup disks are to be placed in drive B. The full pathname of the file follows the drive letter, colon, and a space. Above, the file FILE1.DAT is to be restored. You must specify a full pathname and the file can only be restored to that directory. Wildcards can also be used to restore a group of files.

If you need to restore a subdirectory, then specify that directory's name plus a backslash (\) and star-dot-star:

```
C> RESTORE A: C:\MISC\*.* /S
```

Above, A: indicates the drive containing the backup disk(s). Substitute B: if the backup disks will be placed in that drive. The drive letter is followed by a colon, a space, and then the full pathname of the subdirectory to restore. See how star-dot-star is used above? That restores all files in the subdirectory. Further, a space and a slash-S are added to the command.

I recommend you use a third-party backup program. If you've been using the DOS Backup command anyway, here is how to restore your entire hard drive, use this command:

```
C> RESTORE A: C:\*.* /S
```

That's RESTORE, then A: to indicate the drive containing the backup disks (use B: if you're putting the disks into that drive). That's followed by a space, then C, colon, and star-dot-star, which indicates all files on drive C. If you're restoring to another hard drive, substitute its drive letter for C: above. And finally, a space and a slash-S ends the command.

In all circumstances, you should start restoring by putting the first backup disk into the proper floppy drive. The RESTORE command will tell you when to swap disks; remove the current disk and replace it with the next disk in sequence. This happens until all the files are restored.

✔ Backing up is covered in Chapter 13, starting with the section titled "Backing up."

✔ Refer to Chapter 13 for more information on directories and pathnames.

✔ Refer to "Using *.* (star-dot-star)" in Chapter 14 for information on using that wildcard.

Chapter 17
DOS Error Messages
(What They Mean, What to Do)

. . . .

In this chapter...

▶ Abort, Retry, Ignore?

▶ Access denied.

▶ Bad command or file name.

▶ Bad or missing command interpreter.

▶ Drive not ready error.

▶ Duplicate file name or file not found.

▶ File cannot be copied onto itself.

▶ File creation error.

▶ File not found.

▶ General failure.

▶ Insufficient disk space.

▶ Invalid directory.

▶ Invalid drive specification.

▶ Invalid file name or file not found.

▶ Invalid media, track 0 bad or unusable.

▶ Invalid number of parameters.

▶ Invalid parameter.

▶ Invalid switch.

▶ Non-system disk or disk error.

▶ Not ready, reading drive X.

▶ Write protect.

. . . .

*T*hey stopped putting the canonical list of error messages in the DOS manual, starting with version 4.0. With that version, you had to buy an extra booklet that contained all the error messages, what they meant, and how to deal with each. With DOS 5.0, they have the best DOS manual (so far, which isn't saying much), but they don't have the error messages. (Maybe they're embarrassed at just how many error messages there are!)

This chapter contains 21 common error messages you may see while you're running your PC. Each error message is explained according to its meaning and probable cause with a suggested solution for each. Nothing here is really fatal, though a few of the error messages will scare the bejezus out of you. Never fear, a solution is always at hand.

Note that the text of each error message may vary between DOS versions. The solutions, however, are always the same. Note also that DOS error messages tend to be kind of vague. This is because neither DOS nor the PC hardware are built to perform the kind of defaulted diagnostics that would result in messages like, "There's no disk in drive A; please put one in, or press A to cancel that last command." Oh well.

You'll find extended discussions of some issues or solutions in other chapters. We've cross-referenced them here.

Abort, Retry, Ignore?

Meaning: The latest missile launched by the Air Force is careening out of control toward Moscow. Actually, this is a generic response to a variety of what DOS calls *fatal errors*. DOS has taken its best stab at doing something and just can't figure out what's wrong.

Probable cause: Typically this message is preceded by a line of text explaining what DOS tried to do: read from a disk, write to a disk, touch its toes, etc. Nine times out of ten you'll see this message when you attempt to access a floppy disk in drive A or B and the drive door is open or there is no disk in the drive.

Solution: If you can remedy the situation, such as closing the drive door or putting a disk into the drive, then do so. Then press R to Retry. If nothing can be done, press A for Abort (which means Cancel, but most programmers don't know if Cancel has one or two L's in it). Never under any circumstances should you press I to Ignore.

Tales from real life you don't have to read

Most often I get the "Abort, Retry, Ignore" message when I type A: instead of B: and there is no disk in drive A. My solution is to have a formatted disk (any disk will do) handy. I slip that disk into drive A, then press R to retry. After the DOS command is done (or whatever), I retype the command again specifying B: or whichever letter I originally meant to type.

Skip this only if you don't take the hard drive seriously

When you get the "Abort, Retry, Ignore" message and the error DOS displays seems more drastic, then it's time to worry a bit. Situations such as a "read error," "write error," or "seek error" could be the rumblings of a major disk disaster (especially if the disk you're trying to access is the hard disk). If the errors are consistent, refer to the nearest PC-knowledgeable person and scream "Help" quietly into their ear.

Access denied

Meaning: You've tried to change a file that DOS is not allowed to change.

Probable cause: The file you've specified, or one of several files in a group, has its "read-only" file protection set. You cannot rename the command with REN; you cannot delete it with DEL; and you cannot use any applications to change the file's contents. This error may also occur if you've specified a subdirectory name in a command that normally manipulates files.

Solution: Just ignore the file. Chances are they don't want you to touch it, anyway. (You can refer to "The file! I cannot kill it!" in Chapter 3 if you're desperate about the situation.)

Bad command or file name

Meaning: DOS doesn't understand the command you just typed.

Probable cause: You mistyped a command name, misspelled the name of a program on disk, or DOS cannot find the named program. This is also DOS's typical response when you type in a dirty word or hurl it an insult via the command line.

Solution: Check your typing. You can also refer to "Where is my program?" in Chapter 16 if you're certain the program worked before.

Bad or missing command interpreter

Meaning: DOS cannot locate the file named COMMAND.COM, which contains its basic operations, and so it cannot proceed. Sounds worse than it is.

Probable cause A: One of two catagories are usually the culprit. If you were exiting a program to return to the DOS prompt and you got this message, or a similar one referring to an inability to locate COMMAND.COM, this just means DOS has gotten confused, probably because your program decided to drop DOS off at a different drive than DOS was expecting (like the A, B, or D drive, when the C drive is the one that has the COMMAND.COM program on it).

Solution A: Just reboot (reset, push the reset button) your computer. Everything should be fine at this point, since the program was exiting normally anyway.

Probable cause B: This happens when you're starting your computer. It might mean you left a disk in drive A; or you don't have a disk in drive A and the hard disk hasn't been set up to start DOS; or COMMAND.COM isn't in the root directory of your hard drive where it's supposed to be because it's been moved or deleted (a major no-no).

Solution B: If there's a disk in drive A, take it out and push the reset button. If this isn't the problem, or it doesn't work, get help from a knowledgeable user. This user will probably dig out your original DOS floppy disk and copy COMMAND.COM back onto the hard drive's main directory where it belongs. This assumes you have a "bootable" copy of the DOS disks around. Note that the DOS 5 upgrade kit's disks are not bootable — you can't use them to start the computer! Which means that when you install DOS 5 on your computer, you should make a bootable disk just for such emergencies. Make a bootable disk by putting a fresh floppy in drive A and typing:

```
C> format a:/s/u
```

S stands for "system" which is what COMMAND.COM is part of — the DOS system file group. If FORMAT burps and won't do its job, or you only have a low-density floppy in a high-density drive, refer to "Formatting a disk" in Chapter 10.

Drive not ready error

Refer to "Not ready reading drive *x*" later in this chapter.

Duplicate file name or file not found

Meaning: You've used the REN command to rename a file and something went wrong.

Probable cause: You've specified a new filename with improper characters in it; you've specified the new name and that file already exists; or the file you want to rename doesn't exist.

Solution: Try the command again. Check to see that a file with the new name doesn't already exist. (Refer to "Renaming a file" in Chapter 3 for more information.)

File cannot be copied onto itself

Meaning: You've forgotten something with the COPY command. This isn't a major boo-boo. In fact, nothing bad has happened (which is ironic, given the insincere nature of the COPY command).

Probable cause: You've used the COPY command to duplicate a file and given the duplicate the same name as the original. While COPY will overwrite a file that already exists, you cannot use COPY to overwrite the source file. For example, you typed something along the lines of:

```
C> COPY MYSELF MYSELF
```

or meant to type C> COPY MYSELF B: and you left off the B:.

Solution: Don't specify the same name twice. Refer to "Duplicating a file" in Chapter 3 for the proper ways and means.

File creation error

Meaning: For some unspecified reason, DOS will not make a new file.

Probable cause: Using the COPY command to copy or duplicate a file and the filename is already used by a directory; or if a file already exists by that name, but it's a read-only file; or if the disk or directory is full and can't contain any additional files. This error can also be produced by any program as it saves a file, though "File creation error" is an error message specific to DOS.

Solution: If the filename is already taken by a directory or some other file, try creating the file using a new name. If the file is read-only, refer to the section "The file! I cannot kill it!" in Chapter 3. If the disk is full, delete some superfluous files or try using another disk or making a subdirectory.

File not found

Meaning: DOS is unable to locate the file you've named.

Probable cause: You mistyped the name, or the file isn't on that drive or in the current directory, or on the path you've specified.

Solution: Check your typing. Refer to "Finding a lost file" in Chapter 14.

General failure

Meaning: DOS has lots of specific error messages. When it tosses "General failure" at you, it means something bad has happened but DOS has nothing specific to say about it. This is like DOS saying "all hell's breaking loose," but not that serious.

Probable cause: Typical things that cause DOS to report "General failure" include: an incompatible floppy disk; the floppy drive door being left open; an attempt to read from an unformatted disk; or the absence of a disk from a floppy drive.

Solution: Check to see if there is a disk in the drive or if the drive's door latch is open. Try again by pressing R for Retry. If there is a disk present, then it's not properly formatted; press A for Abort. Use the FORMAT command to format the disk — but make sure the disk is formatted to its proper size and capacity. Refer to Chapter 10 and the sections "What kind of disk is this?," "Formatting a disk," and "Formatting a low-capacity disk in a high-capacity drive."

Insufficient disk space

Meaning: The disk is full. There is no more room left to create or copy any files.

Probable cause: You've used the COPY command to copy too many files to the disk. Various other DOS commands and programs may produce this error.

Solution: Use a different disk, or delete some unneeded files, or start copying to another disk. If you notice that the disk still seems to have ample space available, then you've simply filled up the root directory. Delete a few files (or copy them to another disk), and then create subdirectories for the extra files. Refer to "How to name a directory" in Chapter 14. Run CHKDSK (see Chapter 13) to see if your disk is filled with loose fragments that take up space but don't do any good.

Invalid directory

Meaning: You've specified a directory that doesn't exist. (DOS is big on using the term *invalid*, which it takes to mean illegal.)

Probable cause: You used the CD command to change to a directory that you don't have. If not that, then you may have specified a full pathname to a file or directory and something in the pathname isn't right.

Solution: Check your typing. Refer to "Finding a lost subdirectory" in Chapter 14 for hunting down lost directories.

Invalid drive specification

Meaning: What the hell kind of drive is that?

Probable cause: You've typed in a drive letter that isn't assigned to any disk drive on your system. For example, if you have drives A, B, and C, and you type D:, you'll get this message.

Solution: Check your typing. The colon (:) is a sacred character under DOS. It only follows a drive letter, which can be any letter of the alphabet. If that drive doesn't exist, DOS will spit back a variation of the "Invalid drive specification" error message. P.S. If it gives this message when you try to log (switch) to drive C, that means DOS has lost track of your hard drive. Oops. See Chapter 15, "When it's Time to Toss in the Towel (and Call a DOS Guru)".

Invalid file name or file not found

Meaning: You've specified a filename with an illegal character, one that DOS cannot find.

Probable cause: You've used the REN command to give a file a new name that has an illegal character in it. Also, this error appears when you try to use the TYPE command with a wildcard filename; you can only view one file at a time using the TYPE command. (Refer to "Looking at files" in Chapter 1.)

Solution: Check your typing. Refer to "Use these filenames — go directly to jail!" in Chapter 14. Also see the error message "Duplicate file name or file not found" in this chapter.

Invalid media, track 0 bad or unusable

Meaning: The FORMAT command cannot format the disk. At least, it cannot format it to the specific capacity.

Probable cause: You're trying to format a disk at the wrong capacity, for example, a 360K disk to 1.2MB or a 1.2MB disk at 360K. Or you may have successfully formatted a high-capacity disk at low capacity and now are attempting to reformat it to high-capacity. Or you have a bad disk.

Solution: You can try the FORMAT command again, but add the slash-U (/U) option. If that doesn't work, try taking a bulk eraser, one that you may use to erase a video tape, and erase the disk. That may allow the disk to be formatted — but always format disks to their proper capacity. Refer to Chapter 10.

Invalid number of parameters
Invalid parameter
Invalid switch

Meaning: You typed something improperly at the DOS prompt, left something required out of a command, or mistyped an option.

Probable cause: Usually a typo. If one of these errors pop up you're on the right track, but may need to check the format of the command again.

Solution: Check your typing. You may have forgotten a space. If you've forgotten an option with some DOS command, enter the command again but with its help switch, slash-?, supplied instead. For example:

```
C> FORMAT /?
```

With DOS 5 type:

```
C> HELP FORMAT
```

Either way displays all the options and requirements of the command. Check for the one you want, then specify it properly. Refer to "About the darn command formats" in Chapter 11 for more information.

Non-system disk or disk error

Meaning: You're trying to start the computer from a non-boot disk. It may be formatted, but there is no copy of DOS on the disk.

Probable cause: You've left a floppy disk in your A drive.

Solution: Make sure drive A is empty, or open the drive door latch. Press the spacebar to allow DOS to boot from the hard drive.

Not ready, reading drive X

Meaning: You've tried to access or log to either of your floppy drives and DOS found only air where it expected a disk.

Probable cause: There's no disk in the drive or the drive door latch is open.

Solution: Stick a disk into the drive or close the drive door, then type R to retry.

Write protect

Meaning: You've attempted to write to or alter a disk that's been tagged as write-protected.

Probable cause: The disk has a write protect tab on it, or the 3½-inch disk has its little tile off the hole. This prevents any information from being written to the disk or information on the disk from being changed.

Solution: Answer A for Abort. If you really want to change the information, remove the disk's write protection and try again (press R for Retry instead of Abort). Refer to "Write-protecting disks" in Chapter 10 for additional information.

Section Five
The Section of Tens

The 5th Wave

By Rich Tennant

"OH YEAH, AND TRY NOT TO ENTER THE WRONG PASSWORD."

In this section...

If you love to read trivia, world records, or books containing lists, then this is the part of the book you've been waiting for. These aren't meaningless "lists of tens," such as Ten People Who Have Plunged to Their Deaths Over Niagara Falls, Ten Otherwise Ugly People I've Seen on Geraldo, or Ten Things Liberals Would Like to Do to William F. Buckley. Instead, these are interesting lists of dos and don'ts, suggestions, tips, and other helpful information for people with computers sitting on their desks.

Note that there won't always be ten items in each category, and in some cases there may be more. After all, if one more misguided soul died while going over the falls, why leave him off the list?

Chapter 18
Ten Common Beginner Mistakes

In this chapter...

▶ Assuming it's your own fault.

▶ Mistyping commands.

▶ Buying the wrong thing.

▶ Buying too much software.

▶ Assuming it will be easy (just because it says so).

▶ Incorrectly inserting disks.

▶ Logged to the wrong drive or directory.

▶ Pressing Y too quickly.

▶ Reformatting an important disk.

▶ No organization or housekeeping.

Golly, if there really were only ten common beginner mistakes then life would be so much easier with computers. Sad to say, the following only highlights a few common beginner faults, but nothing that can't be cured. Review this list and reduce your problems.

Assuming it's your own fault

The first thing most beginners assume is that when something doesn't go right it's their own fault. Usually it isn't. Computers don't always work as advertised. If you type in the command exactly as it's listed in the book or manual and it doesn't work, then the manual is wrong, not you. How do you find out what is right? You can check the program's README file, or call the developer for technical support. Or experiment, especially if it's your own computer (so you only delete your own files and not your coworker's).

Mistyping commands

Making typing mistakes is a common problem for all computer users. Beginners typically forget spaces on the command line, sandwiching separate parts of a DOS command together which doesn't make sense to DOS, therefore you get an error message. Also, never end any DOS command with a period. Even though the manual may have a period after the command (in obeisance to English grammar), few if any DOS commands ever end with a period. And be aware of the differences between the forward slash (/) and backslash (\), as well as the colon (:) and semicolon (;).

Buying the wrong thing

Hardware and software must be compatible with your computer. In particular, this means that software must run "under DOS," and your computer must have the proper innards to support the software. The problem primarily exists with PC graphics and memory. If you don't have enough or the proper type of either, some software may not work. Don't try too hard to save money by buying "bargain" hardware from remainder catalogs if you don't know enough about computers to tell the difference.

Buying too much software

It's fun to go crazy in a software store, wielding your VISA card like a samurai sword. Bringing home all those applications and getting started with them takes time, however. Don't give yourself too much to do, or you may neglect some of the programs you've bought. Start buying software with the basics, maybe one or two packages. Learn those, then expand with other programs as needed. Your brain and your monthly VISA bill will be easier to live with.

Assuming it will be easy (just because it says so)

This goes right along with buying too much software. You need time to learn a program, get comfortable with it, and become productive. With today's over-whelming applications, you may never master everything (no one does). Still, give yourself time to learn. You can get your work done far more quickly if you take those extra few days to experiment and play with the software, work the

tutorials, and practice. (Be sure to tell the boss about that.) Most of all, don't buy software on deadline. I mean, don't think you can buy the program on Monday, install it on Tuesday, and produce the divisional report that's due on Wednesday. Programs save time only after you've learned them — until then, they eat time.

A correlary to this is: Don't expect to learn the program if you refuse to look at the manual (or a book about the program). There's no such thing as an intuitive program, no matter what they say. At least take the introductory tutorial.

Incorrectly inserting disks

The handy 3½-inch disks can only fit into a floppy drive one way. Even though you have a potential of eight ways to insert the disk, only one of them meets with success. The 5¼-inch disks are different. You can fit them into a drive on any of four sides both rightside-up and upside-down. The correct method for both types of disks is with the label up and toward you. The notch on the 5¼-inch disk is to the left and the oblong hole on the disk goes in first. Nothing heinous happens if you insert a 5¼-inch disk wrongly, it just doesn't work.

Logged to the wrong drive or directory

As you use the computer, you'll always be using, or "logged to," one directory on one disk drive. Never assume you know where you are. If you do, you may delete files you don't want to delete, or be unable to find files you expect to be there. Refer to "Finding the current directory" in Chapter 13.

Another common variant of this mistake is logging to a floppy drive that doesn't have a disk in it. If you do so, you'll see a "General failure" error; put the proper disk into the drive, then press R to Retry.

Pressing Y too quickly

DOS asks a Y/N (yes or no) question for a reason; what's about to take place has serious consequences. Are you *sure* you want to go ahead? Only press Y if you really do. If you're uncertain, then press N or Ctrl-C and re-examine your situation. This happens more often than not with the DEL*.* command; make sure you're logged to the proper directory before typing DEL*.* to delete all the files.

Reformatting an important disk

Eventually, like all computer users, you will have accumulated some 10,000 or so floppy disks, which you'll keep in a drawer, on a tabletop, in city-scape-like piles on the floor, or tossed onto a shelf. Grabbing one of these and reformatting it is cheaper than buying a new disk. But make sure that old disk doesn't contain anything valuable before you do so. How do you do that? Label the disks properly and do a DIR to see what's there.

No organization or housekeeping

Organization and housekeeping are two duties that the intermediate-to-advanced DOS users learn to take upon themselves. It's routine stuff, actually part of the larger picture of "hard disk management." Not performing housekeeping or being unorganized are things beginners are good at. But over the long run, picking up after yourself now can save you massive problems in the near future.

Unless you want to pick up a good book on hard disk management (which implies taking that first step toward computer nerdhood), my suggestion is to let your favorite computer expert have a crack at your computer. Tell him or her to check out the system, organize things, and clean up your hard drive. (But tell him or her not to get too fancy — you don't want to plow through six layers of subdirectories to find something.) The end result will be a faster system — and maybe even some more disk space. That's a plus, but getting there isn't something beginners need to concern themselves with.

Chapter 19
Ten Things
You Shouldn't Ever Do

● ●

In this chapter...

▶ Don't switch disks.

▶ Don't work from a floppy disk.

▶ Don't take a disk out of the drive with the light on.

▶ Don't turn off the computer when the hard drive light is on.

▶ Don't reset to leave an application.

▶ Don't plug anything into the computer while it's on.

▶ Don't force a disk into the drive.

▶ Never format a high-capacity disk to low-capacity.

▶ Never format a low-capacity disk to high-capacity.

▶ Never load software from an alien disk.

▶ Never use these DOS commands: CTTY, DEBUG, FDISK, FORMAT C:, RECOVER.

● ●

U h-oh. Here is a list of ten big no-nos (okay, there are 11, but who's counting?) Actually, there are a lot of bad things you can do to a nice computer. For some of them I'm hoping you don't need a written warning. For example, it's a bad idea to attempt to fix your own monitor. You can, conceivably, upgrade your computer, but being able to do something and wanting to do it are two different things.

Here then are ten unhealthy things you don't even want to consider doing.

Don't switch disks

This isn't that obvious a warning. Basically, it means don't switch disks while you're still using the one in the drive. For example, suppose you're working on a file in drive A and you haven't yet saved the file back to disk. Then, for some reason, you switch disks and try to save the file on the second disk. The result is that you've ruined the second disk and not truly saved your file.

Always save a file on the same disk from which you've loaded it. If you want a second copy of the file on another disk, use the COPY command once you've returned to DOS. Refer to "Copying a single file" in Chapter 3.

Don't work from a floppy disk

I am often amazed at people whose computers have nice, big, fast hard drives do their work on floppy disks. It's almost impossible to find a program any more that can be run from a floppy, but it's easy to read and write all your data from a floppy. It's slow and floppies are less reliable than hard disks. Back up your data files to your floppies, and use them to move files to another machine — but do your day-to-day work on your hard drive.

Don't take a disk out of the drive with the light on

The drive light is on only when the computer is writing to or reading from the disk. As with humans, the computer becomes annoyed when you remove its reading material while it's reading from it. The result could be a damaged disk and lost information.

If you remove a disk forgetfully, the computer will display a "What's going on?" error message. Replace the disk and press R to Retry the operation.

Don't turn off the computer when the hard drive light is on

The only safe time to turn off the computer is when you're at the DOS prompt. However, if the hard drive light is still on, that means the computer is accessing the hard disk. It's only safe to turn off the system when the hard drive light is off, meaning that the computer is done writing to disk. (You should also refer to "Turning the computer off" in Chapter 1, as well as "Black box program rules" in Chapter 21.)

Don't reset to leave an application

This goes along with not turning off the PC in the middle of something. Always properly quit a program and return to the DOS prompt. From the DOS prompt you can quickly run your next program. Of course, you can reset if the program has run amok and pressing Ctrl-C or Esc can't stop it.

Don't plug anything into the computer while it's on

Connect any external goodies to your computer only when your computer is off. This especially goes for the keyboard, monitor, and printer. Plugging in any of those items while the computer's power is on can "fry" something you've paid a lot of money for. It's best to turn off the computer, then plug in your goodies, then turn the computer back on again.

Don't force a disk into the drive

If it doesn't go in, then the disk is probably pointed in the wrong direction. Or worse, what you're sticking the disk into is probably not a disk drive. Refer to "Changing disks" in Chapter 1 for the details.

Never format a high-capacity disk to low-capacity

First, it's a waste of money. Second, many low-capacity drives can't read high-capacity disks formatted to low capacity. Third, it's hard to force the machine into reformatting the disk back to high capacity later.

Never format a low-capacity disk to high-capacity

Oh, you can try. The results are usually a disk that's riddled with errors, or a disk that fails miserably over time and loses lots of data. Don't be fooled by some huckster into thinking that a $19.95 hole-punching device can do the trick for you; don't be cheap with your disks or your prized data.

Never load software from an alien disk

Only buy software "shrink wrapped" from a reputable computer dealer. Any other program you get, especially those on cheaply-labeled disks, is suspect. Don't trust it! This is how computer viruses are spread, so it's best not to load anything from an alien disk. And, for God's sake, never boot from such a disk.

Never use these dangerous DOS commands

The following commands serve special purposes way beyond the reach of most beginning computer users. It's okay to let someone who knows what they're doing use these commands, but you should never try them yourselves. The consequences are just too horrible to think of.

CTTY   This command unhooks DOS from the keyboard and screen. Don't try it.

DEBUG   This is a programmer's tool used to create programs, modify memory and, if you're careless, mess up a disk drive. Don't run this program. (If you do, type Q to quit.)

FDISK   This command could destroy all information on your hard drive if used improperly.

FORMAT C: The FORMAT command should only be used with drives A and B to format floppy disks. Never format your hard drive C, or any drive letter higher than C.

RECOVER   This command sounds healthy, but RECOVER is dumb and deadly. If you type this command it will destroy all files on your disk and remove all your subdirectories, replacing them with garbage — all without a Y/N warning. Don't try it.

Chapter 20
Ten Programs
That Make Life Easier

● ●

In this chapter...

We review some neat programs (and give them an IQ rating where 100 takes DOS talent — so the lower the better):

▶ COPYCON — a quick text file editor/creator (60).

▶ Direct Access — a menu system (50).

▶ DOS 5 Shell — a free menu system (100).

▶ LIST — a quick file viewer (70).

▶ Magellan — a point-and-shoot disk manager (90).

▶ PC Shell — everything but the kitchen sink (100).

▶ Windows — makes the entire computer easier to use (90).

▶ XTree Easy — an easy file maintenance program (80).

▶ Other cutesy shells, as stated.

● ●

*O*kay. Some people are just going to hate everything. You may hate your car, but you use it. Even so, one of those rolly-bead back things you put on your seat will make driving more comfortable. And a good stereo system will make you forget that everyone else is passing you on the freeway. Enjoy life, be comfortable, and consider some of the following programs that will make life easier for any DOS user (though they're not as cool as fuzzy dice).

COPYCON (IQ:60)

The COPYCON (copy-con) program is used to edit text files (those files you can view with the TYPE command). It gets its name from a handy DOS trick used to create quick-and-dirty text files: You can use the COPY command to copy information from the keyboard (the CON) to a file. For example:

```
C> COPY CON FUNSTUFF
```

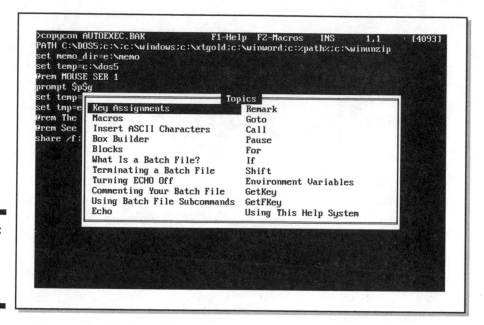

```
>copycon AUTOEXEC.BAK              F1-Help  F2-Macros   INS      1,1     [4093]
PATH C:\DOS5;c:\;c:\windows;c:\xtgold;c:\winword;c:\path%;c:\winunzip
set memo_dir=e:\memo
set temp=c:\dos5
@rem MOUSE SER 1
prompt $p$g
set temp=    ┌─────────────────────────Topics──┐
set tmp=e    │ Key Assignments           Remark  │
@rem The     │ Macros                     Goto    │
@rem See     │ Insert ASCII Characters    Call    │
share /f :   │ Box Builder                Pause   │
             │ Blocks                     For     │
             │ What Is a Batch File?      If      │
             │ Terminating a Batch File   Shift   │
             │ Turning ECHO Off           Environment Variables │
             │ Commenting Your Batch File GetKey  │
             │ Using Batch File Subcommands GetFKey │
             │ Echo                       Using This Help System │
             └───────────────────────────────────┘
```

Figure 20-1:
COPYCON is
a simple,
no-brains
editor.

After pressing Enter you're in a "dumb typewriter" sort of mode. Everything you type goes into a file on disk (FUNSTUFF in example above) or whatever file you specify. You can only backspace to edit, you must press Enter at the end of each line (there is no word processor-like word wrap), and when you're done you press the F6 function key. Nothing big.

The major drawback is that you cannot edit a file with the above COPY command. Remember, COPY always erases the "target" file, so the file FUNSTUFF would be overwritten if you used COPYCON. (Refer to Chapter 3 for more information on the COPY command.)

The COPYCON program takes the simple elegance of DOS's COPY CON and makes it into a real bone-headed editor. I give it a 60 on the DOS IQ chart (where anything over 100 requires real brains to get the work done). With COPYCON on your disk, you can quickly edit files — including CONFIG.SYS or AUTOEXEC.BAT, and never have to learn the DOS editor, EDLIN, or any other gross "text editor." You also don't have to wait 60 seconds while your big, hulking word processor loads.

For example, to edit the file FUNSTUFF, you would type the following:

```
C> COPYCON FUNSTUFF
```

Note that there's no space between COPY and CON above. It's all one word. You're running the COPYCON program. If all goes well, you'll see your file in a handy editing screen, something like Figure 20-1.

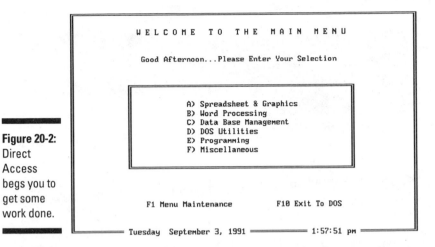

```
        W E L C O M E   T O   T H E   M A I N   M E N U

        Good Afternoon...Please Enter Your Selection

    ┌─────────────────────────────────────────────────┐
    │                                                 │
    │           A) Spreadsheet & Graphics             │
    │           B) Word Processing                    │
    │           C) Data Base Management               │
    │           D) DOS Utilities                      │
    │           E) Programming                        │
    │           F) Miscellaneous                      │
    │                                                 │
    └─────────────────────────────────────────────────┘


        F1 Menu Maintenance        F10 Exit To DOS

    ═══ Tuesday  September 3, 1991 ═══════ 1:57:51 PM ═══
```

Figure 20-2:
Direct
Access
begs you to
get some
work done.

✔ If you get a "Bad command or file name" error, you probably don't have COPYCON on your computer. You can order it directly from the author for $10 at: JB Technology Inc., 28701 N. Main St., Ridgefield, WA 98642. Or you can check with your local computer user group or a national software distributor, such as PC-SIG (dial 800-245-6717, or 800-222-2996 in California, and ask for disk #2029).

✔ Know the differences: the COPYCON program has no space and doesn't erase files; DOS's COPY CON has a space and will erase files. If you don't see COPYCON's screen (Figure 20-1), then press Ctrl-C at once!

✔ Press the F6 key to end editing and save your file.

✔ Press the F1 key for a quickie help screen.

Direct Access (IQ:50)

Direct Access is a menu program, and is probably the simplest and most elegant way to use a PC; no graphics, no beeps and zooming windows, no "486 required," just a list of programs to choose from. Ahhh. Figure 20-2 shows a sample screen from Direct Access.

The beauty of Direct Access is that it lets you use your computer and all your software without having to mess with DOS. Once you set it up (or pull out someone else's hair until they set it up for you), your system is as easy to use as pressing a button. On the DOS IQ scale, Direct Access gets a 50 — less if someone else sets it up for you.

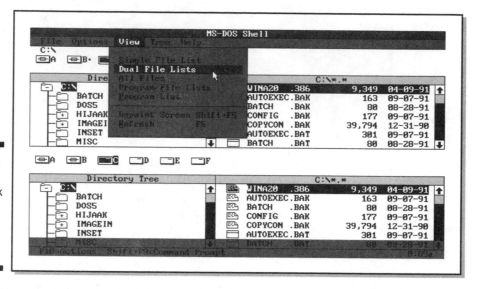

Figure 20-3:
DOS 5 Shell is fun to look at, but may be a tad bit complex to use.

✔ Make sure Direct Access is part of your AUTOEXEC.BAT file, so that it runs each time you start your PC. (Tell your computer expert to set it up that way, or refer to Chapter 2.)

✔ Direct Access is available at nearly all software stores, or you can order it direct from Fifth Generation Systems. Call them at 800-766-7283.

The DOS 5 Shell (IQ:100)

Shells and menu programs are popular ways of avoiding DOS. The most common shell that needs mentioning is the DOS 5 Shell, the program that's included with all versions of DOS (4.0 and greater). Unlike Direct Access, however, the DOS 5 Shell is a bit more technical. It gets a 100 on the DOS IQ scale (see Figure 20-3).

You can use the DOS 5 Shell to circumvent DOS's ugly command line. In the shell, you can copy, move, delete, and rename files. This is all done using the shell's menu system and fancy graphics — plus a mouse if you have one installed. Of course, this may be overwhelming to you. If so, you can have someone configure the shell to show only a list of programs to run. Then you can select which programs you want and entirely avoid DOS.

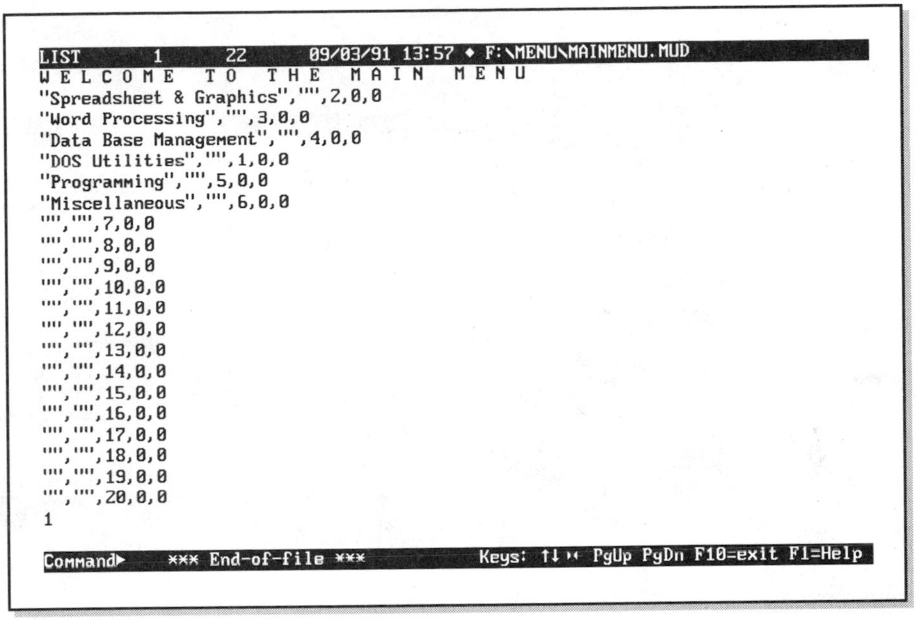

```
LIST        1      22      09/03/91 13:57 ♦ F:\MENU\MAINMENU.MUD
W E L C O M E   T O   T H E   M A I N   M E N U
"Spreadsheet & Graphics","",2,0,0
"Word Processing","",3,0,0
"Data Base Management","",4,0,0
"DOS Utilities","",1,0,0
"Programming","",5,0,0
"Miscellaneous","",6,0,0
"","",7,0,0
"","",8,0,0
"","",9,0,0
"","",10,0,0
"","",11,0,0
"","",12,0,0
"","",13,0,0
"","",14,0,0
"","",15,0,0
"","",16,0,0
"","",17,0,0
"","",18,0,0
"","",19,0,0
"","",20,0,0
1

Command►    *** End-of-file ***           Keys: ↑↓ ►◄ PgUp PgDn F10=exit F1=Help
```

Figure 20-4:
The LIST program beats the pants off of the TYPE command.

✔ The shell is a pain to set up, so make someone else do it for you. Tell them which programs you want installed. Then have them configure the shell so that it shows only the "program list" window on the screen. Further, have them edit AUTOEXEC.BAT so that the DOS 5 Shell always comes up when you start your PC.

✔ Since it comes with every copy of DOS 5, and pretty soon everyone will have DOS 5, I devote Chapter 4 in the book to a rundown of the DOS 5 Shell.

✔ Gotta have a mouse. No mouse, no fun.

LIST (IQ:70)

The LIST program is basically a better version of DOS's TYPE command. Unlike TYPE, however, LIST shows you a file using the entire screen, letting you "scroll" though it using the arrow keys. This is perhaps the best thought-out program ever; just use LIST instead of TYPE. Figure 20-4 shows how LIST displays a file.

LIST gets a 70 on the DOS IQ scale. I would rank it lower (and lower is better), but LIST does more than just look at files, which will make it beneficial to you in

```
Magellan MENU            Use ↑↓→← to navigate              TREE
◄ Tree: F:\QPRO
    DUTB.SFO       A1: [W13]
    DUTI.SFO                 A         B         C         D         E
    EGASPL.PCX     1
    EMSTEST.COM    2
    ENVELOPE.CLP   3                             EXPENSE REPORT FOR ALLISON SPRINGS
    EURO.CHR       4                             WEEK ENDING JUNE 24, 1989
    EUROPE.CLP    •5
    EXPENSES.WQ1   6   DAY OF WEEK    DATE    LOCATION   TRANSPORT   HOTEL
    FANFARE.SND    7   MONDAY        06-18  SAN DIEGO     $89.00    $0.00
    FILELIST.DOC   8   TUESDAY       06-19  SAN DIEGO      $9.00   $67.00
    FONTS.BGI      9   WEDNESDAY     06-20  SAN DIEGO     $27.55   $67.00
    FRANCE.CLP    10   THURSDAY      06-21  SAN DIEGO     $12.50   $67.00
    FRWK!.TRN     11   FRIDAY        06-22  SAN DIEGO      $0.00   $67.00
    FRWK$.TRN     12   SATURDAY      06-23  SAN DIEGO      $0.00   $67.00
    FRWKZ.TRN     13   SUNDAY        06-24  SAN JOSE     $133.00   $67.00
    FRWQ!.TRN     14   TOTAL                             $271.05  $402.00
    FSWK!.TRN     15
    FSWK$.TRN     16
    FSWKZ.TRN     17
    FSWQ!.TRN                                                          READY
  File 36 of 117    ↔   F:\QPRO\EXPENSES.WQ1    Quattro Pro      3,776 Bytes
ALT   F1       F2      F3       F4        F5      F6     F7       F8      F9     F10
    Compose   Move   Mark   Rename    Index   Tree   Macro   Options   Path    Dos
```

Figure 20-5: Magellan is shown here displaying a spreadsheet in context.

the future (if you care to expand your DOS knowledge). Using LIST you can copy, delete, move, and rename files, which gives this program lots of power beyond a simple file viewer.

TIP

✔ If you don't have LIST, you can pick it up from a user group or a shareware library. You can also order it directly from the author (who wants $20 for it): Vernon D. Buerg, 139 White Oak Circle, Petaluma, CA 94952.

Magellan (IQ:90)

Magellan is an interesting tool, but hard to describe. It's like the DOS 5 Shell in that you can copy, move, delete, and rename files. Yet it's also like the LIST program in that you can see a file's contents — even in the same format in which the file was created (which is a real help). Further, Magellan is smart enough to know which program created any file on disk and, at the touch of a key, it will run that program and load your file. How's that for magic?

Figure 20-5 shows Magellan at what it does best. A list of files is on one side of the screen. The highlighted file is a worksheet, which is shown on the other side of the screen as if it were in the program that created it (Quattro Pro). That's remarkable because spreadsheet programs store their files in Greek, so a TYPE or LIST just shows garbage. If you were to press a special "launch" key at this point, Magellan would run Quattro Pro and load the highlighted worksheet.

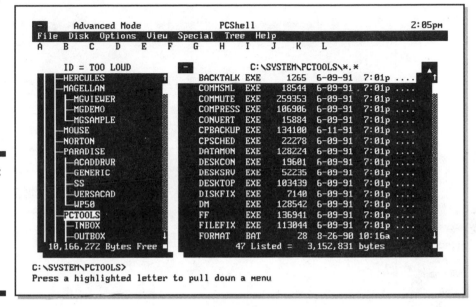

Figure 20-6: PC Tools' PC Shell helps you organize and examine files.

Magellan gets a 90 on the DOS IQ scale, primarily because it can be overwhelming. Even so, Magellan is the best utility for keeping track of all your stuff on your hard drive. It can find lost files, not only by their names, but by what's in them (and that's severely nifty in my opinion). But for some beginners, particularly those who may just want a menu system like Direct Access, Magellan would be a bit much.

> ✔ You can pick up Magellan at just about any software store. Lotus sells it directly, but rather than buy from them, consider picking it up cheaper from a mail-order discount house. Several of these are listed in some of the major, national computer publications.

PC Shell (IQ:100)

Central Point's PC Tools started out as a meek Albania-sized program. Presently, it's bigger than the whole of Eurasia, thanks to dozens of useful little programs, most of which are way beyond the abilities of beginning DOS users. PC Tools is massive. Yet, the shell program, PC Shell, can be a much better way of using a computer than staring at a DOS prompt (see Figure 20-6).

PC Shell gets an IQ rating of 100, which some will consider a bit low. However, with the program in the basic mode, and forgetting the ten thousand other DOS utilities that come in the PC Tools package, PC Shell does rate a 100. It's quite similar to DOS's DOS 5 Shell, but has many more features and abilities.

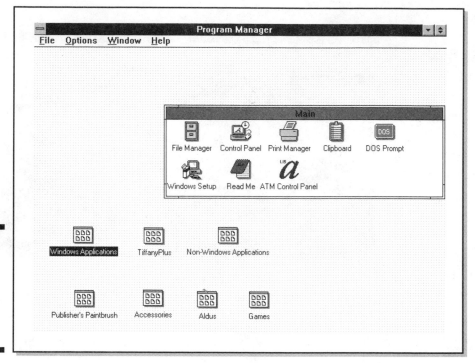

Figure 20-7:
Here is
Windows'
happy,
friendly,
graphical
face.

About the biggest advantage to PC Shell is the sheer immensity of PC Tools. There are lots of useful programs bundled together, including a backup program, computer-to-computer file transfer and modem programs, disaster recovery and prevention, and stuff that will boggle the mind. Impressive, but maybe a bit high on the IQ scale for some of us.

✔ You can get PC Tools at any software store; it's often heavily discounted (and well worth the price). Or you can order it directory from Central Point Software.

Windows (IQ:90)

I've seen the future and it has Windows! Actually, we're all supposed to be using computers graphically in the future. Toss out that old command line and DOS prompt! The computer industry will have everyone using a PC with a mouse soon, and Windows is the way that's done under DOS.

Windows can totally replace DOS. With the WIN command stuck at the end of your AUTOEXEC.BAT file (see Chapter 2), you'll never see a DOS prompt while you use your computer (see Figure 20-7). Want to run an application? Then just point the mouse at it and click. (Mouse stuff is provided in Chapter 8; more info on Windows is raked over in Chapter 21).

Windows gets a 90 on the IQ scale. It should get 100, or even higher, because Windows can at times be quite a load to bear. By itself, Windows is intuitive, obvious, and I'll admit, a little fun to use. It may require someone else to set it up just the way you like, which is why Windows scores a bit high on the IQ thermometer.

✔ Windows can be purchased all over; refer to your local software dealer or a national mail-order house. Note that sometimes Windows is bundled with other products, such as Windows-specific programs, a computer mouse, or other goodies.

✔ Windows works best when it runs Windows-specific programs, such as Word for Windows, Microsoft Excel, Ami, WordPerfect for Windows, and so on. It can run other DOS programs as well, though you won't get all those fancy graphics.

✔ Gotta use a mouse.

✔ Gotta read the manual. Bill Gates (President of Microsoft and Genius) thinks it's intuitive; enough said.

XTree Easy (IQ:80)

XTree Easy is the easiest to use of several XTree-brand programs, all designed to make file management a snap. Using XTree Easy you can copy, delete, rename, and move files all around your hard drive, you can compare two different subdirectories and work with files between them, or you can "prune and graft" various subdirectories to help keep yourself organized.

But forget all that: When you start XTree Easy, it presents you with a list of all the programs on your computer. To run one you just "point and shoot." Nothing could be easier. It even sets all that up for you.

The nice thing about XTree Easy is that it always gives you a visual representation of your files and hard disk's tree structure (see Figure 20-8). This makes it easy to zip around and see where things are, as well as run those programs you have stashed all over the place.

This isn't straightforward like Direct Access, but it's still easy to use. Therefore, XTree Easy gets a big 80 on the DOS IQ scale. Especially if you've been using your computer for years and have no idea what's where, or you prefer a more visual way of working with files; consider it.

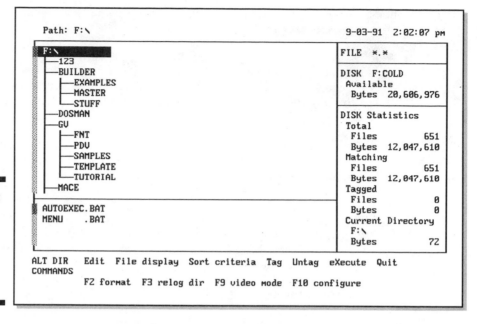

Figure 20-8:
XTree Easy
shows you
the pro-
grams on
your hard
drive.

✔ XTree Easy is available all over — software stores, computer dealers, and
national mail-order places. But beware: XTree Pro, its big brother, is a wee
bit more complex than XTree Easy. If that's what you want, great. But for a
DOS beginner, I'd recommend XTree Easy.

Other cutesy shells

There are many, many programs available that make DOS easier to use. Windows
is the front-runner, followed by Direct Access. Everything else that claims to be a
"menu system" or "DOS 5 shell" falls in between (though Magellan is really an
information management program). Out there in the real world, you'll find even
more programs. I could list about 50 or so here. Instead, the following are some
items you may want to mull over before you decide to buy a program that
professes to make DOS easier to use.

Purpose

Discover what the program does. How does it make DOS easier to use? Is it a
menu program, such as Direct Access? Or is it more along the lines of PC Shell
or the DOS 5 Shell — or even Windows? A menu system lists your programs; a
DOS 5 shell makes it easier to perform basic DOS functions; both usually do some
of each. If what the program does matches your needs, you're halfway home.

The 5th Wave   By Rich Tennant

"OH SURE, $1.8 MILLION DOLLARS SEEMS LIKE ALOT RIGHT NOW, BUT WHAT ABOUT RANDY? WHAT ABOUT HIS FUTURE? THINK WHAT A COMPUTER LIKE THIS WILL DO FOR HIS S.A.T. SCORE SOMEDAY."

Ease of installation

How easy is the program to set up? For example, some menu programs will scan your hard drive for programs and automatically set up your own menu system. That saves you a big step. Also remember to check the program's requirements. For example, Windows makes a computer easy to use, but it's taxing on memory, graphics, and computer horsepower (you really nead a 386). Does your system meet the requirements?

Ease of use

You would think this a redundant category. After all, some of these programs have the word "easy" on the package several times too many. But what the developer thinks is easy and what you find easy could be two different things. Up front, anything is easier than using DOS. So see what else it is the program does and how it makes that one thing so much more "easy."

If you're buying from a software store, try to see a demo of the program. That's the true gauge of whether or not something is easy. And here you can chalk up a big point for Direct Access: It's the program that your typical software store uses to run the other demo programs in.

Support

Support comes from three places: the dealer or computer store, the software developer, and from people who are willing to help you. Sometimes the store can't be counted on; they sell hundreds of software programs and no one can really be an expert in all of them. Instead, take a hard look at developer support. Do they have a phone-in support line? Is it toll free? For how long can you call? Then ask your friends: The best program to buy is the one all your friends have because they know it and can answer questions. Presto, free tech support.

Price

Finally comes the issue of price. The "other cutesy shells" can range in price from a couple of hundred dollars to free. What you're getting for that price is more important than comparing individual prices. After all, programs like PC Tools offer you more than Direct Access, so there's going to be a difference in price.

Just about anything that makes a computer easier to use can be a blessing. Even DOS experts will use shells and menu systems simply because they make things quicker and less painful than using DOS. Finding the right one can be complicated. But it's a big field, full of competition, so there's bound to be a way to make DOS easier to use for everyone. Keep looking.

Chapter 21
Ten Popular Programs
(and How to Fake Your Way Through Them)

● ●

In this chapter...

▶ General rules for using a black box program.

▶ dBase IV

▶ Q&A

▶ Lotus 1-2-3

▶ Quattro Pro

▶ WordPerfect

▶ Microsoft Word 5.5

▶ WordStar

▶ Windows 3

▶ Harvard Graphics

▶ Procomm Plus

● ●

*T*his chapter consists of quick-and-dirty lessons in ten popular programs. It's designed for two groups: Those who find themselves in trouble with programs they use all the time but don't understand completely; and those who suddenly have to make an unfamiliar program do something simple.

Let's face it, there are two kinds of people in the world: computer enthusiasts, and the rest of us. The computer enthusiasts use many different programs and love learning new ones. The rest of us have one, maybe two programs we use often enough to feel comfortable with, and we sincerely hope we never have to learn a third.

If you are lucky and have been very good in a past life, the one or two programs you do use have been set up by one of those computer enthusiasts, and all you have to do is run it. Of course, sometimes they crash, or you push the wrong button and end up in the wrong place, or you badly need to do something the enthusiast didn't think of — and naturally the enthusiast is nowhere to be found. At this point you may wish you knew *just a little bit more* about the program — just enough to get out of trouble and back on track. This chapter is for you. It will show you how to get that macro running again, how to print that worksheet, how to undelete that huge chunk you just erased by accident.

Even if your regular program never crashes, or you know it so well you feel like a bit of a computer guru yourself, nothing will make you feel more like a dummy than trying to run a program you've never used before. The most advanced programmer guru enlightened four-eyes pen-protector Coke-swigging PC jockey can be humbled by a new program in the twinkling of an eye (it's kind of fun to watch, actually). So remember you've got this chapter to refer to when you turn into a whiz yourself.

(By the way, I got a little help from my friends writing this chapter. I've been doing this a long time but even I don't know the ins and outs of all ten of these programs. You will find the credits at the beginning of the book. A tip of the Gookin hat to a great bunch.)

Black box program rules

Before I begin with the popular programs, I need to explain what a "black box" program is.

A "black box" program is a program that runs itself so that you, the user, don't have to know how it works. The details are concealed inside a "black box."

For example, dBASE is a program that can run other programs for you, such as order entry, a customer list, or any number of database programs. Such programs usually prompt you through the things you're to do. Microsoft Windows is a single program that can run a number of other programs. And there are lesser types of programs, usually called *menu systems* that run all the programs on your computer from one handy menu. These are all black box programs; doing the DOS dirty work for you, while you sit back and get work done.

The following are the rules for using a black box program, particularly those that supersede rules already pounded into your head elsewhere in this book. These are general rules you can use on any black box program to get out of trouble.

Basic black box information

Fill in this information if you're using a black box program on your PC. If you don't know the answers, then get the answers; force them out of your PC guru at gun point if necessary (I'm not one to advocate the use of violence to get what's rightly yours, but it's always worked for me). Why get this information? Because when things go wrong, it will help you save yourself, maybe by looking in this book, rather than having to wait for the guru to return from lunch or vacation.

The formal name of your black box program: _____

How that name is pronounced: _____

The command you type to start your black box program: _____

Its drive and directory: _____

(Use this information to locate the program if you ever "lose" it; refer to "Where is my program?" in Chapter 16, for your hunting license.)

Files associated with the black box program that you should never delete:

Filename: **In English:**

_____   _____

_____   _____

_____   _____

_____   _____

_____   _____

_____   _____

_____   _____

_____   _____

Your guru's phone number: _____

Times when it's okay to call: _____

(Just ask them that last question to be nice; feel free to call whenever you need them. Refer to Chapter 20 for information on common bribes.)

Note the names of programs you'll run. For example, if you're in dBASE, you'll probably be running several "do" files. Write down their names here. If you're in Windows, then you're running some programs that have "icons" (little pictures on the screen). Write down their names and what they do below. The same holds true for whichever black box program you're running.

Program Name (do file):	What it does:
_____	_____
_____	_____
_____	_____
_____	_____
_____	_____
_____	_____
_____	_____

Exit from the black box program before turning off or resetting your computer. In a black box program, you can be at a DOS prompt that makes it look all right to reset or turn off your PC. However, that DOS prompt may just be part of the black box program — not a "real" DOS prompt.

If you find yourself at a DOS prompt in a black box program, type the EXIT command:

```
C> EXIT
```

This should return you to the black box program. From there, you should quit the black box program and return to the "real" DOS prompt. At that point it's okay to reset or to shut off your computer.

dBASE IV

Often you will be working on an application program that someone else has written in dBASE IV and are not aware of dBASE's presence at all. You'll turn to this section when something goes wrong and find yourself out of the prepared application and wishing you knew how to get back in.

On the other hand, you may need to use dBASE directly to look at your data or generate simple reports. I give you a few basic tips here.

(This covers dBASE IV; if you can't find the Command Center and stuff like that, you probably have an older version, maybe dBASE III or even II. Most of the parts that don't refer to the Command Center will work equally well in earlier versions, though. And if you ask your programmer nicely, he/she can probably write in the equivalents in those earlier versions for you.)

Starting dBASE and running dBASE applications

If you're using an application (a program written in dBASE for you), the developer may have set it up to start automatically when you turn the computer on in the morning, or may have given you explicit instructions for starting the program. If not, or if you somehow ended up at the DOS prompt (C>) and want to start dBASE, here's how.

You start dBASE by typing at the DOS prompt:

    C> DBASE

✔ If you're missing dBASE, then it's usually found in the \dBASE subdirectory on drive C. Type the following:

    C> C:

Then:

    C> CD \DBASE

If you know the name of the prepared application, you can load it at the same time that you load dBASE; for example, to load a dBASE application called INVOICE, type this:

    C> DBASE INVOICE

A logo screen and ominous sounding licensing message will display as the program loads, demanding that you press Enter to accept the license. If you're using dBASE IV and you didn't specify the name of an application, you should next see the dBASE IV Control Center screen. If all you see is a blank screen with one line at the bottom and a single dot . . . don't panic. To get into the Control Center type:

    ASSIST

To run an application from the dBASE IV Control Center, move the highlight to the application name in the Applications column and press Enter. When the prompt appears asking if you would like to modify or run the application, choose Run.

If you unexpectedly exit a dBASE application, you may find yourself not at the DOS prompt but at the "dBASE dot prompt," which is just a period at the left of the screen with the blinking cursor next to it. To run a prepared application for which you know the name (you made your programmer write it down for you in an earlier chapter of this book, remember?), do this (let's say the application name is again INVOICE):

```
. DO INVOICE
```

The application will load and you're back home.

Loading a dBASE IV database catalog

dBASE IV data and associated reports and applications are grouped into what is known as a catalog. When you start the Command Center it will open the catalog that was in use the last time the program was run. To change catalogs, press Alt-C to activate the Catalog menu at the top of the screen. Choose the Use a Different Catalog option.

You can access the various data files, reports, and forms in the catalog by using the arrow keys to move the highlight to the item you're interested in and pressing Enter.

Canceling a command

The dBASE cancel key is Esc, which will cancel almost any changes you make. The Esc key will also back you out of all menus and operations like browsing files or creating forms.

Undoing commands

When editing data in a form, you can undo changes to the data by selecting the Undo command from the Record menu, as long as you do this before moving to the next record. If you've already moved, you're out of luck . . . the changes are permanent.

The other thing you can undo in dBASE is record deletion. When you choose to delete a record, it's still there — the program just flags the data to signify that it's really not supposed to be there. Depending on how your copy of dBASE is set up, these marked records may disappear from your view of the data completely or they may show but indicate Del in the status line. Either way, you can "undelete" them with the Clear Deletion Mark option on the Record menu.

Getting help

On-line help in dBASE IV is accessed by pressing the F1 key. The help screen gives information on the particular operation you're working on at the time. You can use the window options to view related topics or a table of contents. When viewing the help table of contents, F3 will take you to a more generalized list, while F4 moves to a narrower group of topics.

General advice

The only thing you want to really be careful not to do in either version of dBASE is something called "packing the database." This shows up as a menu option to Erase Marked Records at various places in the system. Do not *ever* choose this option unless you actually know what you're doing. This process really erases the records that are only pretending to be erased when marked for deletion. Once you do this, they are gone forever.

If you ever press the Esc key one too many times and find yourself back at the blank screen with the dot, remember to type ASSIST to get back to the dBASE IV Control Center. If you get to this point and really just want to get out of the program completely, type QUIT. *Never never never* exit dBASE by typing Ctrl-Alt-Del. dBASE files almost always get corrupted when you do this.

Q&A

Ease of use is the byword for Symantec's Q&A, the top-selling flat-file ("every-day") database manager that also includes a word processor. It's easy, yet it can be very powerful too. But let's not worry about that part; we'll just cover the basics here.

Starting Q&A

Load Q&A by typing QA (not Q&A) at the DOS prompt:

```
C> QA
```

If you see "Bad command or file name" error, then type the following:

```
C> C:
```

Then:

```
C> CD\QA
```

Then type QA to start the program.

> ✔ If you still can't find the program, refer to "Where is my program?" in Chapter 16.

Canceling commands

Use the Esc key to return to the previous menu, cancel a command, put a help screen away, or back out of any operation. On the other hand, F10 in Q&A usually means "continue" or proceed to the next action.

Function keys

Most Q&A screens display (along the bottom) the function key combinations you're most likely to need to perform various actions. If function keys pertain to what you're doing, the F1 help screen usually describes what they do when pressed. You can also use a mouse with Q&A.

Adding and updating database records

To open a database, select File from the Q&A main menu, then choose the kind of operation you want to perform — for example, Add Data adds records to the file, or Search/Update to find or edit existing records. Type in the name of the database when Q&A prompts you, and press Enter to open the file.

> ✔ To see a list of all the databases in the directory, press Enter with no filename specified, then highlight the one you want, and press Enter to open it.

> ✔ In Add Data mode, Q&A displays a fresh empty form. Fill in the information blanks, using the Tab, Enter, or arrow keys to move from field to field. When the record is filled out, hitting F10 adds it to the file and displays another one to fill out.

> ✔ In Search/Update mode, Q&A displays the Retrieve Spec screen for the database. Tab to the field that contains the information you want to search on (for example, last name, social security number, or invoice number),

type in the search value or range of values (F1 help can really come in handy here), and press F10 to display the first record in the group that meets your criteria. Edit the record if you like, and press F10 to resave it and bring up the next record in the stack.

✔ The database may contain several previously designed retrieve specifications. At the Retrieve Spec screen you can press Alt-F8 to display and choose from a list of same.

✔ When working on a database record, the F1 help key may display a custom help screen placed there by your friendly neighborhood consultant. To get Q&A's own generic help, press F1 again.

✔ When you're finished adding or updating records, press Esc or Shift-F10 to close the database file and return to the File menu.

The Q&A word processor

Choose Write from the Q&A Main menu, and then Type/Edit to display a blank screen for you to begin typing your letter, memo, or other document. The bottom of the screen shows the function keys that invoke routine word processing operations; F8 displays an options menu, and F1 displays help on editing and using Q&A's Write features, including document formatting. You can do some fancy merge-printing with the word processor (merge-printing is making a mass mailing using the names in a database), but let's leave that exotica for some other day.

Loading an existing document

Choose Write from the Q&A Main menu, select Get, then type in the name of the document and press Enter to display it.

✔ To see a list of documents in the current directory, press Enter with the filename blank, highlight the document you want, and press Enter to bring it onto the screen.

✔ With the document displayed, press F2 and F10 to print it out, or Shift-F8 to save it to disk.

Undoing a text deletion

Shift-F7 restores the last portion of text just deleted.

Running a database report

Choose Report from the Q&A Main menu, and then Print a Report. Enter the name of the database that contains the information you want to include in the report; the list of the report; designs on disk will display. Use your arrow keys to highlight the one you want to run, press Enter, and confirm whether you want to make any one-time changes to the report design. Answer Yes if you want to make temporary changes, and you can then press F1 for information on how to customize the report.

Using the intelligent assistant for queries, reports, and printing

Q&A's Assistant is an unusual database query tool that interacts with you in plain English. To use it, choose Assistant from the Q&A Main menu, and then select the query method that suits you best.

1. If you want to type in a direct command such as "Show me the records where the city is Denver," choose Ask me to do something and enter the name of the database. The Assistant may need to scan the database before prompting you to type your request (with a large file this could take some time). When the Assistant understands your command it presents its plan of action for you to confirm. Select No to edit your command, or press Enter to have the Assistant act on it. Press F1 if you need assistance with the Assistant.

2. If you prefer to sit back and answer questions rather than type out the command, choose Query Guide and enter the name of the database. The Assistant will prompt you to select the kind of operation you want to perform, and then prompt you further until you tell it to execute your request. Follow the directions on screen, pressing F1 if you need more help. You can also use the Query Guide to run predefined reports and file print jobs.

Macros

Q&A macros are stored keystrokes you can play back to automate repetitive tasks. Press Alt-F2 to display the list of available macros, use your arrow key to highlight the one you want, and hit Enter to run it.

✔ Should the macro pause during execution (with a large blinking cursor), it expects you either to type in some variable information, or make a selection from a displayed list or menu. The message at the bottom of the screen will tell you which key resumes execution — it's usually the Enter key.

✔ A Q&A macro invoked from one location in the program, when it was designed to be invoked from a different location, could produce unwanted results. Lengthy macros are usually most safely launched from the position of the Q&A Main menu.

✔ Pressing Esc during macro execution kills the macro, but doesn't undo what the macro has already done.

DOS facilities

You can perform DOS housekeeping chores (delete, copy, or rename files) from inside Q&A. For database files, select Utilities from the Q&A Main menu; for document files, select Utilities from the Write menu. Then choose DOS File Facilities, select the action you want to perform, and enter the name of the file. You can choose List Files rather than type filenames.

Getting help

Pressing F1 from almost anywhere inside Q&A usually displays help related to what you're doing at that moment. At some help screens you'll need to press PgDn to see more.

General advice

Keep an eye out for Q&A system messages appearing near the bottom of the screen — they tell you what your next step is, report on a goof you've just made, or explain why an action you've attempted can't be performed. Q&A also pops up warning screens when you're about to take some action that could result in the loss of information. Read them carefully before proceeding.

Never reboot or turn off your computer without exiting Q&A via the X - Exit selection on the Main menu. Doing so could damage any database or document file that was still open.

Lotus 1-2-3

Release 2.3, 3.1, and earlier (text versions)

Lotus 1-2-3, is the most popular spreadsheet for the PC. Popular, but primitive. Most of the time you won't be using 1-2-3 directly at all. Hopefully, you'll be using special macros to get your work done. (Macros are little programs written by someone who knows what they're doing to make life easier for you.) Still, you might find yourself having to fake your way through a 1-2-3 session. Here are some tips. (If you're using 1-2-3 for Windows, don't worry: Hit the slash key and you'll see the so-called Classic menu appear, which will obey all the instructions listed here.)

✔ 1-2-3 works like this: You hit the slash key, the menu across the top of the screen is activated, then you hit the first letter of the words in the menu that you want to execute. For example, if you want to do a File command, you hit F for File. In the discussions below (except for "Starting 1-2-3"), I spell out the word, but you just hit the capitalized letter in that word.

Starting 1-2-3

You start 1-2-3 by typing 123 at the DOS prompt:

```
C> 123
```

✔ If you're missing 1-2-3, then it's usually found in the \123 subdirectory on drive C. Type the following:

```
C> C:
```

Then:

```
C> CD \123
```

That's the CD command, space, a backslash, and then 1-2-3. Then type 123 to start the program.

✔ If you still can't find 1-2-3, refer to "Where is my program?" in Chapter 16.

Stopping 1-2-3 (safely)

Any time you want to leave 1-2-3, first decide if you want to save your new or changed worksheet. If so, first type: /, FILE, SAVE

That's a slash followed by a comma, space, the FILE command followed by a comma, space, and then the SAVE command. Answer the prompts. Go ahead and save backups.

Once you've saved your file (or decided not to), type this: /, QUIT, YES

That's a slash followed by a comma, space, the QUIT command followed by a comma, and then the word Yes. If you've made changes and haven't saved them, you'll be asked whether you want to quit anyway. If you say Yes, you lose your changes. If you say No, you return to the worksheet. Anything already on disk won't be affected if you abandon a file you changed on screen but didn't save.

Loading a worksheet

You can load a worksheet at the same time that you start 1-2-3. Type 123, a space, a hyphen and a W, and then the name of the file you want to load, like this:

```
C> 123 -WBUDGET
```

This starts 1-2-3 and loads the file named BUDGET, all in one stroke.

Once you're in 1-2-3, you load a worksheet using the /, FILE, RETRIEVE command (by which I mean you press the slash key, then F for File, then R for Retrieve). A list of files appears: Select the file you want to load. You can press F3 to see more filenames displayed.

A new, blank worksheet appears when you first start 1-2-3 without specifying a filename. If you've been working on a worksheet and now you want a new, blank one, use the following command: /, FILE, NEW

That's a slash followed by a comma, space, the FILE command followed by a comma, space, and then the NEW command. Naturally, save the previous worksheet first if it's new or if you made changes you don't want to lose.

Entering stuff on the worksheet

Move the cell cursor to the cell you want to put something in (the whole cell is highlighted).

To enter something just type, then press Enter when you're done. The text appears in the edit line at the top while you're typing it, and in the cell when you press Enter. 1-2-3 usually knows the difference between text and numbers. *Except:* When the text you're typing starts with a numeral (*3RD ANNUAL SOMETHING OR ANOTHER*), it might get mixed up; help it out by starting the entry with a single or double quote mark: '3RD ANNUAL . . . etc. Now it's text for sure.

To enter a number or a numerical formula, just type it in:

    2+2

(Press Enter and you get 4 in the cell.)

Now comes the tricky stuff. To enter a reference to a cell, put it in parentheses:

    (A4+C6)

This adds the values in cells A4 and C6.

To enter 1-2-3's @functions — just type them in: @SUM(B1..B12)

The @SUM is 1-2-3's add-'em-up function, and B1..B12 means from cell B1 down to cell B12," and is, you will notice, in parentheses, just like algebra class.

To edit something that's already in a cell, move the cursor to that cell and hit F2. The contents appear on the edit line. Type, delete, or use the left and right arrow to move back and forth.

Changing width of a column

To change a column's width so it's wider or smaller, type this:

    /, WORKSHEET, COLUMN, SET-WIDTH, #

That's a slash followed by a comma, space, the word WORKSHEET followed by a comma, space, the word COLUMN followed by a comma, the word SET, a hyphen, the word WIDTH followed by a comma, space, and then the number of the width you want. Type in a number where I put the #. The regular width is 9. If you make the column too small, numbers that can't fit in the cells might be replaced by asterisks (or by scientific notation: 1.1E+33, for example).

Recalculating your worksheet

Usually, 1-2-3 will be set up to recalculate everything on a worksheet every time you enter something. But just to be sure, before you print or otherwise use the info on the screen, press the F9 function key to force a recalc. That way you know your data's up to date. Ahhh.

Printing

This can be a pain in the neck in 1-2-3. See if you can get someone to set up a macro to handle this for you. No? OK, here's how to print. I'm not going to show you how to remove borders, print a special subsection, print narrow or sideways, put in headers and footers and that kind of thing, because that's for somebody who actually wants to learn 1-2-3. I'll just show you how to get the whole worksheet out of the computer and onto a printed page, however crudely. Do this:

/, Print, Printer, <Home key — that's usually on the 10-key pad>, . [the period], <End key>, <Home key>, <Enter>, Align, Go, Page

When the printing stops, hit Q to Quit printing and return to the worksheet.

Canceling a command

The 1-2-3 cancel key is the Esc key, which will cancel most things you do. Pressing Esc will also back you out of any 1-2-3 menu, though you may have to press Esc a few times before you're returned to the worksheet.

Undoing commands

You can use 1-2-3's Undo feature to restore your spreadsheet to its previous condition, probably just before you did something you now regret. The Undo key is Alt-F4.

Note that the Undo feature of 1-2-3 must be activated before you can use the Alt-F4 key. If it is active, you'll see UNDO at the bottom of the screen. If you don't, activate Undo by pressing /, Worksheet, Global, Default, Other, Undo, Enable.

Running macros

A macro is several 1-2-3 commands or actions stored as a group so you can automate things. If you're lucky, somebody has already automated things for you by creating macros to handle the worksheets you're using. It's even possible to completely automate the worksheet with macros, so all you do is fill in the blanks, and everything else happens automatically.

If you've got a macro-automated system, make sure the person who created it writes down for you the name of the macro that starts things. Then if you need to, you can start the macro yourself. Or your local guru may have set up a number of handy-dandy macros for specific purposes. Here's how to run them.

Press Alt-F3 to see a list of the names of the macros available for the current worksheet. (After pressing Alt-F3, press F3 to see a more complete list.) Select the macro you want to run by using the arrow keys to highlight the macro's name, then press Enter.

By the way, the macro names that start with a backslash (\S, for example) are Alt-key macros; you can run them by pressing an Alt-key combination instead of just picking them off the list. For example, press Alt-S to run the macro named \S.

How do you know which macros to run? Some you can figure out from the names. Otherwise you need a cheat sheet from your guru.

Getting help

Press F1 to get on-line help in 1-2-3. Select your help topic from the index. Note: The index item @Function Index contains a list of all 1-2-3's functions and their formats.

General advice

The only scary thing that may happen with 1-2-3 is that you may, for some reason, find yourself back at the DOS prompt. Normally, when you exit 1-2-3 (/, Quit, Yes), you'll be told that you haven't yet saved your worksheet. This makes it hard to exit 1-2-3 without realizing it.

If you ever find yourself at the DOS prompt without a warning, you might have accessed the /, System command sequence. This command puts you at the DOS prompt (and quite easily), but you haven't really quit 1-2-3. To return to your worksheet, type the EXIT command:

```
C> EXIT
```

Pressing Enter here returns you to 1-2-3. If it doesn't, then you really did quit 1-2-3.

> ✔ If the program keeps beeping at you when you're trying to enter a command or do something like print, check to see if you're at Ready. If the word READY doesn't appear in the upper-right corner of the screen, that's because 1-2-3 thinks you're in the middle of doing something like entering or editing data in a cell or issuing a command, and it won't accept some kinds of orders. To get back to Ready, hit the Esc key a few times until it appears. Then try your command again.

Quattro Pro

Quattro Pro is a spreadsheet program that reads and writes 1-2-3 files, and offers you a menu system you can customize. You can also choose a menu that imitates 1-2-3's menu system. If your copy of Quattro Pro is set up to mimic 1-2-3, just follow the previous instructions for 1-2-3 in this chapter. Here, however, I'll use the Quattro Pro interface commands, which also consist of a number of slash commands, with keyboard shortcuts where relevant. Since it is so similar to 1-2-3, I'll use the same language in spots, so yes, I am plagiarizing myself, don't write and point it out to my editor.

(By the way, if you know 1-2-3 and want to use Quattro Pro's 1-2-3-style menu, start the program by typing Q123 at the DOS prompt. Or if you're already in Quattro Pro, use this command sequence: /, Option, Startup, Menu-tree — then select 1-2-3. When you hit Return, the menu will switch to accept 1-2-3 commands.)

Starting Quattro Pro

You start Quattro Pro by typing Q at the DOS prompt:

```
C> Q
```

> ✔ If you get the message "Bad command or file name," then Quattro Pro is not in your path. Type the following:
>
> ```
> C> CD \QPRO
> ```

Then type Q to start the program.

✔ If you still can't find Quattro Pro, refer to "Where is my program?" in Chapter 16.

Stopping Quattro Pro (safely)

To leave Quattro Pro, just type this:

```
/, FILE, EXIT
```

(Ctrl-X is the shortcut.)

If you've made changes to the file and haven't saved them, you'll be asked whether you want to quit anyway. If you say Yes, you lose your changes. (Anything already on disk won't be affected if you abandon a file you changed on screen but didn't save.) If you say No, you return to the worksheet. If you say Save & Exit, the changes are saved first, then you exit.

Loading a spreadsheet

Loading a spreadsheet in Quattro Pro can be done easily from within the product by using the /, File, Retrieve command. You also can use /, File, Open to open additional spreadsheets (Quattro Pro allows 32 spreadsheets to be opened at once if you have enough memory.) Select the file to load by using the cursor keys to highlight the file to load. You can press F3 to see more filenames and the Gray + key shows you the size and date of the files.

You can also load a spreadsheet while starting the program by typing a space and the filename you want to load. For example:

```
C> Q BUDGET
```

Above, Quattro Pro is started and the worksheet BUDGET will be loaded and ready to run.

If you start Quattro Pro without specifying a worksheet, you'll get a blank worksheet to use. If you want to get a blank worksheet after using and saving another worksheet, select /, File, New, and press Enter.

Entering stuff on the worksheet

Move the cell cursor to the cell you want to put something in (the whole cell is highlighted).

To enter something, just type it, then press Enter when you're done. The text appears in the edit line at the top while you're typing it, and in the cell when you press Enter. Quattro Pro usually knows the difference between text and numbers. ***Except:*** When the text you're typing starts with a numeral (3RD ANNUAL SOMETHING OR ANOTHER), it might get mixed up; help it out by starting the entry with a single or double quote mark: '3RD ANNUAL . . . etc. Now it's text for sure.

To enter a number or a numerical formula, just type it in:

    2+2

(Press Enter and you get 4 in the cell.)

Now comes the tricky stuff. To enter a reference to a cell, put it in parentheses:

    (A4+C6)

This adds the values in cells A4 and C6.

To enter Quattro Pro's @ functions — just them type them in:

    @SUM(B1..B12)

The @SUM is Quattro Pro's add-'em-up function, and B1..B12 means from cell B1 down to cell B12, and is, you will notice, in parentheses, just like algebra class.

To edit something that's already in a cell, move the cursor to that cell and hit F2. The contents appear on the edit line. Type, delete, or use the left and right arrow to move back and forth.

Changing width of a column

To change a column's width so it's wider or smaller, put the cursor anywhere in the column in question, then type /, STYLE, COLUMN-WIDTH, then use the left and right arrow keys to visually widen or narrow the column. Press Enter when you've got it the way you want it.

> ✔ **Shortcut:** Instead of going through the menu, just hit Ctrl-W, then use the cursor keys as above.

As with Lotus 1-2-3, if you make the column too small in Quattro Pro, numbers that can't fit in the cells might be replaced by asterisks (or by scientific notation: 1.1E+33 for example).

Recalculating your worksheet

Usually, your Quattro Pro will be set up to recalculate everything on the worksheet every time you enter something. But just to be sure, before you print or otherwise use the info on the screen, press the F9 function key to force a recalc. That way you know your data's up-to-date.

Printing

Printing is pretty much the same pain in Quattro Pro that it is in 1-2-3, except that at least the printer module isn't a whole separate program. Now here's how to print an entire worksheet. (If you want to learn how to remove borders, print a special subsection, print narrow or sideways or standing on your head, put in headers and footers and whatnot, dig the manual out and raise your hand and say "I *want to learn* more about this program!" The rest of you follow me.)
Do this:

/, Print, Block, <Home key — that's usually on the 10-key pad>, . [the period], <End key>, <Home key>, <Enter>, Spreadsheet-print.

When the printing stops, if the printer doesn't eject the page, hit /, Print, Adjust-printer, Formfeed.

Canceling a command

The Quattro Pro cancel key is Esc, which will stop most things you do. Remember the Esc key is your friend, if you are in a menu that you want out of, escape. If Quattro Pro is performing an operation that Esc will not cancel, it will display the correct keys to use.

Undoing commands

You can use Quattro Pro's Undo feature to "undo" any accidents that may happen while using the keyboard. The Undo key is Alt-F4.

Note that Undo must be enabled before you can use the Alt-F4 key. To activate Undo select /, Options, Other, Undo, Enable, Update, Quit. Undo will be activated the next time you load Quattro Pro. (Doesn't do you much good this time, though, does it?)

Running macros

Much of the complicated stuff in spreadsheets can be replaced by using macros. If you are using macros in a spreadsheet designed by someone else, go ask them for a list of macros and what they do, and what method to use to run them.

There are two ways to run a macro. Some can be called up by using Alt-key combinations (like Alt-Z, for example). For this you need a list of Alt-key combinations and what they do.

Or you can use the macro execute function: hit Alt-F2, then F3 for a list of "block" names. Pick the block name (using the arrow keys), hit Enter, and that macro executes (if it is a macro). For this you need a list of the block names and what they do.

Getting help

On-line help in Quattro Pro is provided by pressing the F1 key. The F1 key knows where you are in the program, so that the help screen very likely will be of immediate help to you.

General advice

Quattro Pro always keeps the spreadsheet in memory; beware of a power outage. All of the changes you have made since the last time the file was saved will be lost. Saving the file often is very important and it is easy!

Use the Ctrl-S hot key to save a file quickly and easily. When you press Ctrl-S Quattro Pro will give you the option to Cancel, Replace, or Backup. I suggest that you get in the habit of choosing Backup when saving spreadsheets.

Many menu options in Quattro Pro are assigned hot keys that can make working in the spreadsheet much easier. If a menu selection has a corresponding hot key it will be displayed to the right of the menu selection. Next time, you can use that if you remember it.

WordPerfect

WordPerfect is the world's most popular word processor, almost to the point that some people actually use the term "word perfect" instead of "word processor." Yet, WordPerfect is a seriously huge program that goes way beyond simple word processing skills. Most of that power will remain untapped, but that's okay. Writing is supposed to be a simple art.

Starting WordPerfect

You start WordPerfect by typing WP at the DOS prompt:

```
C> WP
```

✔ If you see a "Bad command or file name" error, then type the following:

```
C> C:
```

Then:

```
C> CD \WP51
```

The directory may also be named just \WP. Then type WP to start the program.

✔ If you still can't find the program, refer to "Where is my program?" in Chapter 16.

Stopping WordPerfect (safely)

To quit WordPerfect, press the F7 (Exit) key. If you have a document on the screen, a prompt appears; answer Y for Yes if you want to save the document (then give it a name or accept the name that's displayed if there is one and press Enter). Or press N for No if you don't want to save the existing document.

Either way, WordPerfect then comes back and asks if you want to "exit WP." Press Y to return to DOS. (Or press N to stay in WordPerfect and get a fresh new blank document to write in.)

Loading a document

Loading in a document for work is done by typing that document's full name as part of starting WordPerfect at the DOS prompt:

```
C> WP LETTER.DOC
```

In this example, the command starts WordPerfect and loads the document LETTER.DOC, ready for editing. If a document isn't specified, then WordPerfect starts with the proverbial "blank page" staring at you, ready for you to type on.

✔ If you're in WordPerfect and wish to load a document press Shift-F10, Retrieve. Enter the full pathname of the document you want to load.

✔ You can also press the F5 key (List files) to see a list of files and select one for loading. To do so, highlight the filename using the arrow keys, then press 1 (Retrieve) to load in the file.

Starting a new document

As I said earlier, if you start WordPerfect and don't name a specific document to load, then you get a blank screen and you're ready to start typing. Like that blank sheet of paper curled up in your typewriter, WordPerfect is ready for your thoughts.

If you're done using a document and want to start a new one, press F7 to exit the old document. Answer the prompts to save the document or not. Then press N when asked if you want to exit WP. Once again you get that blank screen, which represents a new document. Start typing.

Formatting stuff

To have your text printed in bold, press F6. Everything you type after that will be in bold. To stop it, press F6 again.

To make text underlined, press F8 instead; press it again to turn it off.

To make text italic, it's not so easy. Press Ctrl-F8, then A for Appearance, and I for Italic. To turn it off, press Ctrl-F8, A, N for normal.

To make text that's already on the screen into bold or underlined or italics, you first must mark it as a "block" of text. Move the cursor to the start of the area you want to block off and press Alt-F4. Use the arrow keys to move the cursor to the end of the block (it lights up behind you). Press F6 to make it all bold, F8 to make it all underlined, or go through that Ctrl-F8, A, I rigamarole for italic.

To center text, press Shift-F6; all the text you type thereafter will be centered, until you press Enter. To center a block of text, first mark it as a block (put the cursor at the beginning of the block, Alt-F4, move the cursor to the end of the block), then press Shift-F6 and Y.

Tab stops: Press Shift-F8, L for Line, then T for Tabs. A "ruler" is displayed on the bottom of the screen. To set a tab, put the cursor at the spot on the ruler where you want the tab and press the L key. To delete a tab, put the cursor on the tab and press the Del key. When you're done fooling with the tab settings, press F7 to accept the settings and return to your document.

To force a new page (page break when printing), press Ctrl-Enter. On the screen you get a row of equal signs, marking the beginning of a new page. (Normal dynamic page breaks are shown as a row of hyphens.)

If you want to learn any formatting secrets beyond these, you'll have to dig out the user manual.

Running the spelling checker

To spell check a document, press Ctrl-F2, then D for Document. The screen splits, showing you the misspelled words it found (or doesn't have in its dictionary) and suggested spellings below. Press the letter of the correctly spelled alternative to replace the misspelled word.

Printing

To print a document showing on the screen, press Shift-F7, then F for Full document. (Remember to save your document after printing.) There are fancier ways to print — parts of documents, documents on disk, multiple files, etc. — but this is the easy one.

Canceling a command

WordPerfect's cancel key is F1—which is easily confused because F1 is the help key with most other DOS programs. Press F1 once to cancel a command, or press F1 to cancel a menu, then keep pressing F1 until you're returned to the document.

Also, the zero and F7 keys will back you out of certain operations in WordPerfect. Starting with version 5.1, though, WordPerfect Corp. has let the world know that the F1 key will be the only cancel key used in the future.

Undoing deletes

Within a document, the F1 key is your undelete command. Press F1 once and you'll see a highlighted block containing the last bit of text deleted. Press 1 or R to restore the deleted text. You can press 2 (or P) to see the previously deleted block of text, then press 2 again to see the block deleted before that.

Note that F1 only "remembers" the last three bits of text deleted. Anything gone before that is gone for good.

Running macros

WordPerfect isn't as heavy into macros as spreadsheets like Lotus 1-2-3. But macros are still available. Some are assigned to Alt-keys, others must be run by typing their names. You should keep a list of macros handy, since there's no real way to tell which macros you have without it.

To run a named macro, press Alt-F10 (Macro) and type in the macro's name.

Getting help

The WordPerfect Help key is F3. Pressing F3 will give you help on whatever command you're currently using. If not, press the first letter of that command — say, M for macro. WordPerfect then displays a list of all help items it has that start with M. Look up the proper keystrokes for that command (Ctrl-F10 for macro, for example), and you'll find your information.

To get an on-screen listing of what all the function keys do (in case you've lost your function-key template), press F3 twice.

Note that to get out of the Help program, you need to press the Enter key.

General advice

Something that's saved me a few times is WordPerfect's timed backup feature. Every five minutes or so, WordPerfect writes my document to a special file on disk. If the system crashes, the most typing I've lost is five minutes worth. To activate this handy feature, type Shift-F1 (Setup), E (Environment), B (Backup Options), and read the instructions. Item 1 is the timed document backup. Turn it on and tell WordPerfect to back up your document every five minutes or so.

It's a good idea to save a document frequently — even if you have automatic backup turned on. I always save before a spell check or whenever I leave the computer for a brief period of time.

To save a document and continue working on it, use F10 (Save). (F7, by contrast, removes the document from the screen.)

Microsoft Word 5.5

Microsoft Word copied its command system from the late unlamented spreadsheet program Multiplan. This meant that to access the menu, you hit the Esc key.

Starting with version 5.5 of Microsoft Word, a stock pull-down menu interface was added for the rest of us. You get at the menu using the Alt key or a mouse.

For this cheater, I'll try to give you the 5.5 pull-down commands and also the Esc-key menu commands from the earlier versions, which I'll call "earlier versions." (If there's no "earlier version" listing, then it's the same in both versions; or else I couldn't figure it out.) Let's hope this doesn't get too confusing.

Starting Word

Microsoft Word begins by typing Word at the DOS prompt:

```
C> WORD
```

✔ If you see a "Bad command or file name" error message, then type the following:

```
C> C:
```

Then type:

```
C> CD\ WORD
```

You can now type WORD to start the program.

✔ However, the directory may also be named \WORD5 or \WORD55, depending on the version of the program you use and on the way it was installed on your computer. If you can't find the program or don't know the directory name, refer to "Where is my program?" in Chapter 16.

Stopping Word (safely)

To exit Word, pull down the File menu and select Exit. You'll be prompted to save your file if you changed it. In earlier versions, the command to exit is Esc, Q; you are also prompted to save if necessary.

Loading a document

You can load a particular document when you start Word:

```
C> WORD LETTER.DOC
```

This loads LETTER.DOC for you to edit. If you don't specify a particular document, then Word loads and takes you to the empty editing screen. There you can begin typing a new document, or you can use the Alt-F key to look at the file menu and follow the instructions to select an existing document to edit.

In earlier versions, loading a document once you were in Word involves using this sequence: Esc, T for Transfer, L for Load (or Ctrl-F7). To select the document from a list, press F1.

On all versions, you use the Tab key to move through the selections on the menus.

To save a document, use File, Save in Word 5.5, or Esc, Transfer, Save in earlier versions.

Starting a new document

In Word 5.5, pull down the File menu (Alt-F) and choose New to get a new blank page (you'll be prompted to save any previous unsaved document). In previous versions, try Esc, T for Transfer, C for Clear, and A for All or W for Window (take your choice).

Formatting stuff

In Word 5.5, the second line from the top of the screen has "Bld Ital Ul" at the right end. Click one or more of these choices to turn on bold, italics, or underline (they highlight when you do that); click them a second time to turn that feature off.

You say you don't see a line like that? Well, pull down the View menu and click where it says Ribbon.

To center, pull down Format, then Paragraph, and when the window pops up, see Alignment and click on Center, then click OK.

To set tabs, see if you've got a third line across the top of the screen that looks like this: L[. . . . .1 . . . . .2 and so on. If not, pull down the View menu and click next to where it says Ruler. To set a tab, click the mouse on the ruler in the spot where you want the tab to appear; an L shows up where the left-tab setting will work. Now here's the trick: That only works for the paragraph you're on at the moment. To make it work for the whole document, you have to highlight (block off) the whole document first; then your tabs apply to whatever existing paragraphs are highlighted at the time.

To change the formatting of a block of text, first block it off: With a mouse, start at one end of the block, hold down the left mouse button and drag the cursor over the text you want to change; release the mouse button when you get to the end. With lots of text, do this instead: Put the cursor at the beginning of the block, move the mouse to the end, hold down the Shift key, and click the left mouse button once. This lights up all the text inbetween.

With the keyboard, start at one end of the block, hold down the Shift key, use the cursor arrow keys to move the cursor to the other end of the block, then let go.

Here are the shortcut keys used with earlier versions of Word: Alt-B for bold, Alt-I for italics, Alt-U for underline, Alt-spacebar to return to normal text, Alt-C to center, and Alt-L to left-align (turn centering off). To highlight blocks so you can apply these formats, use F7 or F8 to select a word at the cursor position, Shift-F7 to highlight the previous sentence, F9 to select the previous paragraph, Shift-F9 to select the line you're on, and Shift-F10 to select the whole document. Or you can put the cursor at the beginning of the block and press F6 to start the block, then use the cursor arrow keys to move the cursor to the other end of the block.

For setting tabs in earlier versions, use Alt-F1 for the tab menu.

Running the spell checker

In Word 5.5 you'll find the spell checker under the Utilities menu. The thesaurus is also there.

In earlier versions, use Alt-F6 to call up the spell checker. The thesaurus is at Ctrl-F6.

Printing

In Word 5.5 printing is found under the File menu. Click on Print and answer OK to the window that pops up.

Besides just calling up Print, you can also see what the document will look like when printed by using Print Preview; pull down the File menu in that view to go ahead and print, or to exit Print Preview.

In earlier versions, the command to print is Ctrl-F8.

Canceling a Command

Word in all versions cancels commands with the Esc key.

Undoing deletes

Alt-Backspace (or Edit, Undo) in Word 5.5, and Shift-F1 in earlier versions, will undo most (but not all) commands and actions. They will also undelete the most recent thing you deleted. In Word 5.5, Alt-Backspace will undo most Edit commands, all Insert commands, all Format commands, and most of the Utilities commands.

Running macros

Microsoft Word has souped-up macro capabilities, but for quick-and-dirty work it's not important for you to master them if all you want to do is get a memo out the door. But if you've been told there's a macro you should use to do something complicated in one keystroke, here's the poop.

Macros live in a special file called a Glossary. Type Alt-M to get the macro menu, then select Edit Macro, and Open Glossary. Select the glossary you've been told has your macro in it.

To use the macro, type Alt-M, select Run Macro, and select the name of the macro you want to run.

Getting help

Type F1 at any point to get Help keyed to whatever you're doing at the moment. Use Esc to get back to your work.

General advice

Word 5.5 has a timed backup facility; use it to keep you from losing data in the event of a power failure. Turn it on by typing Alt-U, Customize, highlight Autosave Frequency, type in a number of minutes (I like 5), and click OK. If the power does go off, when it comes back you can get your backed-up file by using Alt-F (File) to look for a file with the name you were using but with the extension SVD, for example LETTER.SVD. (Whenever you save your document in the regular way through the File (Alt-F) menu, Word erases the now unneeded backup file.)

Word has two main editing modes. One, called graphics, lets you see italics and bold and underline on the screen, although not exactly as they will print. The other, called text, lets you see all your text with enhancements indicated by shading. The text screen is what you will get unless you make a change. It is faster by far than the graphics screen. To change between them, use Alt-U, Customize, Preferences, Display Mode.

WordStar

WordStar invented professional word processing for microcomputers back in the late 1970s. At one time it was on top; now it's given way to Word and WordPerfect. Oh well, it still works just fine. And now that they've added pull-down menus and stuff, it's not even that hard to use anymore. For consistency's sake, however, and because I know it better, I give you the standard WordStar Classic commands.

Starting WordStar

You begin WordStar by typing WS at the DOS prompt:

```
C> WS
```

✔ If you see a "Bad command or file name" error message, then type the following:

```
C> C:
```

Then type:

```
C> CD\ WS
```

You can now type WS to start the program.

✔ However, the director may also be named \WS6 or \WS5, depending on the version of the program you use and on the way it was installed on your computer. If you can't find the program or don't know the directory name, refer to "Where is my program?" in Chapter 16.

Loading a document

You can load a particular document when you start WordStar:

```
C> WS LETTER.DOC
```

This loads LETTER.DOC for you to edit.

If you don't specify a particular document, then WordStar goes to its Opening menu. Hit D (for Document), then type in the name of the document you want. If the name you type is the name of an existing document, it is displayed on the screen. If there is no document by that name, then you get a new blank screen to type on. (If you made a mistake and meant to get a new document but got an existing one, or vice-versa, get back to the main menu by typing Ctrl-K, Q; if it says something about abandoning edits, answer Y.)

Formatting stuff

Ctrl-P, B turns on bold; Ctrl-P, Y is for italics; Ctrl-P, S is for underlining. Repeat the command to turn it off.

By the way, these commands embed invisible codes on the WordStar screen; to see them, try this: Ctrl-O, D. Now you can see, for example, ^PB where you turned boldfacing on. If you put the cursor there and delete it, boldfacing goes off. Handy. But watch out: the ^PB at the other end of the bold section is now active; you have to delete it also, or all the rest of the document will be bold.

To center something, use Ctrl-O, C. If there's already type there, it becomes centered; or anything you type on that line centers.

To set tabs, put the cursor where you want the tab to be set, then use Ctrl-O, I, and in answer to the prompt, press the Esc key. To delete tabs, put the cursor on the soon-to-be-defunct tab position, then hit Ctrl-O, N, and Esc in answer to the prompt.

To format a block of text, you don't have to set the block first, as you do in most other word processors. Just put the cursor at the beginning of the area you want to be, say, boldfaced, and type Ctrl-P, B to insert the ^PB character at that position. Everything following is now bolded. Move the cursor to the end of the block and type Ctrl-P, B again to mark the end point. Now the area between the two control codes is bold. It works the same with italics and underlining.

Running the spell checker

That's Ctrl-Q, L to spell check the rest of the document starting at the cursor position (so move it to the top of the file if you want to check everything). The menu that appears tells you what to do (I for Ignore and E to enter a correction are the two most obvious; or type the number of the suggested alternative spelling if you want it).

Printing

To print the document you're typing, first type Ctrl-K, S to save, then Ctrl-K, P. Answer N when it asks about merge-printing. Type in the name of this file (or hit Ctrl-R to insert the name of the current file automatically), then hit the Esc key (this bypasses all the remaining seven prompts and goes directly to printing).

To print another document, first get out of the document you're in by typing Ctrl-K, D to save it (or Ctrl-K, Q to abandon it). Then from the main menu choose P for Printing, and type the name of the document (there's a list below). Hit Esc to begin printing. Or hit Return to see some options: The ones you're interested in are Number of Copies (enter a number), and Starting Page and Ending Page (enter a number). All the others you can simply hit Return to ignore. Keep hitting Return until the choices run out, and printing begins.

Canceling a command

The WordStar cancel commands use the Esc key and the Ctrl-U key. Multiple Esc keys will back you out of almost every sequence of menus or commands and bring you back to the editing screen. The Ctrl-U key will cancel an operation in process such as search-and-replace or spell check. The Esc key also initiates shorthand macros and the Ctrl-U key implements the undo or unerase feature.

Undoing deletes

Ctrl-U undeletes the most recent word or block deletion.

Using macros

WordStar's macros are short and sweet. They are not likely to be of great value to someone just creating a quick memo or printing a document.

Getting help

F1 gets you help that relates to whatever you are doing at the time. When you finish reading a help screen, return to your work by typing Esc.

General advice

WordStar always keeps a backup of your document when you edit. The backup takes the same name as your document but adds or substitutes a BAK extension to the name. So if you edit LETTER.DOC, WordStar creates LETTER BAK as the backup. If something goes wrong, you can always go to LETTER.BAK.

The new WordStar user interface presents the more modern, hip, with-it pull-down menus accessed with an Alt-letter command. If you see them installed, use them instead of the control-key shortcuts; you can just browse among them to find most of the things you would want to do (which is why people like them so much).

Windows 3

Next to DOS and its ugly command line, Windows is the most popular way to use a PC. Windows offers a graphic look for your computer and your Windows software. Windows programs are shown as graphics and have menus that allow you to easily see your options and manipulate information using a mouse. This is a more fun and relaxed way of using a computer than the terse DOS command line.

Starting Windows

Windows should start automatically on your computer. If not, you can start Windows at the DOS prompt by typing WIN:

```
C> WIN
```

> ✔ If you want Windows to automatically run each time you start your computer, you need to add the WIN command to the end of your AUTOEXEC.BAT file. Refer to Chapter 2 for details.

> ✔ If you get a "Bad command or file name" error when you start Windows, refer to "Where is my program?" in Chapter 16.

Running a program in Windows

There are three ways to run a program in Windows. The first is to locate that program's icon (little graphic picture) in the Program Manager's window. Double-click on that icon with the mouse and the program runs. But this method only works for Windows programs and those applications someone has already installed for you in the Program Manager's window. You're best off if you can browbeat your guru into doing this for you. The following two methods aren't as nice.

The second method is to use the File Manager program, which shows you a list of files on disk. Look for the program names that end in the COM or EXE extension to find the program you want to run, then double-click on it and the program will start.

The third method is to type in the program's name, just as you would at the DOS prompt. This is done by selecting the File menu, then Run in either the Program Manager or File Manager. Type in the full pathname of the program to run it. Hmm, just like DOS.

✔ Note that only Windows-specific programs will show up as graphics. Everything else will look the same way it does when you run the program under DOS. But don't be fooled: You're still in Windows. (Which also means don't just quit the program and shut off the computer when you're done; return to Windows by typing EXIT and quit gracefully from Windows.)

✔ If you're running Windows on a '386 computer, you can press Alt-Enter to make a DOS text program run in a smaller window. (Or maybe it will hang at that point. Give it a try. Take a chance in life.)

Loading Windows and running a program at the same time

Some programs can only run under Windows. Two of the most popular are Word for Windows (WinWord) and Microsoft's Excel spreadsheet. Normally you would run these programs by double-clicking the mouse on their icons when you're in Windows. However, it's possible to start Windows and load these programs at the same time.

For example, if you want to run Word for Windows at the DOS prompt, type:

```
C> WIN WINWORD
```

This loads Windows into memory and immediately runs the WINWORD program, which is Word for Windows.

To run Excel, you could type the following:

```
C> WIN EXCEL
```

This loads Windows and launches the Excel program, so you're ready to work with your spreadsheets.

✔ Of course, if you're already in Windows, you simply click on the proper icon to run the program.

Switching programs

In Windows you can "run" several programs at once. You only work on the program whose window is up in front (or filling the entire screen). To switch to another program you have several options.

The quickest way to switch is to grab the mouse and click in another program's window, if it's visible. If not, then use the second method: press Alt-Esc. This switches you to the next program you have active (in the order in which you started the programs).

The third method is to hit Ctrl-Esc, which calls up the Task List window, which shows you a list of the programs currently running. Double-click on a program in the list and you are immediately switched to it. (You can also bring up the Task List by double-clicking on the "desktop" or background.)

Stopping a Windows program (safely)

You end a Windows-compatible program by selecting Exit from the program's File menu. You can also exit by double-clicking on the slot-like doohickey in the upper-left corner of the window, or by single-clicking on said slot-like device and selecting Close from the menu that appears.

Non-Windows programs under Windows must be quit in the same way as you'd quit them under DOS: Press F7 for WordPerfect— /, Quit for 1-2-3, etc.

To exit Windows itself, double-click on the slot-like icon in the upper-left of the Windows Program Manager window. Answer OK to the prompt. (Now you can turn off the machine.)

> ✔ Just because you're no longer using a program in Windows doesn't necessarily mean that you've quit it. It's possible to switch between programs without quitting; refer to "Switching programs" above.

> ✔ Just don't exit by shutting off the machine. See "General advice," below, for more.

The general UNDO command

Windows-specific programs all share a common UNDO key: Alt-Backspace, which is also the UNDO menu item in every program's Edit menu. UNDO undoes just about anything you can do: unchange edits, replace cut graphics, fix up a bad marriage, and so on.

Note that the UNDO command is not shared with non-Windows programs. For example, if you're running Lotus 1-2-3 under Windows, then your Undo key is still Alt-F4.

Getting help

Windows has an incredible help system and all Windows-specific programs share it. Help is always activated by pressing the F1 key. From there you're shown the help "engine" that allows you to look up topics, search for topics, or see related items of interest all by properly using your mouse. Here are some hints:

✔ Green text can be clicked on to see related topics.

✔ Green underlined text (with a dotted underline) can be clicked on to see a pop-window defining the term. (Press and hold the mouse button to see the pop-up information.)

✔ Browse forward or backward through the help topics to see an index or to look up a specific item.

General advice

Use your mouse. If you don't have a mouse you can still use Windows, but not as elegantly.

Have someone organize your Program Manager for you so you can click on any program or file you want to run, and have him or her get rid of all those other programs you don't use that clutter up your screen.

Windows is a "black box" program in that a lot is going on in the background that you might forget is going on (see "Black box program rules" earlier in this chapter). Never reset while you're running Windows. And before you quit Windows itself, make sure you've properly quit from all the programs you're running under Windows.

Keep in mind that Windows can run several programs at once. Use the Task List (Ctrl-Esc) to see if a program is already running before starting a second copy. (Yes, you can run several copies of a program under Windows, but you probably only need to run one.)

Be wary of seeing a DOS prompt when you're in Windows. The DOS program may simply be one of Window's "programs"; seeing it doesn't mean that you've quit Windows, nor is it a sure sign that you can reset or turn the computer off. To be sure, type the EXIT command:

```
C> EXIT
```

If that doesn't return you to Windows, then you're out of Windows and it's safe to reset.

If a program crashes under Windows, big deal! Windows is constructed so that one dead program won't topple the whole computer. You simply close that program's window and keep on working — you can even start the program again after it's been properly disposed of. This is one of the neater aspects of Windows. (When it works.)

Harvard Graphics

Harvard Graphics is the most popular presentation package for the PC. It allows you to create charts that can be combined into a presentation. You can display the presentation on your computer screen, print it, or turn it into 35mm slides or $8\frac{1}{2}" \times 11"$ view foils. The charts you can build include text charts in title, bullet, and table formats; graphic charts in pie, bar, line, area, and high/low/close formats; and organization charts. You can also use the Draw component of Harvard Graphics to enhance another chart or create a unique chart.

This summary will help you when you are desperate to throw together a quick presentation or a few charts.

Starting Harvard Graphics

You start Harvard Graphics by typing HG at the DOS prompt. *Note:* If you have the more recent version of Harvard Graphics, you have to type HG3 instead of just HG.

```
C>HG
```

press Enter.

> ✔ If that did not work, you need to change to the directory in which Harvard Graphics is stored on your hard disk. This is usually named HG or HG3. Do that by typing the following commands:
>
> ```
> C> C:
> ```
>
> and press Enter,
>
> ```
> C> CD\HG
> ```
>
> and press Enter.

(Replace HG with HG3 for that version.) Then type HG (or HG3) to start the program.

> ✔ If that still did not work, refer to "Where is my program?" in chapter 16.

Using Harvard Graphics

First the Main menu is displayed. You select an option from that or any Harvard Graphics menu by typing the number or letter to the right of the option. You can also use the cursor (arrow) keys to move the highlight to the option and press Enter or, in later versions, click the left mouse button on it.

At the top of the Harvard Graphics screen is the title bar. Initially it tells you the program's name. As you use the program, the title bar tells you the general thing you are doing, such as Bullet Chart or Pie Chart. Below the title bar is a list of function keys and what they do. This list will change depending on what you are doing, but four function keys will remain constant:

F1   Gets help about what you are currently doing.

F2   Displays the current chart.

F6   Displays the Main menu.

F10   Completes the current task and prepares for the next one.

Canceling a command

You can usually press Esc (or click the right mouse button in later versions) to cancel a task or command or to close a window. You may need to press Esc several times to back all the way out.

Working with charts

Charts are the principle product of Harvard Graphics. There are five tasks that are common to all charts, as follows:

Creating a chart

Press F6 to open the Main menu, and select Create chart (1), select the chart type (Text, Pie, XY, Organization). For a text chart select the text type (Title, Bullet, Table); for an XY chart select type of x-axis data, type titles, type text, or enter labels and values; and press Enter to go from one text or data line to the next.

Saving a chart

Press Ctrl-S or F6, select File (4), select Save chart (4), type the directory and filename, and press Enter.

Retrieving a chart

Press Ctrl-G or F6, select File (4), select Get chart (1), select or type the directory and filename, and press Enter.

Editing a chart

Press F6, select Edit chart (2), press Enter or Tab to go from item to item, and type changes as necessary.

Printing a chart

Press F6, select Output (5), select output device, set options, and press F10 to begin printing.

Working with presentations

A presentation is a list of up to 175 charts. You create a presentation by adding chart files to this list. That and the other principle tasks dealing with presentations along with the commands to implement them are:

Creating a presentation

Press F6 to open the Main menu, select Presentation (6), select Create presentation (1), press Ctrl-Insert or F7, select Add file (1), select or type the directory and filename, and press Enter.

Saving a presentation

Press F6, select Presentation (6), select Save presentation (5), type the directory and filename, and press Enter.

Retrieving a presentation

Press F6, select Presentation (6), select Get presentation (4), select or type the directory and filename, and press Enter.

Printing a presentation

Press F6, select Output (5,) select Presentation (5), select output device, set options, and press F10 to begin printing.

Getting help

Besides getting context-sensitive help by pressing F1 as described above, you can press Shift-F1 and get a help index. You can see further detail on an index entry by using the cursor (arrow) keys to move the highlight to the entry and pressing Enter. You can do this a number of times. To return to the previous level of help, press Esc. Finally, you can get a list of "speed keys" (like Ctrl-S to save a chart) by pressing Ctrl-F1.

General advice

Harvard Graphics allows you to create many types of charts with many options. It is very easy to become overwhelmed by the variety available. Start out by using only the most rudimentary types and options. Become familiar with those and then, on a slow basis, begin to add enhancements and apply options. Main rule: If you're in a rush, keep it simple.

Using Procomm Plus

Procomm is a popular telecommunications program that lets your computer use the telephone to call and talk to another computer. Why? Usually so you can download (transfer to your computer) or upload (send to the other computer) files or messages. People use such packages to send mail through MCI Mail, or files through CompuServe.

Fair warning: Telecommunications is not simple, and nothing I can do in writing will make it simple. Why? Because the modem and communications vendors have come up with fifty million different ways to do things, and some of the most arcane jargon this side of high-order physics to describe it. Which port is your modem plugged in to? What is its speed? What duplex mode, start and stop bits, transmission protocol, and other gobbledygook is the other modem expecting? It's a nightmare.

The best possible way to do this is to get somebody else to set you up from soup to nuts, including preparing a dialing directory, then walking you through the basics for the kinds of things you need to get done. Here we'll just review the basics, in case it helps.

What is a telecommunications program?

A telecommunications program is software that controls the connection between your computer and some other remote computer system, such as an on-line service (like CompuServe, GENie, or MCI Mail).

(Some on-line services, such as Prodigy or America OnLine, require special software, rather than a general-purpose program like Procomm.)

Before you start

The Procomm software has to be installed in your system, a modem must be properly connected to your computer, and you need certain information about your modem and computer and about the system you're calling. Let's assume your modem is hooked up right. To call another system, you need to know the following about the other system:

- the phone number to call

- any password or log-in procedure the other system requires

- the baud rate (for example, 1200 bps, 2400 bps)

- number of data bits (usually 7 or 8)

- the number of stop bits (usually 1)

- the parity (odd, even, or none)

If you're talking to another personal computer user, rather than a communications service, the important thing is for both ends to agree on the same answers to these questions, but *which* answers doesn't usually matter. Baud rate ought to be as fast as both modems can handle, but data bits, stop bits, etc., are up to you. For calling a service, if you don't know the baud rate, data bits, etc., you can always fake it by setting these things randomly and hoping for the best. You can't break the modem, and you can change the settings while you're on line, hoping to find something that works before the other computer breaks the connection in disgust.

The most common sources of problems

Once you get going, telecommunications can be easy. You may encounter some problems, however. The most common sources of problems are:

- Not having the right cable between your computer and your modem (this needs to be a standard RS232 serial cable).

✔ Not having the modem connected to the correct port on your computer (for most machines, this will be either COM1 or COM2; naturally, they won't be labeled).

✔ Not having the right telephone cable hookup between your modem and your telephone line (most modems use standard RJ11 cable, but many business phone systems use cables that are different from this).

✔ Having the modem device configured improperly (many modems have hardware jumpers, other modems can be configured by software commands alone).

✔ Using a modem that is not fully "Hayes" compatible (the set of commands for the Hayes brand of modems is now a defacto industry standard for all modem devices, but many older devices are not fully Hayes compatible).

✔ Trying to connect to a system that has an incompatible modem at the other end of the line (rare). (By the way, an IBM PC compatible can talk via modem to any Macintosh, Amiga, Apple II, and most other personal computers. There, at least, the computers are compatible.)

✔ Trying to connect to a system using communications settings that don't match (baud rate, stop bits, parity, the stuff mentioned above).

✔ Trying to dial out over an internal phone line that requires special phone connections or signals (Rolm phones are the bane of the telecommuter's existence; a dedicated external phone line makes life a lot easier).

See? Easy, like I said.

Starting Procomm

Type:

```
C> PROCOMM
```

Owners of Procomm Plus type:

```
C> PCPLUS
```

(Thanks, guys.)

To confirm you are now talking to your modem, type the letters AT and then press the Enter key. The modem should reply by sending the letters OK to the screen. If it doesn't, check the problem list above, then call your guru.

Getting help

Most commands in Procomm are accessed by Alt-key combinations. Help is Alt-F10.

Setting up

Alt-P gets you the Parameter list. If the system has been set up for you, forget this because when you select a phone number from the dialing directory, these are set to the right values for that phone number. If not, pray they're right.

Dialing a number

Alt-D brings up a list of phone numbers. Pick the one you want, and Procomm will make the call.

After one or more rings, the modem you're calling should answer the phone and send its distinctive warble. The pitch of the warble will vary as the two modems compare notes, then will fall abruptly silent, and (if all goes well) you will see the word CONNECT on your screen. Wait a second or two, and then follow the instructions of the service you're calling.

For CompuServe, for example, you press Ctrl-C to get a prompt asking for your password and ID. For MCI Mail, you press Enter to get the prompt. At this point you need to have some information on how to sign in and log on.

If you're just calling another person who's expecting you, just type something and see if you get a response.

If when you type you get double letters or no letters at all, then press Alt-E to toggle "Duplex" between Half and Full (?). That should fix it.

If you do not get a response, or if you get a long stream of "garbage" characters across the screen, try changing the line parameters if you know how (it's a long story). If not, call your guru.

Capturing what happens on the screen

While you're on line you usually want to keep a record of what goes by on the screen. With MCI Mail, for example, when you ask to read your mail, it's displayed on the screen. At 2400 bits per second (nearly 300 characters a second), it's hard to read it as it goes by; better to save it to print and read later.

To do this, turn on the log feature by typing Alt-F1, then give a filename (any DOS filename will do). You'll see a prompt on the bottom of the screen "Log file on." Everything that goes by on your screen is now being saved to a disk file.

When you're done with your session, hit Alt-F1 again to close the file and store it. You can look at it with your word processor later.

Uploading and downloading a file

If you want to transfer a program by modem, you can't just display it on the screen; it's full of dingbats, and the file that arrived wouldn't work right. Instead, you want to "download" the file using a "protocol." This means you tell the modem to get the file, and the transfer takes place invisibly, creating a file on your hard disk. (If you have the file sent to your computer, that's downloading; if you send the file from your computer to another one, that's uploading. No, it doesn't really matter.)

You have to upload or download program files, spreadsheet data files, graphics files, compressed or zipped files, or formatted word processing files.

Every on-line service has a different method of initiating the download operation. But basically, you select the file you want to transfer, and specify a protocol (a technique for controlling the mechanics of the transfer operation). Common protocols are: XModem, YModem, CompuServe B, and Kermit. Different systems have different protocols available. Some are faster or more reliable, but as long as both your local computer and the remote system are using the same protocol, you will be OK.

Once you have initiated the transfer on the remote system, you will see a message; if you are downloading (taking info in), the message will be like "Starting transfer. Please set up your local system to receive data." At that point, press the PageDn key on your keyboard. If you are sending a file, the remote system's message will be something like "Ready to receive data." In that case, press the PageUp key.

In either case, Procomm will display a menu of available protocols, such as XModem. Pick one. Then give the name of the file to be uploaded, or with some protocols you will be asked for a filename to store incoming data in. (Other protocols know what filename to create all by themselves.)

Once the transfer is underway, Procomm displays a progress indicator. *Large files can take a long time to transfer,* as much as 30 minutes or more for a 100K or larger file! This depends on the speed of your modem (2400 is the most popular now, 9600 is the next higher but is very expensive). Calculate by dividing your modem's transmission speed (1200, 2400) by 8, then dividing that number into your file size in bytes (100K is 100,000 bytes), which gives you the number of seconds transmission time; divide this by 60 to get minutes. So at 1200 bps, your modem is transmitting something under 150 characters per second, so a 150K file will take 1,000 seconds, or over 16 minutes (boy is AT&T happy!).

Logging off and hanging up

When you're done, you have to figure out what special word your on-line service wants before it will let you hang up. MCI Mail wants Exit, CompuServe insists on Bye. Try also Quit, Logout, LO, and Off. Don't just hang up without trying, because if you're being charged, the line will stay open for a few more minutes until it dawns on the mental midgit computer at the other end that you're not there hanging breathlessly on its every byte.

If you give up, type Alt-H to cause Procomm to hang up the phone — or in a panic, turn the power off the modem.

To exit Procomm, type Alt-X.

There, wasn't that fun?

Chapter 22
Ten Otherwise Worthless Acronyms to Impress Your Friends

In this chapter...
▶ ASCII
▶ DOS
▶ EGA
▶ EMS
▶ ESDI
▶ FUD
▶ IDE
▶ SCSI
▶ VGA
▶ WYSIWYG

*T*ired of talking about IRAs, RBIs, and STDs at your local YMCA or YWCA? Get in the loop; learn a little computerspeak. Amaze and delight your friends at your next social by talking about the real issues of today — FUDs, IDEs, and VGAs, for example. Use some of the following acronyms to impress your friends. (After all, what are friends for if not to bolster your image by making them appear ignorant?)

ASCII

What it stands for: American Standard Code for Information Interchange.

Pronunciation: ASK-ee.

Meaning: Usually used to identify a type of file that contains only readable text, one that can be displayed with the TYPE command and read by a human.

As used in a sentence: Here is the ASCII version of that file because I know you're too lame to buy WordPerfect.

Please don't read this

ASCII is a coding scheme used to identify characters in a computer. Each character, letter, number, or symbol is assigned a code number from zero through 127. All personal computers use the same coding scheme to represent these characters, which means that basic (text-only) files can be transferred between two computers without the need for translation.

DOS

What it stands for: Disk Operating System.

Pronunciation: It rhymes with boss. (Don't pronounce it "dose.")

Meaning: The main program that controls all PCs; your computer environment on the computer.

As used in a sentence: "DOS is definitely not for dummies."

EGA

What it stands for: Enhanced Graphics Adapter.

Pronunciation: Letters only; E-G-A.

Meaning: A type of graphics monitor/card on a PC; not as fancy as the VGA standard, but fair. (Refer to "Graph-a-bits soup" in Chapter 7.)

As used in a sentence: "Ha! You only have EGA graphics? Jeez, wake up to the '90s, pal."

EMS

What it stands for: Expanded Memory Specification.

Pronunciation: Letters only; E-M-S.

Meaning: Extra memory in a PC, particularly memory that can be used by graphics programs, spreadsheets, and most applications that are severe memory hogs. *Note:* 386 computers can turn "extended" memory into EMS memory automatically.

As used in a sentence: "I have four megabytes of EMS memory, so I can run bigger spreadsheets." Ha ha.

ESDI

What it stands for: Enhanced Small Device Interface.

Pronunciation: EZ-dee; or letters only, E-S-D-I.

Meaning: A type of hard drive on a computer, usually fast. (See IDE and SCSI.)

As used in a sentence: "How much for that 100MB ESDI drive? Oh. When will it be going on sale, then?"

FUD

What it stands for: Fear, Uncertainty, Doubt.

Pronunciation: FUD, rhymes with dud.

Meaning: The reasons why people don't buy computers, or hesitate to upgrade. It's the FUD factor.

As used in a sentence: "Naa, there's no point in the company laying down hard cash to buy a laser printer. I'm just too full of FUD."

IDE

What it stands for: Integrated Drive Environment.

Pronunciation: Letters only, I-D-E.

.Meaning: A type of fast hard drive, typically found on most laptop computers. (See ESDI and SCSI.)

As used in a sentence: "Golly, those IDE drives are cheap and fast."

SCSI

What it stands for: Small Computer System Interface.

Pronunciation: Scuzzy (believe it or not).

Meaning: It's like a fast and versatile serial port, onto which you can "chain" a variety of devices: hard drives, scanners, tape backup systems, CD ROM drives, etc. The standard for hard drives on Macintoshes, less common on PCs. (See ESDI and IDE.)

As used in a sentence: "I never thought I'd pay that kind of money for a SCSI WORM drive."

VGA

What it stands for: Video Graphics Array (not Video Graphics *Adapter*).

Pronunciation: Letters only, V-G-A.

Meaning: The current, top-o'-the-line in PC graphics. (Refer to "Graph-a-bits soup" in Chapter 7.)

As used in a sentence: "These VGA graphics are fantastic!"

WYSIWYG

What it stands for: What You See Is What You Get.

Pronunciation: WIZZY-wig (yup, it's true).

Meaning: The stuff you see on the screen looks identical to the way it will appear when printed. Sort of.

As used in a sentence: "The more you pay, the more WYSIWYG lives up to its name."

Section Six
DOS Reference for Real People

The 5th Wave   By Rich Tennant

In this section...

Is there really a need for a DOS reference for DOS beginners? Yes. Don't think this is your standard DOS reference, such as those endless pages with cryptic notations muddling through your DOS manual. This reference contains two chapters: Chapter 23 has ten common DOS commands you may be using every day, with information on how they work. Chapter 24 contains commands beyond the everyday use of DOS beginners. This information is simply an explanation of what the command does; formatting and command examples have been cheerfully omitted.

Chapter 23
DOS Commands You Can Use (the Top 10)

● ●

In this chapter...

▶ CD.

▶ CLS.

▶ COPY.

▶ DEL.

▶ DIR.

▶ DISKCOPY.

▶ FORMAT.

▶ MORE.

▶ REN.

▶ TYPE.

● ●

*T*here are a few DOS commands mentioned more than once in this book. I've added a few more to round it out to ten.

You'll probably use other DOS commands with as much frequency as some of these. They're listed in the following chapter, along with every other DOS command whether you'll use it or not. But here are the ones most people find the most useful.

The CD command

Purpose: To display the pathname of the current directory.

Sample: CD

Comments: Type CD and you'll see the name of the current drive and directory — the pathname — displayed. That tells you where you are in the maze of your hard drive structure.

Other purpose: To change to another directory.

Sample: CD \WP51\DATA

Comments: The CD command is followed by a space and the full name of the directory to which you're changing. The directory's pathname usually starts with a backslash but doesn't end with a backslash.

Where to look: "Changing directories" in Chapter 1; almost all of Chapter 13; "Finding a lost subdirectory" in Chapter 14.

The CLS command

Purpose: It clears the screen.

Sample: CLS

Comments: CLS clears the screen, erasing the display and any embarrassing error messages that may be glowing therein. Simple enough.

The COPY command

Purpose: To make a copy or duplicate of a file.

Sample: COPY C:FILE1 A:FILE2

Where to look: "Duplicating a file," "Copying a single file," "Copying a file to you," "Copying a group of files," and "Moving a file" all in Chapter 3; and you might also want to check "What is a pathname?" in Chapter 13 and "Wildcards (or, poker was never this much fun)" in Chapter 14.

The general rule here is: First comes the location and name of the file you're copying; then the location and name of the copy you're making. If you're already logged onto the source or the destination, then you can leave that location off, but if that's confusing, just give the entire location for both halves of the command.

Give the entire pathname; for example: Copy C:\WP51\DATA\FILE\ A:\FILE1 (to copy FILE1 from drive C to drive A). You can change the name of the copy — and if you're making a copy to the same place, you *have* to change the name.

The DEL command

Purpose: To delete one or more files, eliminating them from a disk and freeing up the space they used.

Sample: DEL USELESS.TXT

Or: DEL *.BAK

Comments: The DEL command totally zaps a single file (or a group of files if you use a wildcard). This is necessary to eliminate older files and to give yourself more disk space.

Where to look: "Deleting a file," "Deleting a group of files," and "Moving a file" in Chapter 3; also in Chapter 3 you might want to peek at "Undeleting a file"; check out "What is a pathname?" in Chapter 13 and "Wildcards (or, poker was never this much fun)" in Chapter 14; also "The perils of DEL *.*" in Chapter 16.

The DIR command

Purpose: To display a list of files on disk.

Sample: DIR

Or: DIR C:

Or: DIR C:WP51

Comments: DIR is probably the most common DOS command, and the only way to look at the files you have on disk. You can see a list of files on any drive or in any subdirectory by following the DIR command with that drive letter or subdirectory pathname.

Where to Look: "The DIR command" in Chapter 1; "That funny <DIR> thing" in Chapter 13; "Using the DIR command," "The wide DIR command," and "Displaying a sorted directory," all in Chapter 14.

The DISKCOPY command

Purpose: To make an exact duplicate of a floppy disk.

Sample: DISKCOPY A: B:

Or: DISKCOPY A: A:

Comments: This command makes an *exact* copy of a disk. Both drives A and B have to be the same kind (physical size and capacity). If not (or if you only have one floppy drive), type DISKCOPY A: A:; DOS will copy part of the disk in drive A, then prompt you to put in a blank disk.

Where to look: "Duplicating disks (the DISKCOPY command)" in Chapter 10.

The FORMAT command

Purpose: To prepare floppy disks for use.

Sample: FORMAT A:

Comments: All disks must be formatted before you can use them. The FORMAT command must be followed by the drive letter (and colon) of the floppy drive containing the disk to be formatted. *Never* use the FORMAT command with any drive higher than B.

Where to look: "Formatting a disk" and "Formatting a low-capacity disk in a high-capacity drive" in Chapter 10. Also look up "Reformatting disks," in Chapter 10.

The MORE command

Purpose: The MORE command can be used to view text files one screen at a time.

Sample: MORE < FILENAME

Comments: The MORE command is followed by a space, a less-than symbol (<), another space, and then the name of a text file you want to view. At the end of each screen you'll see the "more" prompt; press the spacebar to see the next screen. Press Ctrl-C to cancel.

Where to look: Refer to "Looking at files" in Chapter 1; "The tree structure" in Chapter 13 has another interesting use of the MORE command; also look at the TYPE command in this chapter.

The REN command

Purpose: To rename a file, giving it a new name without changing its contents.

Sample: REN OLDNAME NEWNAME

Comments: What's to comment? Just follow the DOS naming rules. DOS will object if you try to give the file the same name as another file in the same directory.

Where to look: "Renaming a file" in Chapter 3; also "Name that file!" in Chapter 14.

The TYPE command

Purpose: To display a file on the screen, allowing you to read its contents.

Sample: TYPE STUFF.DOC

Comments: The TYPE command displays any file you name, though only files that contain readable text can be understood by humans. If the file displays as "garbage," then press Ctrl-C to cancel the TYPE command.

Where to look: "Looking at files" in Chapter 1.

Chapter 24
Beyond DOS Commands You Can Use (the Other 51)

● ●

Here is a list of some more DOS commands. You may want to use some of these from time to time (but they didn't make the "top ten" list in the previous chapter). The rest of these commands others can use. They're useful, but they won't be covered here as they are beyond the scope of the book.

Each command is briefly described. If necessary, a reference is made to the command elsewhere in this text. Otherwise, I just poke fun at it and leave it at that.

● ●

Commands you may occasionally use

BACKUP   This command is used to *archive* files from your hard disk to a series of floppy disks. Using it is covered in Chapter 13, beginning with the section "Backing up." This is something you should do often, but better you should get somebody else to set it up.

CHKDSK   This command reports the status of a disk, how many files are on it and how much of the disk is used by what. It can also check to see if there are lost file clusters, which you should immediately destroy. CHKDSK is covered in "Checking the disk (the CHKDSK command)" and "CHKDSK says I have lost files in clusters or something" in Chapter 13.

COMP   The COMP command is short for compare; it compares the contents of two files line by line and tells you if they're identical. This goes into detail beyond just comparing a file's name and its size by looking at it using the DIR command.

DATE   This command displays the current date (according to the computer, at least) and gives you the opportunity to enter a new date. See "The date and time" in Chapter 5.

MD   The MD (also MKDIR) command is used to make a subdirectory. Refer to "How to name a directory" in Chapter 16.

MODE

The MODE command configures a variety of things on your computer: the screen, keyboard, serial ports, printer, etc. Refer to "Which do I have?" and "Funky display" in Chapter 7; "Controlling the keyboard" in Chapter 8; and "The serial connection" in Chapter 9.

PATH

The PATH command creates the DOS *search path*, which is a list of one or more subdirectories in which DOS will look for programs to run. It goes in your AUTOEXEC.BAT file that runs when you turn on the computer.

PROMPT

This command changes the appearance of the DOS prompt. Refer to "Prompt styles of the rich and famous" in Chapter 2.

RESTORE

The RESTORE command is used to copy files from a backup disk back onto your hard drive. Refer to "I just deleted an entire subdirectory!" and "Restoring from a backup" in Chapter 16.

TIME

This command displays what DOS thinks is the current time and gives you the chance to enter a new time whenever you want. Refer to "The date and time" in Chapter 5.

VER

The VER command displays DOS's name and the version number. Refer to "Names and versions" in Chapter 2.

VOL

This command displays a disk's volume label. Refer to "Changing the volume label" in Chapter 10.

XCOPY

This is like a super COPY command; much faster and smarter than the plain old COPY command. You can use XCOPY as a straight-across substitute for the COPY command if you like. It even copies subdirectories! Wow, this modern age.

Commands you may see others use

APPEND

Weird command. Like the PATH command (above), this command allows DOS to look in other subdirectories to find data files. It's not really as keen as it sounds, and generally causes more trouble than it's worth. An older command best avoided.

ASSIGN

The ASSIGN command forces DOS to ignore one disk drive, replacing it with another. For example, if you don't have a B drive, yet some idiot program insists on saving stuff there, you can use the ASSIGN command to tell the program to look on drive A instead. Programs can be so dumb.

ATTRIB   This command changes a file's attributes, which describe how
              DOS can treat a file. Refer to "The file! I cannot kill it" in Chapter 3.

BREAK   The BREAK command turns special Ctrl-C and Ctrl-Break testing on
              or off. With it on, Ctrl-C might be a little more responsive; with it
              off, your computer runs faster.

CALL   This is a batch file command used in batch file programming. The
              CALL command runs a second batch file from within another batch
              file.

COMMAND   The COMMAND command is actually DOS, the program you use
              when you work on your PC (it's COMMAND.COM). Never delete this
              program.

DISKCOMP   This command compares two disks to see if they're identical.
              Since the DISKCOPY command is very reliable, this command is a
              colossal waste of time.

ECHO   This is a special batch file command that displays information on
              the screen, usually the line of text following ECHO. You can use
              this command to eject a page of paper from your printer; refer to
              "Form feeding" in Chapter 9.

EXIT   The EXIT command is used to quit from DOS — actually, the
              COMMAND program that DOS runs (see COMMAND above). Refer to
              "How do I get back?" in Chapter 16.

FC   FC stands for File Compare, which makes this command redun-
              dant with the COMP command. Unlike COMP, however, FC offers
              more detailed descriptions of the differences between two files,
              and it's not as chicken about looking at files as the COMP com-
              mand is.

FIND   This command is used to find text in a file, or it can be connived
              to search for text in a DOS command. A sample of this feat is
              offered in, "Finding a lost subdirectory" in Chapter 14.

FOR   This is a special batch file programming command. Even in books
              I've written on batch file programming it's hard to explain what
              this command does. Best leave it alone.

GOTO   Yet another batch file programming command, which is only
              useful inside a batch file; there's really nothing to "go to" at the
              DOS prompt.

IF   IF is a special batch file command used in making decisions. For
              example: IF THE COMPUTER EXPLODES, I SHOULD WEAR A HAT. That's
              computer logic for you.

MEM   The MEM command tells you about memory in your computer and how it's used. Refer to "Conventional memory" in Chapter 6.

PAUSE   This is a special batch file command that displays a "press any key" message and (surprise) waits for you to press a key before going on.

REM   This is a batch file command that allows you to put comments or remarks into a batch file program.

RMDIR   The RMDIR command (also RD) is used to delete a subdirectory. The subdirectory has to be empty first.

SET   The SET command is used in two ways: First, by itself SET displays the contents of DOS's *environment*. Secondly, SET can be used to place items into the environment or to remove them. Yawn.

SHIFT   Another batch file command. This one does something so complex I'd have to tell it *twice* to Mr. Spock.

SORT   This command is used to sort the output of some other DOS command or text file.

SYS   The SYS command is used to make a disk bootable. It transfers the DOS system files to a disk, so that disk can be used thereafter.

VERIFY   This command turns on double verification of all the information DOS writes to disk. With the command on, you'll be certain that the information is properly stored. On the down side, it slows down your computer. Normally, VERIFY is off.

Commands no one uses more than once

FDISK   The FDISK command is used when you first set up a hard disk. It prepares the disk for formatting. Using this command after the disk has been prepared could damage your hard drive. Do not use this command; only let an expert play with FDISK.

GRAFTBL   This is one of DOS's many "code page" commands. GRAFTBL loads a code page (foreign language character set) into the memory on your computer's screen (graphics adapter).

GRAPHICS   The GRAPHICS command works with IBM and Hewlett-Packard printers, allowing them to accurately print graphics.

JOIN   The JOIN command is used to fake DOS into thinking one of your disk drives is really a subdirectory. Weird. Also dangerous.

KEYB
The KEYB command loads a foreign language keyboard driver into memory, allowing you to type using special foreign language characters. (Ooo, la, la!)

SUBST
The SUBST command is used to fake DOS into thinking a subdirectory is actually a disk drive. And dangerous, too.

Commands not worth bothering with

CHCP
This is the change code page command, which allows you to switch in an alternate character set for the screen. (Sounds like fun, but setting up a PC to do that is complex and confusing.)

EDLIN
This is DOS's old command-line editor. Yuck! Refer to Chapter 2 where I make my real feelings clear about using this cruddy old program.

EXE2BIN
This is a programmer's tool. (DOS used to come with another programmer's tool, LINK. Don't ask why. DOS dry.)

FASTOPEN
This is a program used to speed up access to files on disk. I've heard nothing but problems with it, especially with switching floppy disks. Don't use this command.

NLSFUNC
Yet another "code page" program. This adds "natural language support" to DOS, allowing foreigners (mostly cab drivers) to type in their own native lingo.

REPLACE
Interesting command: It will search out and replace all files on the hard disk with newer versions on a floppy disk. This command is used when updating older versions of DOS.

SELECT
This was the program that installed DOS 3.3 and 4.0. Don't use it.

Commands no one in their right mind uses

CTTY
The CTTY command is interesting, but typing it can disconnect your keyboard and monitor, forcing you to reset the computer in order to regain control. It's more of a curiosity than a command you can get any mileage out of.

RECOVER
This command is not as pleasant as its name might suggest. RECOVER tries too hard. Using this command can permanently damage all files on disk and instantly rob you of your subdirectories. Under no circumstances should you ever use this command. In fact, delete it from your hard disk.

Glossary

• •

'386

This number refers to all computers that have an 80386, 80486, or any higher-numbered 80×86 microprocessor or "brain" in their computer.

80286

This is the number of a microprocessor or "brain" in an AT or 286 computer. It's one notch less than an 80386 and one notch greater than an 8086.

80386

This number refers to the microprocessor or "brain" in all 80386 computers. There are two types: the 80386DX and the 80386SX. The SX is simply a cheaper version of the DX model, with all the caffeine but only half the calories.

80486

This number refers to the brains found in an 80486 computer. It's a notch better than an 80386 system, and will put a bigger dent in your wallet.

8086/8088

These two numbers refer to the first processors in the first line of PCs produced. While a lot of these models were sold, and many are still up and running, few are sold today.

Alt-key

A key combination involving the Alt key plus some other key on the keyboard such as a letter, number, or function key. When you see Alt-S, it means to press and hold the Alt key, type an S, then release both keys. Note that Alt-S doesn't imply Alt-Shift-S; the S key by itself is fine.

applications

This is a term applying to computer programs, generally programs of a similar type. For example, you can have word processing applications, spreadsheet applications, etc. There are several computer programs that fit into each application category. And everything is generally referred to as "software," which makes the computer do its thing.

arrow keys

These are keys on the keyboard that have directional arrows on them. Note that some keys, such as Shift, Tab, Backspace, and Enter, also have arrows on them. But the traditional arrow keys are used to move the cursor. See *cursor keys*.

ASCII

An acronym for American Standard Code for Information Interchange. ASCII (ASK-ee) uses code values from 0 to 127 to represent letters, numbers, and symbols used by a computer. In DOS, you'll often see ASCII used to refer to a plain text file, or one that can be viewed by the TYPE command and read by a human.

backslash

The \ character, a backwards-slanting slash. Under DOS, the backslash character is used as a symbol for the root directory, as well as a separator between several items in a pathname.

backup

A method of copying a whole gang of files from a hard drive to a series of floppy disks (though other devices, such as tape systems, can also be used). It could also refer to a duplicate of a single file — an unchanged original — used in case anything happens to the copy you're working on.

baud

Part of the old computer cliché, "Byte my baud," it actually refers to a technical description of a "signal change." With computers, people often use the term Baud to refer to bits per second or BPS, the speed of a modem. See *BPS*.

bit

A contraction of "binary digit," a bit refers to a single tiny switch inside the computer, which contains the value 1 or 0. There are millions of such switches — bits — inside the typical PC. They form the basis of all the memory and disk storage.

boot

The process of turning on a computer that, surprisingly enough, doesn't involve kicking it with any Western-style footwear. When you turn on a computer, you are "booting" it. When you reset a computer, you are "re-booting" it or giving it a "warm boot."

byte

A group of eight bits, all clustered together to form one unit of information inside a computer. Conceptually speaking, a byte is one single character stored inside a computer. The word "byte" would require four bytes of storage inside your PC. Bytes are also used as a measure of capacity; refer to kilobyte and megabyte.

capacity

The amount of stuff you can store; the total number of bytes that can be stored in memory or, more likely, on a disk. Some hard disks have a capacity of 100MB. Floppy disks have storage capacities ranging from 360K on up through 2.8MB.

CD-ROM

An acronym for compact disc-read only memory. It's a special optical storage device that contains millions of bytes of information. Like the musical CDs, you can use the appropriate CD-ROM hardware to access the volumes of information stored on a CD disc.

CGA

An acronym for color graphics adapter. The CGA was the first video system for the PC that offered both color text and graphics. The text was lousy and graphics only good for the chintziest of games. CGA was soon replaced by the EGA graphics standard.

clone

Clone is a term used to describe an imitation of an original. It doesn't appear much these days, but nearly all PCs are clones of the first IBM micro-computers, the original PC and PC/AT systems.

CMOS

This acronym refers to special memory inside the computer. The CMOS memory stores information about your PC's configuration and hard drive, and keeps track of the date and time. This is all maintained by a battery, so when the battery goes, the computer becomes terribly absent-minded.

compatible

A term used to refer to a computer that can run DOS software. This used to be an issue a few years ago. But today, nearly all PCs are completely compatible with DOS and all its software.

Control key

A key combination involving the Ctrl (Control) key plus another key on the keyboard, typically a letter, number or function key. When you see Ctrl-S, it means to press and hold the Ctrl key and type an S, after which you release both keys. Note that

Ctrl-S shows a capital S, but you don't have to press Ctrl-Shift-S.

conventional memory

The basic type of memory in a PC where DOS runs and all your programs are located. There can only be a maximum of 640K of conventional memory.

CPU

An acronym for central processing unit, CPU is another term for a computer's microprocessor or "brain." See *microprocessor*.

Ctrl

The name of the Control key as it appears on the keyboard.

cursor keys

These are special keys on the keyboard used to control the cursor on the screen. The four primary keys are the up, down, left, and right arrow keys.

cursor

The blinking underline on the screen. The cursor marks your position on the screen, showing you where any new text you type will appear. Cursor comes from the Latin word for "runner."

data

Information or stuff. Data is what you create and manipulate using a computer. It can really be anything: A word processing document, a spreadsheet, a database of bugs your daughter has collected, etc.

default

This is a nasty term computer jockeys use to mean the standard choice, option, or selection automatically taken when you don't choose something else.

directory

A collection of files on disk. Every disk has one main directory, the root directory. It can also have other directories or subdirectories. Files are saved to disk in the various directories. You view the files using the DIR, or directory, command.

disk

A storage device for computer information. Disks (also called diskettes) are of two types: hard disks and floppy disks. The floppy disks are removable and come in two sizes, 3½-inch and 5¼-inch.

display

The computer screen or monitor. The term display is rather specific, and is used to refer to what is displayed on the screen as opposed to the monitor (which is hardware).

document

A file created by a word processor. The term document means something you've saved with your word processor, usually a file that contains formatting information, various text styles, and so forth. This marks the line between a file created by a word processor (the document) and a plain text file, which lacks the formatting information (and can be viewed by the TYPE command).

DOS

An acronym for disk operating system. DOS is the main program that controls all of your PC, all the programs it runs, and anything that saves information to or loads it from disk.

DOS memory

This is another term for conventional memory, the basic 640K of memory in a PC. See *conventional memory*.

dot matrix

A type of printer that uses a series of pins to create an image on paper. Dot matrix printers are a cheap, quick, and noisy way to print computer information, not as slow as the old daisy wheel printer, and not as fast, expensive, or as cool as a laser printer.

dump

Dump is an old computer term that means to wash out one thing and dump it into another. For example, a screen dump takes the information displayed on the screen and literally dumps it out to the printer. See *screen dump*.

EGA

An acronym for enhanced graphics adapter. The EGA was the second graphics standard for the PC, after CGA. It offered many more colors than CGA, plus it has the benefit of easy to read text. EGA has since been superseded by the VGA standard. See *VGA*.

EMS

An acronym for expanded memory specification. The EMS, or more precisely, the LIM EMS (LIM for Lotus-Intel-Microsoft) is a standard for accessing extra memory on all types of PCs. This expanded memory is directly used by DOS and most DOS applications. See *expanded memory*.

Escape key

The name of a key on the keyboard, usually labeled "Esc." The Esc key is used by many programs as a cancel key.

expanded memory

This is extra memory in a PC, useful to DOS and lots of DOS applications. To get expanded memory you must add expanded memory hardware and software to your PC. (For a '386 system, you need only the software.) But, once installed, your computer will have access to lots of extra memory, which can be put to immediate use by many applications.

expansion card

This is a piece of hardware that attaches to your computer's innards. An expansion card expands the abilities of your PC, allowing you to add new devices and goodies that your computer doesn't come with. Expansion cards can add memory (such as expanded memory), a mouse, graphics, a hard disk, or external devices like CD-ROM drives, scanners, plotters, and so on.

expansion slot

This is a special connector inside most PCs that allows you to plug in an expansion card (see *expansion card*). The typical PC has room for five to eight expansion cards, allowing you to add up to that many goodies.

extended memory

This is extra memory in an 80286 or '386 computer; it's not expanded memory. Extended memory is primarily used by operating systems other than DOS. On an 80286, it's better to have expanded memory. On a '386 system, you can add extended memory — as much as you like — then convert it to the more usable expanded memory using special software.

file

A collection of stuff on disk. DOS stores information on disk in a file. The contents of a file could be anything: a program for DOS, a word processing document, a database, a spreadsheet, a graphics image, you name it.

floppy disk

A removable disk in a PC, usually fitting into a 3½-inch or 5¼-inch disk drive. See *disk*.

font

A typesetting term used in computer desktop publishing or word processing. The term really should be "typeface," or a specific style of text. For example, this book uses the Cheltenham typeface or font.

format

The process of preparing a disk for use by DOS. All disks come "naked" out of the box. For DOS to use them they must be formatted and prepared for storing files or information. That's done under DOS by the FORMAT command.

function keys

These are special keys on the keyboard, labeled F1 through F10 or F12. Function keys perform special commands and functions, depending on which program you're using. Sometimes they're used in combination with other keys, such as Shift, Ctrl, or Alt.

geek

A nerd with yellow Cheetos stuff between their teeth.

gigabyte

This is a perilously huge number, typically one billion of something. (And that's billion with a B.) A gigabyte is one billion bytes or 1,000MB.

graphics adapter

This is a piece of hardware that controls your monitor. There are three common types of graphics adapters on the PC: CGA, EGA, and VGA. The graphics adapter plugs into an expansion slot inside your PC.

hard disk

A high speed, long-term storage device for a computer. Hard disks are much faster and store lots more information than a floppy disk.

hardware

This is the physical side of computing, the nuts and bolts. In a computer, hardware is controlled by the software, much in the same way an orchestra plays music; the orchestra is the hardware and the music is the software.

I/O

An abbreviation for Input/Output; the way a computer works. Computers gobble up input and spit out output.

i486

This is a common way of describing the Intel 80486 microprocessor. They write "i486" on the top of the chips, so many folks write "i486" when they refer to that microprocessor. See *80486*.

K

Abbreviation for kilobyte.

keyboard

The thing you type on when you're using a computer. The keyboard has a standard type-writer-like part, plus function keys, cursor keys, a numeric keypad, and special computer keys.

kilobyte

One thousand bytes or, more accurately, 1,024 bytes. This is equal to about half a page of text. Note that kilobytes are abbreviated as K. So 24K is about 24,000 bytes (more or less).

laptop

A special, compact type of computer, usually running off of batteries, that you can take with you. Laptops are popular additions to a desktop system, allowing you to compute on the road. They are, however, expensive.

laser printer

A special type of printer that uses a laser beam to create the image on paper. Most laser printers work like a copying machine, except they use a laser beam to help form the image instead of smoke and mirrors. Laser printers are fast and quiet, and they produce excellent graphics.

LCD

An acronym for liquid crystal display, a type of computer screen particular to laptop computers. Most LCDs are compatible with a desktop system's VGA display, though they're limited to black-and-white display or shades of gray.

load

To move information (a file) from disk into the computer's memory. Only after you've loaded something, say a worksheet or document, into memory can you work on it. See *save*.

MB

An abbreviation for megabyte. See *megabyte*.

macro

A program within a program, usually designed to carry out some complex function, automate a series of commands, or make life easier for anyone who doesn't want to hassle with a program's complexities. Macros exist in just about every application — even DOS — to make routine things easier. (Under DOS, the macros are called "batch files.")

math coprocessor

This is a special companion chip to a computer's microprocessor, specifically designed to perform complex arithmetic and to do it faster than the microprocessor can by itself. The math coprocessor chip is numbered similarly to the microprocessor, save for the last digit which is a 7 instead of a 6. Note that the 80486 microprocessor has its math coprocessor built-in.

megabyte

One million bytes, or 1,024K. A megabyte is a massive amount of storage. For example, *War and*

Peace could fit into a megabyte with room to spare. Typically, hard drive storage capacity is measured in megabytes, with about 40MB being a popular size.

memory

Where the computer stores information as it's worked on. Memory is temporary storage, usually in the form of RAM chips. The microprocessor can only manipulate data in memory. Once that's done, it can be saved on disk for long-term storage.

memory-resident programs

These are programs that hide in memory, working only when you call them or when special situations arise. A common type of memory-resident program is the "pop-up" application. For example, pressing Alt-C may cause a memory-resident calculator to display on your screen — right on top of the program you're already using. Note that some nerds call these types of programs "TSRs."

menu

A list of commands or options in a program. Some menus are displayed across the top or bottom of the screen, giving you one-word commands or choices. Some fill the screen, asking you "What next?" Some menus are graphical pull-down menus that display a hidden list of items or commands. Fun, fun, fun.

MHz

An abbreviation for megahertz. This refers to how fast a computer's microprocessor can compute. The typical PC zips along at 20MHz. The typical human brain, scientists have discovered, works at about 35MHz — or 40MHz after six cups of coffee.

microprocessor

The computer's main brain, the control center for the entire computer where all the calculations take place. Microprocessors are also called "processors" or CPUs. They're given numbers such as 80386, 80286, etc. (Refer to the numbers at the start of this glossary.)

modem

A contraction of modulator-demodulator, a modem is a device that takes electronic information from your computer and converts it into sounds that can be transmitted over phone lines. Those sounds can be converted back into electronic information by the other computer's modem.

monitor

The computer's display or video system. The monitor is like a TV set, showing you information. It's actually only half of your computer's video

system. The other half is the graphics adapter plugged into an expansion slot inside your PC.

monochrome

A type of computer display that shows only two colors, black and white (or green and white). Some monochrome systems will display shades of gray, substituting them for the various colors.

mouse

This is a small, hand-held pointing device primarily used in graphics programs to manipulate stuff on the screen. A mouse has two parts: the hard part, consisting of the mouse unit itself connected to a mouse card in your computer (or a serial port), and the software part, which is a program that controls the mouse and allows your applications to access it.

MS-DOS

This is the long, formal title for DOS, the Microsoft disk operating system.

network

Several computers hooked together. When your computer is on a network, you can share printers with other computers, easily send files back and forth, or run programs or access files on other computers. It sounds neat, but in practice a network can be a hassle to set up and a pain to maintain. (See *NBC.*)

on-line

To be on and ready to go. When a printer is on-line, it's turned on, contains paper, and is all ready to print.

option

An item typed after a DOS command that isn't required. You type an option after a command to control the way the command performs. Most options typed after a DOS command are in the form of "switches," which are slash characters typically followed by a letter of the alphabet.

parallel port

See *printer port.*

pathname

The full, exact name of a file or directory on a disk. The pathname includes the drive letter, a colon, all directories up to and including the directory in question, and a filename. Pathnames are an extremely specific way of listing a file on disk.

PC

An acronym for personal computer. Before the first IBM PC, personal computers were called "microcomputers," after the microprocessor —

the computer's brain. The "PC" in IBM PC means personal computer and since that time all microcomputers — even non-DOS computers — have been called PCs.

PC-DOS

This is the IBM-specific brand of DOS, the personal computer operating system. The differences between this brand of DOS and MS-DOS are slight, and you can run PC-DOS on non-IBM computers.

peripheral

Any item attached to the outside of the computer, such as a printer, modem, or even a monitor or keyboard.

pixel

An individual dot on the computer's display, used to show graphics. A graphic image on a computer is made up of hundreds of dots or pixels. Each pixel can be a different color or in a different position, which creates the image you see on the screen. The number of pixels horizontally and vertically on the display give you the graphics resolution.

port

Essentially, this is a connection on the back of the computer to which you attach various external items (peripherals). There are two primary ports on each PC, a serial port and a printer port, though what the keyboard and monitor plug into could also be considered ports.

printer

This is a device that attaches to your computer and prints information. A printer is necessary to give you "hard copy," or printed output of the information inside your computer.

printer port

This is the connection on the back of the PC into which you plug a printer cable, thereby attaching a printer to your computer. Most PCs have the ability to handle several printers, though you need to add special hardware to give your system the extra ports. The printer port is also known as the parallel port or sometimes you'll hear some dweeb call it a Centronics port.

program

This is a special file on disk that contains instructions for the computer. Under DOS, all programs are stored in files with their second part named either COM, EXE, or BAT. To run a program, you need only type in the first part of the filename.

prompt

This is the ugly C> thing you see when you use DOS, telling you to "type that ridiculous command line here." The DOS prompt is the most familiar of all the prompts. Other programs may use their own prompts, each of which is designed to show you where information is to be entered on the screen. Handy.

RAM

An acronym for random access memory, this is the primary type of memory storage in a PC. RAM = memory.

resolution

This refers to the number of dots (pixels) on the screen. The higher the resolution, the greater the number of dots vertically and horizontally, and the finer the graphics image your computer can display.

RGB

This is an acronym for red-green-blue, or the three primary colors. These colors are used in all computer displays to show you all colors of the rainbow and from which graphics are created. In the old CGA days of computing, RGB also referred to a type of monitor for use with a PC.

ROM

An acronym for read-only memory. These are special chips on the computer that contain instructions or information. For example, the computer's BIOS is stored on a ROM chip. ROM chips are accessed just like regular RAM memory, but unlike RAM they cannot be changed; they're read-only.

root directory

The primary directory on every DOS disk. Other directories, or subdirectories, branch off of the root directory. The symbol for the root directory is the single backslash (\).

save

The process of transferring information from memory to a file on disk for permanent, long-term storage.

screen dump

An ugly term for taking the information on the screen and sending a copy of it to your printer. A screen dump is performed on a PC by pressing the Print Screen key, which may be labeled Print Scrn, PrtSc, or something along those lines.

SCSI

An acronym for small computer system interface, it's like a very fast and versatile serial port. I only mention it here because it's pronounced "scuzzy" and I think that's cool.

serial port

A special type of port into which a variety of interesting devices can be plugged. The most common item plugged into a serial port is a modem (which leads some to call it a modem port). You can also plug in a computer mouse, printer, or scanner. Most PCs have one or two serial ports.

shareware

This describes a category of software that's not free, yet is stuff you don't have to buy before you try it. Generally, shareware consists of programs written by individuals and distributed hand-to-hand, through user groups, via modem, or by national software clearing houses. You try the software and, if you like it, you send the author the required donation.

software

This is what makes a computer worth having, the vast collection of programs that control the hardware and let you get your work done. Software controls computer hardware.

source

The original from which a copy is made. When you copy a file or duplicate a disk, the original is called the source. The source drive is the drive from which you're copying. The destination, or the location to which you're copying, is referred to as the target.

string

In computer lingo, this term applies to any group of characters. A string of text is a line of text, a command you type, or any other nonnumeric information.

subdirectory

A term for a directory in relation to another directory. All directories on a disk are subdirectories of the root.

syntax

The format of a DOS command: what you type, the options, what order they go in, and what they do. When you goof up and specify something out of order, DOS tosses you back a "Syntax error." Not fatal, it just means you need to find the proper syntax and retype the command.

target

The location of a copy or duplicate of an original file. A target can be a filename, a subdirectory, or a disk drive — the final destination of the file.

text editor

A special type of word processor that creates or edits text files only, often called ASCII, unformatted, or non-document files. A text editor lacks most of the fancy formatting features of a word processor.

user

The person who operates a computer or runs a program. The computer is then the usee.

VGA

An acronym for video graphics array, the current top-of-the-line in PC graphic systems. VGA offers you stunning color graphics, great resolution, and crisp text, and is much better than its predecessor, EGA. A SuperVGA (also known as SVGA) is available, which extends the powers and abilities of VGA.

window

An area on the screen where special information appears. It can be a graphic window, such as Microsoft's Windows program, or it can be a text window, outlined with special graphic text characters.

word wrap

The ability of a word processor to move a word from the end of one line to the beginning of the next while you're typing. Word wrap allows you to type an entire paragraph of text without having to press Enter at the end of each line.

write-protect

A method of protecting information on disk from being accidentally changed or erased. This is done by putting a write-protect tab on a 5¼-inch disk, or by sliding the little tile off the hole of a 3½-inch disk. Once that's done, the disk is write-protected and you cannot change, rename, delete, or reformat the disk.

WYSIWYG

An acronym for what-you-see-is-what-you-get. It refers to a program's ability to display information on the screen in exactly the same format in which it will be printed. Sometimes this works, sometimes it doesn't. Generally speaking, if a program is WYSIWYG, what you see on the screen will be close enough to what you get when it's printed.

Index

* (asterisk)
  . (star-dot-star), 164, 180-181
  copying groups of files with, 32-33
  deleting groups of files with, 34-35
  in filenames, 155
  as multiplication operator, 81
  as wildcard, 32-35, 163-164
  See also wildcards
\ (backslash)
  in directory names, 14-15, 84, 143
  displayed at the command line, 22
  in filenames, 155
  as root directory symbol, 14, 84, 140
  See also slash (/)
[] (brackets)
  in command formats, 128-129
  in filenames, 155
^ (caret), 26, 86
: (colon)
  with drive letters, 13
  in filenames, 155
, (comma) in filenames, 155
- (dash) in command formats, 129
$ (dollar sign) in DOS prompt, 27
= (equals sign) in filenames, 155
> (greater-than sign)
  in DOS prompt, 27
  in filenames, 155
  in I/O redirection, 40
< (less-than sign)
  in DOS prompt, 27
  in filenames, 155
. (period)
  dBASE dot prompt, 221-222
  in DIR output, 143
  in filenames, 155
  typing at DOS prompt, 22-23
  in user manuals, 24
| (pipe)
  in command formats, 129
  in DOS prompt, 27
  in filenames, 155
+ (plus sign) in filenames, 155
? (question mark)
  copying groups of files with, 32-33
  deleting groups of files with, 34
  in filenames, 155
  as wildcard, 32-34, 162-163
  See also wildcards
" (quotation marks) in filenames, 155
; (semicolon) in filenames, 155
/ (slash)
  in command formats, 129
  in filenames, 155
  functions of, 83
  See also backslash (\)
  (spaces)
  in filenames, 155
  typing at DOS prompt, 22-23
1-2-3. *See* Lotus 1-2-3
1.2MB disks. *See* floppy disks
1.4MB disks. *See* floppy disks
2.8MB disks, 107, 113
  See also floppy disks

3.5-inch disks. *See* floppy disks
5.25-inch disks. *See* floppy disks
360K disks. *See* floppy disks
640K barrier, 67
720K disks. *See* floppy disks
8088/8086 computers, expanded memory with, 68
80286 computers, expanded memory with, 68
80386 computers, DX vs. SX, 55-56

—A—
"Abort, Retry, Ignore?" error message, 186-187
"Access denied" error message, 35-36, 187
access errors, 171, 187
access-protected files
  deleting, 35-36
  making read-only files, 36
acronyms, 263-266
  ASCII, 10, 263-264
  BPS, 60
  CGA, 73
  CPU, 54-55
  DOS, 264
  EGA, 73, 264
  EMS, 69, 264-265
  ESDI, 265
  FUD, 265
  G or GB, 65
  IDE, 265-266
  K or KB, 65
  LIM 4.0 EMS, 69
  M or MB, 65
  MDA, 73
  OEM, 21
  RAM, 63
  SCSI, 266
  TSRs, 170
  VGA, 73, 266
  WYSIWYG, 266
  XMS, 69
address, memory, 65
/ALL switch for UNDELETE command, 37
Alt key
  key combinations, 85
  location of, 82-83
American Standard Code for Information Interchange (ASCII), 10, 263-264
analog-to-digital (A-to-D) port, 57
angle brackets. *See* greater-than sign (>); less-than sign (<)
any key, 81
APPEND command, 274
applications, 7
  See also software
arrow keys, 80
ASCII (American Standard Code for Information Interchange), 10, 263-264
ASCII files. *See* text files
Ashton-Tate Control Room, 55
ASSIGN command, 274
asterisk (*)
  copying groups of files with, 32-33
  deleting groups of files with, 34-35

  in filenames, 155
  as multiplication operator, 81
  star-dot-star (*.*), 164, 180-181
  as wildcard, 32-35, 163-164
  See also wildcards
A-to-D (analog-to-digital) port, 57
ATTRIB command
  deleting access-protected files, 35-36
  described, 275
  making files read-only, 36
attributes, 36
AUTOEXEC.BAT file, 131-138
  Direct Access in, 208
  editing with DOS 5 EDIT, 132-135
  editing with EDLIN, 132, 135-137
  prompt command in, 27
  resetting after editing, 138
  serial printer setup in, 96
  troubleshooting, 169
  warning about editing, 131

—B—
backing up, 149-152
  EDLIN backup files, 137
  a file, 151-152
  modified files, 152
  restoring files, 182-183
  third-party programs for, 150, 183
  today's work, 152
  using DOS BACKUP, 150-151
backslash (\)
  in directory names, 14-15, 84, 143
  displayed at the command line, 22
  in filenames, 155
  as root directory symbol, 14, 84, 140
  See also slash (/)
BACKUP command
  backing up a single file, 151-152
  backing up modified files, 152
  backing up the hard drive, 150-151
  backing up today's work, 152
  described, 273
backup filename extension, 154
"Bad command or file name" error message, 8-9, 21, 187-188
"Bad or missing command interpreter" error message, 188
BAK filename extension, 154
Basic programming language, 21
Basic programs, running, 179
BAT filename extension, 7, 154, 156
batch files
  ECHO command in, 40
  filename extension for, 7, 154, 156
battery
  for clock, 61, 170-171
  for hard drive information, 171
baud rate
  for modems, 60, 258, 262
  for serial printers, 95
  See also bits per second (BPS)
bits, 66
bits per second (BPS), 60
  See also baud rate

black box programs
  defined, 218
  rules for using, 218-220
blackouts, 169
booting
  resetting the computer, 17-18
  turning the computer on, 3-4
  See also resetting the computer
BPS (bits per second), 60
brackets []
  in command formats, 128-129
  in filenames, 155
BREAK command, 275
brownouts, 169
Buerg, Vernon D., 210
buttons
  form feed button, 97
  line feed button, 97
  mouse buttons, 91
  printer on-line or select button, 96
buying
  beginner errors, 198-199
  DOS shells, 214-216
  floppy disks, 106-108
  preventing virus infections, 204
  software, 121-122, 198-199, 204, 214-216
bytes, 65-66

— C —

cables
  checking connections, 168
  D-shell connectors for, 58
  plugging in, 94, 203
  serial printer cable, 96
CALL command, 275
canceling
  dBASE commands, 222
  DOS commands, 18, 26
  Harvard Graphics commands, 255
  Lotus 1-2-3 commands, 231
  Q&A commands, 224
  Quattro Pro commands, 236
  Word commands, 245
  WordPerfect commands, 241
  WordStar commands, 249
  See also deleting; undoing
CapsLock key, 82-83
caret (^), 26, 86
carriage return character, 84, 100
carriage return/line feed (CRLF), 84
CD (CHDIR) command
  changing directories, 14-15, 145-146
  described, 269-270
  finding the current directory, 144
Central Point Backup, 150
Central Point PC Tools. *See* PC Tools
Central Processing Unit (CPU), 54-55
Centronics port, 58
CGA (Color Graphics Adapter), 73
characters. *See* signs and symbols; special char-
    acters
CHCP command, 276
CHDIR command. *See* CD (CHDIR) command
check disk command. *See* CHKDSK command
child directories, 141
CHKDSK command
  checking amount of memory, 66, 148
  checking hard disk size and free space, 147-148
  deleting garbage files created by, 149, 174
  described, 273
  fixing lost files with, 149
  running after resetting, 174-175

clearing the screen, 270
clicking the mouse, 91-92
clock
  batteries for, 61, 170-171
  setting date and time, 60
  viewing date and time, 60-61
CLS command, 270
clusters, lost, 149, 174-175
colon (:)
  with drive letters, 13
  in filenames, 155
color display
  described, 71-72
  determining if you have it, 72
  resolution vs. colors, 74
  store version vs. your version, 77
  See also monitors
color graphics adapter (CGA), 73
columns displayed on monitor, 74-75
COM1, 96
COM filename extension, 7, 154, 156
comma (,) in filenames, 155
COMMAND.COM file, 33, 275
COMMAND command, 275
command line
  defined, 22
  entering commands, 22-25
  repeating commands, 25
  See also DOS prompt
commands. *See* DOS commands
COMP command, 273
Compaq DOS, 19-20, 21
computer
  80386 family, 55-56
  basic components, 53-55
  cables, 58
  clock, 60-61
  configuring software for, 124
  getting lost in, 177-179
  international computer symbols, 4
  keyboard, 79-90
  leaving on all the time, 16, 17
  locked or frozen, 173
  locking and unlocking, 169
  math coprocessor, 56
  memory, 63-70
  microprocessor type, 54-55
  modems, 59-60
  mouse, 90-92
  plugging equipment into, 94, 203
  ports, 57-59
  printer, 93-104
  resetting, 17-18
  turning off, 15-16, 202
  turning on, 3-4
  See also disk drives; keyboard; memory; mouse;
      printer; resetting the computer; trouble-
      shooting
CON device, 76
CONFIG.SYS file, 131-138
  editing with DOS 5 EDIT, 132-135
  editing with EDLIN, 132, 135-137
  mouse installation, 90
  resetting after editing, 138
  troubleshooting, 169
  warning about editing, 131
configuring. *See* installing
console device, 76
control key. *See* Ctrl key
Control Room, 55
conventional memory, 66
  See also memory
coprocessor, math, 56

COPY command, 29-33
  copying a single file, 30-31
  copying groups of files, 32-33
  copying to the current directory, 31-32
  described, 270
  moving files, 38
  printing text files with, 39-40
  star-dot-star (*.*) with, 164
COPYCON program, 205-207
copying
  all files in directory, 164
  duplicating disks, 116-117
  duplicating files, 29-30
  files to current directory, 31-32
  files to printer, 39-40
  files with DOS shell, 46
  groups of files, 32-33
  moving files, 38
  single files, 30-31
cords. *See* cables
CPU, 54-55
CRLF (carriage return/line feed), 84
CRT. *See* monitors
Ctrl key
  caret (^) symbol for, 26, 86
  key combinations, 85-88
  location of, 82-83
  WordStar key diamond, 87-88
Ctrl-Alt-Del key combination, 17-18
Ctrl-Break key combination, 26
Ctrl-C key combination, 18, 26, 86
Ctrl-L character, 40, 97
Ctrl-P key combination, 101-102
Ctrl-S key combination, 86
CTTY command, 204, 276
cursor, mouse, 91
cursor control keys, 80
cursor movement
  cursor control keys, 80
  moving between DOS shell panels, 45
  WordStar key diamond for, 87

— D —

dash (-) in command formats, 129
data bits, 258
  See also data word format
"The data contained in the first cluster of this
      directory has been overwritten or cor-
      rupted" error message, 37
data word format
  defined, 59
  for serial printers, 95
  See also data bits
database filename extension, 154
database programs. *See* dBASE IV; Q&A
date
  clock battery and, 170-171
  format for, 61
  setting, 60
  viewing, 60-61
DATE command, 60-61, 171, 273
dBASE IV, 220-223
  canceling a command, 222
  directory for, 221
  dot prompt, 221-222
  Erase Marked Records options, 223
  getting to the Control Center, 220, 221, 223
  help, 223
  loading a database catalog, 222
  packing the database, 223
  quitting, 223
  running, 5-7, 179, 221-222
  running dBASE applications, 221-222
  undoing commands, 222

DBF filename extension, 154
DEBUG command, 204
DEL command
   as command format example, 129
   deleting access-protected files, 35-36
   deleting garbage files created by CHKDSK, 149, 174
   deleting groups of files, 34-35
   deleting lost files found by CHKDSK, 149
   deleting single files, 33-34
   described, 270-271
   moving files, 38
   star-dot-star (*.*) with, 164, 180
delay before key repeats, 88-89
deleting
   access-protected files, 35-36
   all files in directory, 164
   files with DOS shell, 47
   garbage files created by CHKDSK, 149, 174
   groups of files, 34-35
   restoring deleted directories, 181-182, 183
   single files, 33-34
   text when typing at DOS prompt, 22
   undeleting files, 36-37, 180-181
   Wordstar key diamond for, 87
   See also canceling; undoing
DESQview
   locked or frozen computer and, 173
   running, 5-7
diapers, changing, 15
dip switches, printer, 99
DIR command, 157-162
   described, 271
   <DIR> symbol, 142
   directories in output of, 142
   displaying sorted directories, 159
   finding lost files with, 159-161
   finding lost subdirectories with, 161-162
   for floppy drives, 8
   listing a single file, 157
   listing files, 7
   listing groups of files, 157
   misspelling, 8-9
   pausing after every screenful, 7-8, 158-159
   periods in output of, 143
   printing directories, 102-103
   simple listing format, 9
   wide (five-column name-only) display, 8, 158
<DIR> symbol, 142
Direct Access menu program, 207-208
directories
   changing directories, 14-15, 48-49, 145-146
   child directories, 141
   for dBASE, 221
   in DIR command output, 142
   finding lost subdirectories, 161-162
   finding the current directory, 144
   for Harvard Graphics, 254
   housekeeping, 200
   logging to root directory, 132
   for Lotus 1-2-3, 228
   naming, 156
   parent directory, 141, 146
   pathnames, 143-144
   printing, 102-103
   for Procomm Plus, 259
   for Q&A, 224
   for Quattro Pro, 233
   restoring deleted directories, 181-182, 183
   root directory, 14, 132, 140
   for software installation, 124
   subdirectories, 14, 140
   tree structure, 146-147

viewing, 7-9, 157-159, 161-162
   when copying files, 31
   for Word, 243
   for WordPerfect, 238
   for WordStar, 247
disk drives
   changing drives, 13, 48
   in command formats, 128-129
   currently logged drive, 145
   in DIR command, 8
   drive letters for, 13
   drive light, 57
   floppy drive sizes and capacities, 106
   hard drive, 139-153
   inserting floppy disks, 12, 199, 203
   labeling, 54
   logging to drives, 13-14, 199-200
   removing floppy disks, 11, 57, 202
   switching disks inappropriately, 201-202
   types of, 57
   See also floppy disks; hard drive
Disk Operating System. *See* DOS
"Disk unusable" error message, 108
DISKCOMP command, 275
DISKCOPY command, 116-117, 271
diskettes. *See* floppy disks
disks. *See* floppy disks; hard drive
displaying. *See* viewing
DOC filename extension, 154
dollar sign ($) in DOS prompt, 27
DOS
   acronym deciphered, 264
   printing output from, 101-102
   versions of, 19-20, 21
DOS commands
   APPEND, 274
   ASSIGN, 274
   ATTRIB, 35-36, 275
   BACKUP, 150-152, 273
   BREAK, 275
   CALL, 275
   canceling, 18, 26
   CD (CHDIR), 14-15, 144-146, 269-270
   CHCP, 276
   CHKDSK, 66, 147-149, 174-175, 273
   CLS, 270
   COMMAND, 275
   command formats, 128-129
   COMP, 273
   COPY, 29-33, 164, 270
   CTTY, 204, 277
   dangerous commands, 204
   DATE, 60, 171, 273
   DEBUG, 204
   DEL, 33-36, 129, 149, 164, 174, 270-271
   DIR, 7-9, 102-103, 142, 143, 157-162, 271
   DISKCOMP, 275
   DISKCOPY, 116-117, 271
   DOSSHELL, 41
   ECHO, 40, 97, 275
   EDIT, 132-135
   EDLIN, 132, 135-137, 276
   entering commands, 22-25
   ERASE, 33
   EXE2BIN, 276
   EXIT, 275
   FASTOPEN, 276
   FC, 275
   FDISK, 204, 276
   FIND, 161-162, 275
   FOR, 275
   FORMAT, 108-110, 128, 271-272
   FORMAT C:, 204

GOTO, 275
GRAFTBL, 276
GRAPHICS, 276
IF, 275
JOIN, 276
KEYB, 276
LABEL, 114
MD (MKDIR), 156, 273
MEM, 66-67, 276
mistyping, 8-9, 198
MODE, 72, 74-77, 88-89, 95-96, 274
MORE, 10-11, 125, 147, 272
NLSFUNC, 276
PATH, 274
PAUSE, 276
PROMPT, 26-27, 274
RD (RMDIR), 181, 276
RECOVER, 204, 277
REM, 276
REN, 38-39, 164, 272
repeating commands, 25
REPLACE, 276
RESTORE, 181-183, 274
SELECT, 276
SET, 276
SHIFT, 276
SORT, 276
SUBST, 276
SYS, 276
TIME, 60, 171, 274
top ten, 269-272
TREE, 146-147
TYPE, 9-10, 272
UNDELETE, 36-37, 181
VER, 20, 274
VERIFY, 276
VOL, 114, 129, 274
XCOPY, 274
   See also specific commands by name
DOS prompt
   appearance in this book, 24
   in black box program, 220
   custom prompts, 26-27
   described, 20
   error messages, 21
   in Lotus, 1-2-3, 232-233
   repeating commands, 25
   special characters in, 27
   typing at, 22-25
   unexpected reappearance of, 178
   in Windows, 253
   See also command line
DOS shell, 41-49, 208-209
   changing directories, 48-49
   changing drives, 48
   copying files, 46
   deleting files, 47
   described, 208-209
   display options, 43-45
   finding lost files, 48
   illustrated, 44-46
   mouse requirement, 42
   moving between panels, 45
   moving files, 47
   quitting, 42-43
   renaming files, 47
   running programs, 49
   starting, 42
DOSSHELL command. *See* DOS shell
dot. *See* period (.)
dot prompt (dBASE), 221-222
double-clicking the mouse, 92
downloading files, 261-262
   See also Procomm Plus; telecommunications

dragging the mouse, 92
"Drive not ready error" message, 189, 193
drives. *See* disk drives
DS/DD floppy disks, 107
D-shell connectors, 58
"Duplicate file name or file not found" error message, 189
duplicating. *See* copying

— E —

ECHO command
 in batch files, 40
 described, 275
 ejecting printer page with, 40, 97
Ed (extended density) disks, 107, 113
 See also floppy disks
EDIT program
 editing CONFIG.SYS or AUTOEXEC.BAT file with, 132-135
 illustrated, 133
 quitting, 135
 saving files, 134
 using menus, 134-135
EDLIN program
 adding a line at the end of the file, 136-137
 background information about, 136
 backup files made by, 137
 described, 276
 editing CONFIG.SYS or AUTOEXEC.BAT file with, 132, 135-137
 quitting, 137
 saving the file, 137
EGA (Enhanced Graphics Adapter), 73, 264
EMM.SYS driver, 69
EMS (Expanded Memory Specification), 69, 264-265
enhanced 101-keyboard, 80-81
 See also keyboard
Enhanced Graphics Adapter (EGA), 73, 264
Enhanced Small Device Interface (ESDI), 265
Enter key, 84
equals sign (=) in filenames, 155
ERASE command. *See* DEL command
erasing. *See* deleting
error messages
 common error messages, 185-194
 with DIR command, 8
 at DOS prompt, 21
 when formatting disks, 108
 See also troubleshooting; *specific messages by name*
Esc key
 canceling program commands with, 26
 location of, 81
 when typing at DOS prompt, 22
ESDI (Enhanced Small Device Interface), 265
Excel, running, 5-7
EXE2BIN command, 276
EXE filename extension, 7, 154, 156
EXIT command, 275
exiting. *See* quitting
expanded memory, 68-69
expanded memory cards, 68
Expanded Memory Specification (EMS), 69, 264-265
extended memory, 68-69
extended-density disks, 107, 113
 See also floppy disks
extensions. *See* filename extensions
external modems, 60

— F —

F3 key
 quitting DOS shell with, 42-43
 repeating commands with, 25
FastBack, 150

FASTOPEN command, 276
fatal errors, 186
FC command, 275
FDISK command, 204, 276
"File cannot be copied onto itself" error message, 189
"File creation error" error message, 190
"File not found" error message, 21, 190
 with COPY command, 30
 with DEL command, 34
 with TYPE command, 10
filename extensions
 common extensions, 154-155
 DIR listing format for, 9
 of programs, 7, 154, 156
 for text files, 10, 155
filenames
 characters forbidden in, 155-156
 in command formats, 129
 creating names, 153-156
 DIR listing format for, 9
 pathnames, 143-144
 of popular programs, 6
 renaming files, 38-39, 47
 warning about overwriting files, 30
files, 29-40, 153-164
 access-protected files, 35-36
 backing up, 149-152
 batch files, 40
 copying, 29-33, 46
 date- and time-stamping, 61
 deleting, 33-36, 47
 DOS shell functions for, 46-48
 downloading, 261-262
 finding lost files, 48, 159-161
 housekeeping, 200
 lost files found by CHKDSK, 149, 174-175
 moving, 38, 47
 naming, 30, 153-155
 printing text files, 39-40
 read-only, 36
 renaming, 38-39, 47
 restoring backed-up files, 182-183
 text files, 10
 undeleting, 36-37, 180-181
 uploading, 261-262
 viewing files and directories, 7-9, 157-162
 viewing text file contents, 9-11
 See also directories; disk drives; floppy disks; hard drive; *specific files by name*
FIND command, 161-162, 275
finding
 amount of memory you have, 66-67
 compatible software, 121-122
 current directory, 144
 lost files in DOS shell, 48
 lost files with DIR command, 159-161
 lost programs, 179-180
 lost subdirectories, 161-162
 when you're lost in the computer, 177-179
 See also viewing
floppy disks, 105-117
 buying, 106-108
 changing disks, 11-12
 DS/DD disks, 107
 duplicating, 116-117
 extended-density (Ed) disks, 107, 113
 formatting, 108-111
 as hardware, 106
 high-capacity disks with low-capacity drives, 203
 inserting, 12, 199, 203
 labeling, 111-112

low-capacity disks with high-capacity drives, 109-111, 203
 quad density disks, 107
 removing, 11, 57, 202
 sizes and capacities, 106-108
 switching inappropriately, 201-202
 telling low-capacity from high-capacity disks, 112-113
 unformatting, 182
 viewing files on, 8
 volume labels, 112, 114
 working from, 202
 write-protecting, 115
 See also disk drives
floppy drives. *See* disk drives
FON filename extension, 155
font filename extension, 155
FOR command, 275
form feed, 97-98
 button, 97
 Ctrl-L for, 40, 97
FORMAT command
 as command format example, 128
 described, 271-272
 FORMAT C:, 204
 formatting floppy disks, 108-110
 formatting hard drives, 204
 QuickFormat option, 115-116
 reformatting floppy disks, 115-116
 unconditional format option, 110, 116
formatting floppy disks, 108-111
 beginner error, 200
 error messages, 108
 high-capacity disks as low-capacity disks, 203
 low-capacity disk in high-capacity drive, 109-110
 low-capacity disks as high-capacity disks, 110-111, 203
 reformatting, 115-116, 200
 unformatting, 182
 when backing up, 151
 when duplicating disks, 117
friends, impressing, 263-266
 See also acronyms
FUD (Fear, Uncertainty, Doubt), 265
function keys
 described, 80
 F3 key, 25, 42-43
 in Harvard Graphics, 255
 in Q&A, 224

— G —

G (gigabyte), 65
games, why they don't work, 75-76
Gates, Bill, 213
GB (gigabyte), 65
"General failure" error message, 190
gigabyte, 65
glossaries. *See* macros
GOTO command, 275
GRA filename extension, 155
GRAFTBL command, 276
GrandView, running, 5-7
graphics
 filename extensions for, 155
 IBM graphics characters don't print, 103
 Print Screen key and, 101
 store display vs. your computer, 77
graphics adapters
 choosing, 76
 defined, 72
 screen modes, 74-75
 text display resolutions, 74-75

types of, 73-74
See also monitors
GRAPHICS command, 276
greater-than sign (>)
in DOS prompt, 27
in filenames, 155
in I/O redirection, 40

— H —

hanging up, 262
hard disk management. *See* directories; hard drive
hard drive
backing up, 149-152
checking the disk, 147-149, 174-175
formatting, 204
hard disk management, 139-153, 200
life expectancy of, 171
missing, 171
troubleshooting, 171-172, 187
working from floppy disks, 202
See also directories; disk drives
hardware. *See* computer; *specific components by name*
Harvard Graphics, 254-257
canceling commands, 255
directory for, 254
function keys, 255
help, 257
learning to use, 257
menus, 255
running, 5-7, 254-255
rush jobs, 257
title bar information, 255
working with charts, 255-256
working with presentations, 256
help
dBASE IV, 223
Harvard Graphics, 257
Lotus 1-2-3, 232
Procomm Plus, 260
Q&A, 227
Quattro Pro, 237
Windows, 253
Word, 246
WordPerfect, 241
WordStar, 249
See also troubleshooting
Hercules adapter, running color graphics with, 77
high-capacity disks. *See* floppy disks; formatting floppy disks
HIMEM.SYS file, 69
housekeeping, 200

— I —

IDE (Integrated Drive Environment), 265-266
IF command, 275
inserting floppy disks, 12, 199, 203
installation programs, 123-124
installing
checking connections, 168
defined, 123
DOS shells, 215
mouse setup, 90
printer connection, 94-96
serial port setup, 59, 95-96
software, 123-125
"Insufficient disk space" error message, 191
Integrated Drive Environment (IDE), 265-266
internal modems, 60
international computer symbols, 4
"Invalid directory" error message, 15, 191
"Invalid drive specification" error message, 191
"Invalid file name or file not found" error message, 192

"Invalid media, track 0 bad or unusable" error message, 192
"Invalid number of parameters" error message, 192-193
"Invalid parameter" error message, 192-193
"Invalid switch" error message, 192-193
IQ for software, 205

— J —

JB Technology, 207
JOIN command, 276
joystick port, 57

— K —

K (kilobyte), 65
KB (kilobyte), 65
KEYB command, 276
keyboard, 79-90
Alt key combinations, 85
any key, 81
beeping from, 89-90
checking connections, 168
Ctrl key combinations, 85-88
cursor control keys, 80
described, 79-80
enhanced 101 keyboard layout, 80-81
function keys, 80
illustrated, 80
keys of state, 82-83
lights, 82
locked, 90
numeric keypad, 81
spilling things into, 176
typematic control, 88-89
typewriter keys, 80
WordStar key diamond, 87-88
See also specific keys by name
keys of state, 82-83
kilobyte, 65

— L —

LABEL command, 114
labeling disks
with sticky labels, 111-112
volume labels, 112
LapLink III, running, 5-7
laser printer
ejecting a page, 40, 97-98
paper jams, 98-99
See also printers/printing
leaving the computer on, 16, 17
left angle bracket. *See* less-than sign (<)
less-than sign (<)
in DOS prompt, 27
in filenames, 155
LIM 4.0 EMS, 68, 69
line feed
button, 97
dip switch for, 99
ending printer lines, 100
Enter key generation of, 84
lines displayed, 74-75
LIST program, 209-210
listing. *See* viewing
loading
described, 64
high, 68
See also running
logging
currently logged drive, 145
defined, 145
to drives, 13-14

logging off with Procomm Plus, 262
to wrong drive or directory, 199-200
looking at. *See* viewing
lost files or clusters, 149, 174-175
Lotus 1-2-3, 228-233
activating menus, 228
canceling commands, 231
changing column widths, 230-231
directory for, 228
DOS prompt from, 232-233
entering data, 230
help, 232
loading a worksheet, 229
macros, 228, 232
printing, 231
quitting, 229, 232-233
recalculating a worksheet, 231
releases of, 228
running, 5-7, 228
undoing commands, 231
Lotus Magellan. *See* Magellan
low-capacity disks. *See* floppy disks; formatting floppy disks
LPT1, LPT2, and LPT3, 94-95

— M —

M (megabyte), 65
macros
Lotus 1-2-3, 228, 232
Q&A, 226-227
Quattro Pro, 237
Word, 245-246
WordPerfect, 241
WordStar, 249
Magellan
described, 210-211
running, 5-7
Manifest, 55
manuals, 127
math coprocessor, 56
mathematical operators, 81, 83
MB (megabyte), 65
MD (MKDIR) command, 156, 273
MDA (Monochrome Display Adapter), 73
megabyte, 65
MEM command, 66-67, 276
memory, 63-70
640K barrier, 67
conventional memory, 66
described, 63-64
expanded memory, 68-69
extended memory, 69
finding how much you have, 66-67
microprocessor and, 55
required amount, 64-65
terminology, 65
turning off or resetting the computer and, 64
upgrading, 70
upper memory, 68
memory-resident programs, 170, 178
menu system
Direct Access program for, 207-208
running, 5
messages. *See* error messages
mice. *See* mouse
microprocessor, 54-55
Microsoft Windows. *See* Windows
Microsoft Word. *See* Word
Microsoft Word for Windows, running, 5-7
mistyping commands, 8-9, 198
MKDIR command, 156, 273
MODE command
described, 274

for keyboard typematic control, 88-89
MODE 40 command, 72, 74, 77
MODE 80 command, 72, 74, 77
MODE MONO command, 77
serial printer settings, 95-96
testing for color display with, 72
for text display resolutions, 74-75, 76
modem port, 59
modems, 59-60
checking connections, 168
troubleshooting, 258-259
See also Procomm Plus; telecommunications
monitors, 71-77
checking, 168
clearing the screen, 270
color vs. monochrome, 71-72
graphics adapters for, 72, 73-74, 76
nothing on screen after computer turned on, 4
printing the screen, 99-101
screen dimming programs, 16
screen modes, 74-75
text display resolutions, 74-75
See also graphics adapters
monochrome display
described, 71-72
determining if you have it, 72
games and, 75-76
running color graphics on, 77
See also monitors
monochrome display adapter (MDA), 73
MORE command
described, 272
viewing directory tree using, 147
viewing files using, 10-11
viewing README files using, 125
mouse, 90-92
DOS shell requirement, 42, 209
droppings, 92
installing, 90
mouse pad, 90
port for, 59, 90
serial mouse, 59
terminology, 91-92
using, 90-91
Windows requirement, 42
moving
files from command line, 38
files with DOS shell, 47
See also cursor movement
MS-DOS, 19-20
See also DOS
MultiMate, running, 5-7

N

names. See directories; filenames
NLSFUNC command, 276
"Non-system disk or disk error" message, 193
Norton Backup, 150
Norton SysInfo, 55
"Not ready, reading drive X" error message, 193
numeric keypad, 81
NumLock key, 82-83
NumLock key, 82-83

— O —

OEMs (Original Equipment Manufacturers), 21
organization, 200
Original Equipment Manufacturers (OEMs), 21

— P —

panels (DOS shell), moving between, 45
parallel port, 58

parent directory, 141, 146
parity, 258
PATH command, 274
pathname, 143-144
PAUSE command, 276
Pause key, 86
pausing
with DIR command, 7-8, 158-159
with Pause key, 86
PC. See computer
PC Shell, 211-212
PC Tools
Backup program, 150
PC Shell, 211-212
running, 5-7
SI (System Information) program, 55
PC-DOS, 19-20
See also DOS
PC-SIG, 207
period (.)
dBASE dot prompt, 221-222
in DIR output, 143
in filenames, 155
typing at DOS prompt, 22-23
in user manuals, 24
PIC filename extension, 155
pictures. See graphics
pipe (|)
in command formats, 129
in DOS prompt, 27
in filenames, 155
pixels, 74
plus sign (+) in filenames, 155
pointer, 91
ports, 57-59
analog-to-digital (A-to-D) port, 57
described, 57
joystick port, 57
mouse port, 59, 90
printer port, 58, 94-95
serial port, 58-59, 95-96
power switch
turning computer off, 15-16, 64
turning computer on, 3-4
Print Screen key, 99-101
printing graphics, 101
printing the screen, 99-100
with Windows, 101
Print Scrn key. See Print Screen key
printer drivers, 103-104
printer port, 58, 94-95
See also serial port
printers/printing, 93-104
connecting to the computer, 94-96
dip switches, 99
double-spaces printed for everything, 99, 100
everything prints on one line, 99, 100
first page has odd characters, 104
form feed (ejecting a page), 40, 97-98
in Harvard Graphics, 256
IBM graphics characters don't print, 103
in Lotus 1-2-3, 231
paper jams, 98-99
printer drivers, 103-104, 124
printing directories, 102-103
printing DOS's output, 101-102
printing text files, 39-40
printing the screen, 99-101
Q&A reports, 226
in Quattro Pro, 236
screen lines and boxes, 101
selecting (going on-line), 96-97
serial port setup for, 95-96

in Word, 245
in WordPerfect, 240
in WordStar, 248-249
PRN device
copying file to, 40
printer ports and, 94
sending DIR output to, 102-103
sending form feed to, 40, 97
sending TREE output to, 147
problems. See troubleshooting
Procomm Plus, 257-262
before you start, 258
capturing what happens on the screen, 261
described, 257-258
dialing a number, 260
directory for, 259
downloading, 261-262
hanging up, 262
help, 260
logging off, 262
quitting, 262
running, 5-7, 259-260
setting up, 260
time required for file transfers, 262
troubleshooting, 258-259
uploading, 261-262
Prodigy, running, 5-7
programs. See software
prompt. See DOS prompt
PROMPT command, 26-27, 274
Prt Scn key. See Print Screen key
punctuation marks. See signs and symbols; special characters; specific punctuation marks by name
purchasing. See buying

— Q —

Q&A, 223-227
adding and updating records, 224-224
canceling commands, 224
database reports, 226
directory for, 224
DOS facilities, 227
function keys, 224
help, 227
intelligent assistant, 226
macros, 226-227
messages and warning screens, 227
quitting, 227
running, 5-7, 223-224
word processing, 225
quad density disks, 107
Quarterdeck Manifest, 55
Quattro Pro, 233-238
canceling commands, 236
changing column widths, 235-236
directory for, 233
entering data, 235
help, 237
hot keys, 237-238
loading a spreadsheet, 234
macros, 237
printing, 236
quitting, 234
recalculating a worksheet, 236
running, 5-7, 233-234
saving frequently in, 237
undoing commands, 237
question mark (?)
copying groups of files with, 32-33
deleting groups of files with, 34
in filenames, 155
as wildcard, 32-34, 162-163
See also wildcards

Quicken, running, 5-7
quitting
    dBASE IV, 223
    DOS 5 EDIT, 135
    DOS shell, 42-43
    EDLIN, 137
    exiting DOS prompt in Windows, 253-254
    exiting DOS prompt within a program, 178, 220
    Lotus 1-2-3, 229, 232-233
    on-line services, 262
    Procomm Plus, 262
    programs in Windows, 252
    Q&A, 227
    Quattro Pro, 234
    resetting vs., 203
    turning off the computer, 15-16
    Word, 243
    WordPerfect, 238-239
quotation marks (") in filenames, 155

— R —

RAM. *See* memory
rate. *See* speed
RD (RMDIR) command, 181, 276
read errors, 171, 187
README files, 125
read-only files
    deleting, 35-36
    making, 36
RECOVER command, 204, 277
reformatting floppy disks, 115-116, 200
REM command, 276
removing floppy disks, 11, 57, 202
REN command
    described, 272
    renaming files, 38-39
    star-dot-star (*.*) with, 164
renaming
    files with DOS shell, 47
    files with REN command, 38-39
    using wildcards, 164
REPLACE command, 276
reserved memory, 68
resetting the computer, 17-18
    after editing CONFIG.SYS or AUTOEXEC.BAT
        files, 138
    after installing software, 126
    to leave an application, 203
    for locked keyboard, 90
    memory and, 64
    for mouse droppings, 92
    what to do after, 174-175
    when computer is locked or frozen, 173
    when lost, 178
    Windows and, 253
resolution of text display, 74-75
RESTORE command
    described, 274
    restoring backed-up files, 182-183
    restoring deleted directories, 181-182, 183
restoring
    backed-up files, 182-183
    deleted directories, 181-182, 183
Return key, 84
right angle bracket. *See* greater-than sign (>)
RMDIR (RD) command, 181, 276
root directory
    described, 14, 140
    logging to, 132
    See also directories
rows displayed on monitor, 74-75
RS-232 port, 59

running
    DOS shell, 42
    menu system, 5
    programs from command line, 5-7
    programs in DOS shell, 49
    starting the computer, 3-4
    See also specific programs by name

— S —

saving files
    described, 64
    with EDIT, 134
    with EDLIN, 137
screen. *See* monitors; viewing
screen dump, 100, 101
scrolling, 87
    See also cursor movement; viewing
ScrollLock key, 82, 83
SCSI (Small Computer System Interface), 266
searching. *See* finding
seek errors, 171, 187
SELECT command, 276
selecting
    with mouse, 92
    printer (going on-line), 96-97
    See also buying
semicolon (;) in filenames, 155
serial port, 58-59
    configuration, 59
    printer setup, 95-96
SET command, 276
SETUP program, 172
shell
    buying a shell, 214-216
    defined, 41
    See also DOS shell; *specific shell programs by
        name*
SHIFT command, 276
Shift keys with CapsLock and NumLock keys, 83
SI (System Information), 55
SideKick, running, 5-7
signs and symbols
    <DIR>, 142
    drive letters, 13
    forbidden in filenames, 155-156
    international computer symbols, 4
    mathematical operators, 81, 83
    See also special characters; wildcards
SIMMs. *See* memory
slash (/)
    in command formats, 129
    in filenames, 155
    functions of, 83
    See also backslash (\)
Small Computer System Interface (SCSI), 266
software, 121-129
    backup programs, 150
    black box program rules, 218-220
    buying, 121-122, 198-199, 204, 214-216
    configuring for your computer, 124
    filename extensions for programs, 7, 154, 156
    finding compatible software, 121-122
    finding lost programs, 179-180
    getting lost in, 177-179
    installation programs, 123-124
    installing, 123-125
    IQ for, 205
    names of popular programs, 6
    README files, 125
    running Basic programs, 179
    running continuously, 170
    running programs, 5-7, 49, 179
    ten programs that make life easier, 205-216

time required to learn, 126-127, 198-199
    updating, 127-128
    using, 126-127, 198-199
    viruses, 204
    weird acting, 169-170
    See also files; *specific programs by name*
SORT command, 276
sorting directory listings, 159
spaces
    in filenames, 155
    typing at DOS prompt, 22-23
special characters
    in DOS prompts, 27
    Enter-key-generated characters, 84
    forbidden in filenames, 155-156
    mistyping, 198
    printer line endings, 100
    wildcards, 32-35, 39, 152, 162-164
    See also signs and symbols; wildcards; *specific
        characters by name*
speed
    baud rate, 60, 95, 258, 262
    bits per second, 60
    typematic rate, 88-89
spreadsheet programs. *See* Lotus 1-2-3; Quattro
    Pro
star. *See* asterisk (*)
starting
    DOS shell, 42
    the computer, 3-4
    See also running; *specific programs by name*
stop bits, 258
stopping. *See* quitting
subdirectories
    defined, 14, 140
    See also directories
SUBST command, 276
SuperVGA, 73
switches (mechanical)
    power switch, 3-4, 15-16, 64
    printer dip switches, 99
switches in command formats, 129
switching between programs in Windows, 251,
    253
switching disks inappropriately, 201-202
symbols. *See* signs and symbols; special charac-
    ters
SYS command, 276
SYS filename extension, 155
SysInfo, 55
System Information (SI), 55

— T —

Tab key, 85
Tandy DOS, 19-20, 21
telecommunications
    about, 257-258
    troubleshooting, 258-259
tens of things (more or less)
    acronyms, 263-266
    common beginner mistakes, 197-200
    DOS commands you can use, 269-272
    popular programs, 217-262
    programs that make life easier, 205-216
    things you should never do, 201-204
terabyte, 65
text files
    described, 10
    filename extension for, 10, 155
    printing, 39-40
    viewing contents of, 9-11
    See also files

time
  clock battery and, 170-171
  for file transfers, 262
  format for, 61
  setting, 60
  viewing, 60-61
TIME command, 60-61, 171, 274
"Track 0 bad" error message, 108
TREE command, 146-147
tree directory structure, 146-147
troubleshooting, 167-204
  basic steps for narrowing problem, 167-169
  brownouts, 169
  CapsLock key working backwards, 82
  checking connections, 168
  common beginner mistakes, 197-200
  dangerous DOS commands, 204
  date or time is wrong, 170-171
  error messages, 185-194
  finding
    lost files, 48, 159-161
    lost programs, 179-180
    lost subdirectories, 161-162
    your way back, 177-179
  getting lost in the computer, 177-179
  hard drive errors, 171-172, 187
  hard drive missing, 171
  hardware problem checklist, 167-169
  keyboard
    beeping, 89-90
    locked, 90
    things spilled into, 176
  locked or frozen computer, 173
  modems, 258-259
  mouse droppings, 92
  printing
    everything double-spaced, 99, 100
    everything on one line, 99, 100
    first page has odd characters, 104
    IBM graphics characters don't print, 103
    laser printer didn't print, 98
    paper jams, 98-99
    screen lines and boxes, 101
  random characters on screen, 170
  resetting the computer, 17-18
    what to do after, 174-175
  SETUP program, 172
  software problem checklist, 169-170
  starting the computer, 4
  telecommunications, 258-259
  things never to do, 201-204
  undeleting files, 180-181
  viruses, 204
  when you need help, 175-176
  See also error messages
TSRs (memory-resident programs), 170, 178
turning computer off, 15-16
  with hard drive light on, 202
  memory and, 64
  resetting, 17-18
turning computer on, 3-4
TXT filename extension, 10, 155
TYPE command
  alternative to, 209-210
  described, 272
  pausing after every screenful, 10
  viewing file contents, 9-10
typematic, 88-89
typewriter keys, 80

— U —
UNDELETE command, 36-37, 181
undoing
  dBASE commands, 222
  Lotus 1-2-3 commands, 231
  Quattro Pro commands, 237
  restoring backed-up files, 182-183
  restoring deleted directories, 181-182, 183
  undeleting files, 36-37, 180-181
  undeleting text in Q&A Write, 225
  undeleting text in Word, 245
  undeleting text in WordPerfect, 241
  undeleting text in WordStar, 249
  unformatting floppy disks, 182
  Windows UNDO command, 252
  See also canceling; deleting
updating software, 127-128
upgrading memory, 70
uploading files, 261-262
  See also Procomm Plus; telecommunications
upper memory, 68

— V —
Ventura Publisher, running, 5-7
VER command, 20, 274
VERIFY command, 276
version number of DOS, 20, 21
vertical bar. *See* pipe (|)
VGA (Video Graphics Array), 73, 266
video display. *See* monitors; viewing
Video Graphics Array (VGA), 73, 266
viewing
  clearing the screen, 270
  date and time, 60
  disk volume labels, 114
  DOS shell display options, 43-45
  file contents, 9-11
  files and directories, 7-9, 157-162
  pausing information scrolling on screen, 86
  printing the screen, 99-101
  README files, 125
  WordStar key diamond scrolling keys, 87
  See also DIR command
viruses, 204
VOL command
  as command format example, 128-129
  described, 274
  viewing volume labels, 114
volume labels
  changing, 114
  sticky labels vs., 112

— W —
warm boot, 18
wildcards, 162-164
  asterisk (*), 163-164
  backing up with, 152
  copying groups of files with, 32-33
  deleting groups of files with, 34-35
  question mark (?), 162-163
  renaming files with, 39
  star-dot-star (*.*), 164
Windows, 250-254
  described, 212-213
  DOS prompt in, 253
  help, 253
  loading and running a program at the same time, 251
  locked or frozen programs in, 173
  mouse requirement, 42
  Print Screen key with, 101
  quitting programs, 252

running, 5-7, 250
  running programs in, 250-251
  switching programs, 251, 253
  UNDO command, 252
WKS filename extension, 155
Word, 242-246
  activating menus, 242
  canceling commands, 245
  directory for, 243
  editing modes (graphics and text), 246
  formatting text, 244
  help, 246
  loading a document, 243
  macros, 245-246
  printing, 245
  quitting, 243
  running, 5-7, 242-243
  spelling checker, 245
  starting a new document, 243
  timed backup feature, 246
  undoing deletes, 245
Word for Windows, running, 5-7
word processing programs. *See* Q&A; Word; Word
  for Windows; WordPerfect; Wordstar
WordPerfect, 238-242
  canceling commands, 241
  directory for, 238
  formatting text, 239-240
  help, 241
  loading a document, 239
  macros, 241
  printing, 240
  quitting, 238-239
  running, 5-7, 238
  spelling checker, 240
  starting a new document, 239
  timed backup feature, 242
  undoing deletes, 241
WordStar, 246-249
  activating menus, 249
  backup documents, 249
  canceling commands, 249
  directory for, 247
  formatting text, 247-248
  help, 249
  key diamond, 87-88
  loading a document, 247
  macros, 249
  printing, 248-249
  running, 5-7, 247
  spelling checker, 248
  starting a new document, 247
  undoing deletes, 249
worksheets. *See* Lotus 1-2-3; Quattro Pro
write errors, 171, 187
"Write protect" error message, 193-194
write-protecting floppy disks, 115
WYSIWYG, 266

— X —
XCOPY command, 274
XMS driver, 69
XTree Easy, 213-214

— Y, Z —
Y, pressing too quickly, 200
YUK filename extension, 155

IDG Books Worldwide Registration Card
DOS for Dummies

Fill this out — and hear about updates to this book and other IDG Books Worldwide products!

Name _____

Company/Title _____

Address _____

City/State/Zip _____

What is the single most important reason you bought this book? _____

_____

Where did you buy this book?
- ❑ Bookstore (Name _____)
- ❑ Electronics/Software store (Name_____)
- ❑ Advertisement (If magazine, which? _____)
- ❑ Mail order (Name of catalog/mail order house _____)
- ❑ Other: _____

How did you hear about this book?
- ❑ Book review in: _____
- ❑ Advertisement in: _____
- ❑ Catalog
- ❑ Found in store
- ❑ Other: _____

How many computer books
do you purchase a year?
- ❑ 1　　　❑ 6-10
- ❑ 2-5　　❑ More than 10

How would you rate the overall content of this book?
- ❑ Very good　　❑ Satisfactory
- ❑ Good　　　　❑ Poor

Why? _____

What chapters did you find most valuable? _____

What chapters did you find least useful? _____

What kind of chapter or topic would you add to future editions of this book?_____

_____

Please give us any additional comments. _____

_____

Thank you for your help!

❑ I liked this book! By checking this box, I give you permission to use my name and quote me in future IDG Books Worldwide promotional materials.

Fold Here

Place
stamp
here

IDG Books Worldwide, Inc.
155 Bovet Road
Suite 610
San Mateo, CA 94402

Attn: Reader Response